Eric —

Here's a souvenir of the pre-spam Internet.

TRAVELS WITH SAMANTHA

Travels with Samantha

Philip Greenspun

ArsDigita Press
Cambridge, Massachusetts
Berkeley, California

Yonie Overton	Vice President, Production & Manufacturing
Elisabeth Beller	Senior Production Editor
Ross Carron Design	Cover and interior design
Technologies 'N Typography	Composition and map scans
Ken DellaPenta	Copyedit
Henry Wu	Photograph at p. 7; repeated on back cover
Hemlock Printers, Ltd.	Four-color scans and printing
Lincoln and Allen Binding	Bindery

Corporate Headquarters:
ArsDigita Corporation
80 Prospect Street
Cambridge, MA 02139

Editorial Office:
ArsDigita Press
2311 LeConte Avenue
Berkeley, CA 94709

Printed in Canada

05 04 03 02 01 00 5 4 3 2 1

The full text of ArsDigita Press books is available to online readers at http://www.arsdigita.com/books.

Library of Congress Cataloging-in-Publication Data is available for this book.
ISBN (paper): 1-58875-001-9 — ISBN (caseside): 1-58875-000-0

This book is printed on acid-free paper.

Contents

Dramatis Personae

Alan	Buddhist philosopher in Telluride, Colorado
Ali and Michelle	Australians on a post-college world tour (Glacier National Park)
Alison	"I've never dated a man who wore a suit to work" (Alaska Marine Highway)
Amber	16-year-old clutching doll in Theodore Roosevelt National Park (North Dakota)
Arleigh	crushed my long-cherished delusions of irresistibility (Yellowstone)
Arthur	HIV+ for nine years (Moab, Utah)
Bruce	old friend and business partner
Carl	Mormon engineer demonstrating True Manhood in Yellowstone with wife and five kids
Charles	ironworker, scholar, Macintosh wizard (Anchorage)
Charles	struggling in Aspen to fund a round-the-world bike trip
Chicca	Italian girlfriend, lives in Rome
Cid	left husband to teach school in Eskimo village (Homer)
Claire	Francophone Montrealer with no Anglophone friends
Christina	visiting from Germany on a Marlboro cigarettes tour (Utah)
Darryl and Leif	"You can get anything you want if you have a pure desire" (Jasper)
Dave	78-year-old wildlife photographer (Katmai)
David, Doug, Sue	praying for the Jews to return to Israel (Salt Lake City)
Dawn	wistful 22-year-old-super-Midwesterner-but-dying-to-live-the-adventurous-Western-life (Missoula, Montana)
Denise	demonstrated just how far up the wall a woman can drive me in two days (Portland)
The Dukes	British family making their fourteenth journey across North America (Whitehorse)
Dwight, Emily, Karla	superhosts in Portland
Eero	old friend, former MIT grad student, professor at Penn
Elder Pomeroy	answered polygamy questions in Salt Lake City
Elke	East German Fulbright Scholar (Vancouver)
Emma	striving "cupcake" at Katmai
Eric and Laurel	fled the rat-race in Minneapolis
Erika	stunning Hungarian single mother (Whitehorse)
Frank	moved back to the ghost town in Montana where he was born in 1912
Gil and Shavit	Israelis who thought Alaska was the Promised Land (Alaska Marine Highway)

George	Samoyed dog, died June 1991
Glynn	left an assortment of wives, girlfriends, and children to be single in Homer
Brenda Griffin	George's last veterinarian
Harry	my brother, an anesthesiologist in Baltimore
Heather	21-year-old divorcée in Montana
Henry	old friend and business partner from Hong Kong
Walter Holland	walked across America; walked from Mexico to Tok, Alaska
Jackie	completely invested in victimhood (Cambridge)
Jennifer	beautiful Jewish woman in Boulder
Jim	Baptist Army chaplain who wants to shoot all the wolves (Denali)
Jim	professor at University of British Columbia
Jo-Anne	Australian actuary living in Vancouver
Jody and Eric	"We're probably the only Jews on this boat" (Seward)
John	selling insurance to polygamists (Monticello, Utah)
John and Judy	Northern and Southern Ireland meet in Calgary
Joel	old friend from MIT (Seattle)
Joseph	Blackfoot Indian with a taste for Ted Kennedy jokes (East Glacier, Montana)
Judy, Jason, Justin	tough, beautiful single mother and her sons from Memphis (Skagway)
Kaarin	Arctic biologist living in a condemned house in Whitehorse
Karin and Walter	"In Europe, old people look old" (Denali)
Keiko and Kazuyo	inscrutable Japanese girls, my companions from Banff to Lake Louise
Keith	"I'd rather face a charging grizzly bear than start a conversation with a strange woman" (Homer)
Keith	bum in Salt Lake City: "[the Mormons] are better at helping their own"
Kelly	truck driver on the Alaska highway: "Why would anyone call himself 'Jewish'?"
Kelly	a mother at age 12 (Kansas City)
Kirk	"Can't wait to get out of Duluth"
Ted Kerasote	author of *Bloodties*: "Don't go to the supermarket; shoot a deer" (Katmai)
Kleanthes	physicist and urban philosopher at MIT
Lavonne	living Christian in Petersburg, Alaska
Lily	first love (Cincinnati)
Lisa	Jewish ranger in Katmai, half of local production of *Dido and Aeneas*
Lisa	New York artist moved to Telluride
Liz	old friend from MIT, professor in Boulder
Lloyd	heavy equipment operator straightening the Alaska Highway (Whitehorse)
Maple	Chinese-Canadian college student in Ottawa

Marcia and Tony	my hosts in Fairbanks
Mark	writer and social worker (Denali)
Michael	engineer/photographer met in Egypt (Vancouver)
Michael	German university student: "Germany is full of Jews. In my life, I've actually met five" (Moab, Utah)
Mike	gave up $100,000/year paramedic job in Anchorage for the simple life
Patrick	managing 600 fish-gutters in Petersburg, Alaska
Ralph	teaches British Columbia school-by-mail (Lake Louise)
Randy	fell in love with Yellowstone 14 years ago and couldn't leave
Randy and Cathy	Fairbanks attorney and transplanted Chicagoan
Ranger Lisa	Jewish park ranger in Katmai
Rebecca	second love (Seattle)
Richard and Cindy	itinerant preachers (Petersburg, Alaska)
Roland	rehabilitates the homeless, Mormon style (Katmai)
Ronen	torn between American blonde and home in Israel (Glacier)
Sadie	just your average Indian transvestite fisherman (Seldovia)
Sallie and Ben	hot dog roasters on the Alaska Highway
Samantha	Macintosh PowerBook 170 computer
Sam and Ken	frontier woman and oil worker in Skagway
Scott and John	iron ore miners in Marquette, Michigan
Stan	grizzled bush pilot in Homer
Stefan	biked LA/Yellowstone in the rain
Stephanie	trophy wife singing the praises of the Midwestern WASP woman (Homer)
Steve	New Age avalanche skier in the Canadian Rockies
Steve	moved from Montana because of the fences (Katmai)
Dr. Stobie	veterinarian
Susan	a free spirit living for today in Homer
Susan	woman in Boston who couldn't bear to hear of a world without AIDS
Teddy	nightclub owner in Aspen
Terry and Rebecca	serving espresso in 100° heat in Moab, Utah
Thomas	Danish superman in Lake Louise
Tom and Lisa	quit their yuppie jobs to roam the continent in a motor home (Alaska Marine Highway)
Wendy and Angie	high school graduates in Sauk Centre, Minnesota
Woody	"If it didn't fit into my backpack, it didn't fit into my life" (Denali)
Yvonne	came all the way from London to see Head-Smashed-In Buffalo Jump

1

White Fur, Red Blood

It started with a nosebleed: red blood dripping from a pink nose onto the floor, leaving the white fur unstained. George was a 65 lb. Samoyed dog, 7 years old, and the very picture of Stoic good health. I brought him to my local veterinarian, who said, "I can't find anything wrong with him. He is only bleeding from one nostril so he probably just has a piece of grass stuck in his nose. Wait three days and, if he is still bleeding, take him down to Angell Memorial where they can look inside his nose. They have CAT scanners, ultrasound, and everything else you'd find at a hospital for humans."

George seemed sluggish and it made me uneasy. I drove straight to Angell Memorial Animal Hospital, the best in Boston, where Dr. Daniel Stobie was able to see him after 30 minutes. Dr. Stobie felt around George's undercarriage and said, "I don't like the feel of his abdomen; he could have a serious problem." His clinical and detached tone chilled me. He removed George's collar and leash and handed it to me, putting a plastic ID collar around the dog's neck instead. I had a fleeting sinking feeling that this would be all of George that would come out of the hospital. It was Thursday afternoon.

After a nervous, nearly sleepless Thursday night, Friday was a day of nail-biting and bad news. Testing seemed to me to proceed at a snail's pace, and I beseeched Dr. Stobie to hurry up with the diagnostic tests so that George could be treated. Somewhat annoyed with my impatience, he called me several times, each time deepening my gloom. By late Friday, he announced that George was in disseminated intravascular coagulation (DIC), a condition induced by various disorders, including heat stroke, cancer, and infection. Small clots form inside the dog at a rapid pace so that the blood's clotting factors are used up. Thus, the thinned blood can pour out of the dog's nose, though usually not from just one nostril. Dr. Stobie said that 75% of the dogs in DIC die and that the remaining 25% often suffer permanent organ damage. X-rays revealed an enlarged liver and spleen, but not the underlying source of George's DIC and were therefore useless for treatment.

"George probably has cancer. There isn't anything we can do for him at the moment other than give him an IV with plasma and fluids to bring him out of DIC." Dr. Stobie didn't sound as though he had much hope.

Visiting hours in the intensive care unit (ICU) are brief, so I rushed down to Angell to take full advantage of them. Bruce and Neil, old friends from work and college, accompanied me. Seeing George in intensive care was heartbreaking. The place was about as nice as could be expected, but it killed me to see animals suffering. Hospitals for humans never bothered me as much, perhaps because the patients can at least comprehend their plight. George was in a cage about 4′ × 6′, lying in a sedated fog. He was happy to see us and struggled to get to his feet.

I cried to see him brought so low and in such a cold place. Neil and Bruce felt awkward seeing me break down. I've never been the politically correct, emotionally sensitive Cambridge Man. I probably hadn't cried in 15 years. George was always tough, aloof, and very much his own dog. He'd jump into bed with me, but would eventually retire to his private corner. This is the dog who hit a trip wire in Harvard Yard while running at a full 30 miles/hour, sailed and tumbled 20 feet through the air, landed on his head, and kept running without yelping. Nothing in my seven years with George prepared me to see him in such a state.

After holding his head and crying into his neck fur for 15 minutes, I let Neil and Bruce get closer to George and looked around the ICU, which was a good recipe for heartache. A magnificent black Newfoundland slept in the adjacent cage. A little farther was a sweet-looking Golden Retriever panting in a closed cell with clear plastic doors so that he could breathe oxygen-enriched air. I felt sorriest for him, little imagining that my own baby would be in his place in two days.

We were kicked out at 7:00 PM, and Bruce followed me home. Bruce and I moved furniture and did some carpentry. George was never out of our minds, but I stopped crying. After Bruce left, I called my brother Harry, an anesthesiologist in

Baltimore, who'd lived with me and George one summer and well understood the potential tragedy.

Harry explained DIC a little more thoroughly—it was definitely something you didn't want to have—and tried to give me a lot of medical advice. He floated the idea that there might be better animal hospitals for canine cancer. It occurred to me that everyone in our family is obsessed with the idea of getting the right specialist. There is no medical problem so serious that it cannot be cured by the genius that cured some cousin's brother-in-law ("everyone said he was going to die and look at him now, five years after he saw that wonderful Dr. Smith"). After I plaintively said, "Harry, I'm calling you as a brother, not a doctor," he was quite sympathetic.

Then I called Chicca, my Italian girlfriend, the only woman I'd ever dated who'd been introduced to me by George. Meeting women with a Samoyed by one's side is like shooting fish in a barrel, but I'd never followed up any of the casual conversations until Chicca interrupted her tour of the U.S. to pet the "poppy." George had good taste, for Chicca probably loved me as much as any woman could. She wanted to jump on the next plane, but I restrained her. "You can't leave school until July and, besides, my parents will be here next week. My local friends can pull me through until Mom and Dad arrive."

I don't remember getting into bed, but I do remember an overwhelming loneliness. I stared up through my bedroom skylight at the empty sky and cried until I fell asleep at about 4:00 AM. Despite my predisposition to sloth, I woke at 8:00 AM without an alarm and wasn't tired. I moved some more heavy things and arrived at Angell Memorial at 11:30 sharp for the only visiting hour on Saturday. Hardly anyone was there, and the quiet was reassuring.

Before I entered the ICU, I could see George through the window sitting up in his cage. He greeted me wildly and seemed to have his energy and health fully restored. The IV plasma had had a miraculous effect on George, and I began to hope. I held him for 30 minutes, and then Rebecca came by.

Rebecca had dumped me a year before. "I'm going to be on CSPAN this weekend," I had said on the phone. "Not only do I not want to see you on television, I don't want to see you in person anymore" was how she had closed the door on our three years together. I had it coming to me, but I would have been mired in despair if not for George's companionship.

Rebecca had a difficult time believing that George was in immediate danger and spoke of breeding him once he'd recovered so that his unique personality would be preserved. She'd never liked dogs and still didn't like them in general, but had grown powerfully attached to George. She was warm with George, but a bit cold and almost bitter with me. We parted from George in a reasonably optimistic mood. He exhibited no signs of illness or depression, and it seemed that he'd be one of the lucky 25%.

Bruce and Henry, my partners in an engineering consulting business, spent Saturday afternoon with me. I wrote some software, relying on my natural obsessive characteristics to take my mind off George. Saturday afternoon, Dr. Stobie gave me some bad news: an ultrasound-guided hunt through George's interior revealed malignant-looking bone marrow cells. However, he promised me no definitive verdict until Monday when a senior pathologist could look at the cells.

Neil, Melissa, and Mara came over in the evening, and we stayed up until 5:15 AM looking at photographs, moving heavy things, talking, watching a movie, listening to Arthur Grumiaux (the Belgian violinist) records, and relaxing on the living room couch. When I met Neil in 1982, just after we graduated from MIT, he struck me as the warmest, sweetest, most sympathetic person I'd ever met. We've been friends ever since, and he is one of the few men that I really feel comfortable touching; sitting close on my couch (hemmed in by the women) was the best time that I had that weekend.

I awoke in a nervous state at 9 on Sunday morning and paced through the hours until 11:30 visiting time. Henry and Bruce met me at the hospital, and we found George in the Golden Retriever's oxygen cage. He looked weak and sick, but when he saw me, he pressed his face against the glass so hard that his features were distorted, like a 5-year-old child smushing his nose and lips against a window. It would have been funny if George had done it while healthy. Now he whimpered and cried, probably from a combination of loneliness and pain. Dr. Stobie had gone on vacation, and Dr. Brenda Griffin came by to take his place. She seemed just as capable, but was infinitely warmer and more sympathetic ("call me Brenda").

Without anyone saying anything, Brenda sensed that George was not just a backyard dog to be played with when work and family responsibilities allowed, but rather a best friend, constant companion, and partner in life. She let George out of the cage, and I held him on the floor trying in vain not to cry. I could have cried freely alone, in front of old friends, or in front of someone who wouldn't have cared, but it seemed cruel to burden Brenda.

George was short of breath from being outside the oxygen cage, but when we put him back in he seemed agitated about being separated from me. We had to leave before the end of visiting hours to keep him from tiring himself. I wasn't sorry to leave anyway; it was killing me to see him in that state. Out in the hallway, Brenda was in the middle of assuring us that she was doing everything possible when three fraternity boys came rushing in to check on the progress of their cat. They accosted Brenda, who had nothing to do with their case, and demanded to know how much they would be charged.

Once out of the hospital, I felt free to collapse. Henry noted my despair and kindly drove me in my car back to Cambridge. "Those guys were archetypical fraternity jerks," Henry fumed. Only his proper Hong Kong upbringing had kept him from exploding on the spot. This conversation drew my own attitudes about George and money into sharp focus. I realized how easy it would be to give up everything material if it would save George. Comparing the pain of losing money when one of my start-up companies went belly-up to the pain of losing Rebecca, I knew that there were many things I loved more than money. However, losing George hammered home the utter impotence of money under the most trying circumstances.

We all sat down to brunch in Harvard Square and tried to remember all the good times we'd had with George. Bruce and Henry chuckled that, even in his last days, George was irresistible to beautiful women (Brenda had expressive green eyes set in fine soft features, framed by long blond hair). Wherever I went, women would stop me so they could pet George, unless I was running fast or in New York City, where people are afraid of their own shadows. "How old is he?", "What's his name?", and "What kind of dog is he?" everyone would ask. We used to have fun answering the last question with "Arctic Pitbull."

We all laughed when we remembered the two saleswomen from an advertising agency who came by our plush new Cambridge offices. They were showing us their book when George, who was lying near one woman, started to make whooping noises.

"What's that?" asked the woman.

"He's going to throw up," I responded while quickly marshaling *Wall Street Journals* to place underneath his mouth.

The women shrieked and closed themselves into a windowless, unlit, 2′ × 2′ closet, refusing to emerge for several minutes.

Trying to numb myself with fatigue, I ran six miles through the woods near my house, up and down hills that overlook the city and ocean. The run, which I'd done a hundred times with George, was a painful reminder that things weren't the same. I missed the joy of admiring his powerful athleticism in jumping over rocks and fallen trees or in plunging through thickets. It used to make me happy just to look at George, sleeping, lying down, walking, or running.

My friend Mark came over with some Chinese food for which I had little appetite. He'd been in psychoanalysis for years and had absorbed a healthy dose of psychology theory, yet couldn't say much to comfort me. Halfway through dinner Brenda called from her house with the bad news: she'd convinced the senior pathologist to come in, and he'd diagnosed liver cancer that had metastasized (spread to other tissues). George wouldn't live more than a few days and would do so in pain.

"He's crying now, and I don't think he should have to endure the night. Some people wish to remember their dog as he was; you don't have to come back in."

The thought of George dying alone made me shudder, and I was very grateful that Brenda was willing to meet me at the hospital.

I couldn't eat another bite of food, but I did manage to take a shower and put on some decent clothes. I drove hurriedly to Angell Memorial, my mind blank of everything but the worry that George might die of weakness before I arrived. I didn't want George to die in the noisy intensive care unit with so many other pathetic cases all about. I carried George, who was too weak to walk at this point, and walked with Brenda to a quiet grassy area outside. I used to pick George up and hug him all the time, and even carried him around the Lincoln Memorial for 15 minutes once ("you are allowed to bring dogs in the Memorial as long as you carry them"). Despite having lost a few pounds in the hospital, George seemed heavier than expected.

We all lay down on the grass together. It was a perfect June night, warm and clear. I held George in my arms and talked to him. I told him how I'd always felt that I had to do something exceptional for him to repay him for the love he'd given me. I told him I was sorry for saying, "I'll be finished with my start-up companies and Ph.D. soon and then we can spend a year exploring North America together." (George loved hiking through the woods more than anything else.) He gave a mournful yelp every few seconds; it was an eerie, utterly unfamiliar sound. This was a dog who would, in turning around to investigate a cellophane package being opened, hit his head on a sharp table corner so hard that everything on the table flew six inches into the air; not only would he not yelp, but he would not appear to have noticed. Every cry now felt like a physical slash to my chest.

I asked Brenda to give him the barbiturate overdose. I was cradling him and could feel his heart and lungs working hard. I felt them stop a few seconds after the injection.

Lying down and holding his body, I felt freer than I had in days and was able to talk with Brenda for 10 minutes without straining not to cry. I wanted desperately to tell her about George so that she didn't think of him the way she'd met him: weak, helpless, and sickly. Although it was very comforting to be with Brenda and what was left of George, I didn't want to impose on her generosity. I carried George's body, which felt twice as heavy now, back into the hospital and cried all the way home. It had been only 78 hours from the time I suspected anything was wrong with George until he was dead. I fell asleep at 3:00 AM.

My mother woke me Monday morning with a phone call from my Aunt Marge's in New Jersey. Marge was in tears, and my parents expressed their regret. However, they would not be coming up to Boston; my father had caught a cold, and they were driving back to Washington.

If my parents weren't exactly the resources I'd hoped they'd be, my friends more than made up for it. Bruce and Henry called all my friends and told them the bad news so that I'd be spared awkward moments in the weeks ahead ("by the way,

how's George?"). Most of them called back and offered their sympathy. For the next two weeks, I couldn't go one hour without someone offering me dinner, a shoulder to cry on, or their assistance in any task.

Best of all, friends offered happy memories of George. Mitzi remembered the night he was running into the sun and rammed a thin aluminum pole in Harvard Yard. He gave a surprised cry, then staggered back 50 feet to meet me and lay down at my feet, bleeding profusely from the nose. George wanted me to hold him for a few minutes before he resumed walking around. I recalled that, rather than get off the bed after 10 minutes to lie on the cold floor, he lay in my arms that entire night.

Cathy remembered the time we were walking through the suburbs and were set upon by an angry 100 lb. Dalmatian that had escaped from someone's backyard. She froze and hid a bit behind her female German Shepherd, but noticed that I instinctively got in front of George and her, prepared to give the Dalmatian a discouraging kick. "I couldn't believe that your first impulse was to worry about George and not yourself."

Although George in his later years was ready to fight with big male dogs, he never killed anything and shrugged off small threats. Cats who attacked him never got worse than a punch in the face or a mouth-hold then a toss. Small dogs who attacked were basically ignored. Children who pulled his hair and tried to ride him were suffered in silence, although he did try to escape them. Just two weeks before George died, exploring with his sister Sky, he approached and sniffed a baby bird that had fallen out of its nest and was walking around the ballfield a few blocks from my house. They let it pass unmolested, and it walked under a fence into a yard where two Siberian Husky bitches killed it within seconds, then didn't bother to eat it. George wasn't that kind of dog.

I remembered our first swim. I took him up to the reservoir on top of a forested hill, about 10 minutes walk from my house. Arctic dogs know that water is deadly, and he wanted no part of it. I dragged him in and then blocked his return to shore. He eventually learned to love swimming and would come when called to the middle of the lake. George would even go swimming on subzero days. His outer fur was so well-insulated from his body heat that it would freeze, eventually thawing into a filthy mess inside the house.

My happiest thought was that I'd spent more hours with George in seven years than most people spend with dogs that live a full life. It took us a year to really get close to each other, but after that George was always with me at work, at home, on many trips, at most parties (my friends would invite him and not me!), at MIT, etc. I gave up sports that I couldn't do with George. I was reluctant to go on trips of any length if I couldn't take him.

George felt the same way about me. To look at him eat, you'd think he loved nothing more than food. Yet if I carried something out to the car while he was eating, he'd leave his food and rush out the door, afraid of being left behind.

Hurt though I was, I remained thankful for a few things. Foremost was that I was not responsible for George's death. If I'd left the gate open and he'd been hit by a car, I never would have forgiven myself. I had taken him to his regular vet just two months ago for a checkup. Even if he had found something, it would only have meant prolonged agony for me and complex, perhaps painful, and certainly ultimately futile treatment for George. I was thankful that I only spent four days worrying that my baby might die. I was thankful that Fate sent us Brenda Griffin to be with us during those last moments. I was thankful that my friends proved to be so loyal and caring.

Bereft of George, I couldn't understand how a lot of people make it through the day. Without a dog, child, or spouse, why don't they ache inside? Friends only go so far, families are often spread far apart, and most love affairs don't last long enough these days to become deep and rich in understanding.

That was in June, 1991. Two years later, I was still asking myself the same questions. I felt kind of stupid grieving over a dog, but then I read a short piece in *Harvard* magazine that claimed it might well be more difficult to get over the loss of a dog than of a family member. "One often has mixed feelings about relatives, but few people could identify serious problems in their relationships with dogs."

I'd go away on a trip or fall in love with a woman and say, "OK, now I've recovered from George's death." Then Life would throw me a curve, and my reaction revealed to me how fragile George's death had left me. I decided to take the trip we were going to take together, Boston to Alaska and back, rather than wait until I finished my Ph.D. This book is about the summer I spent seeing North America, meeting North Americans, and trying to figure out how people live.

Just Married

2

Boston to Montreal, Ottawa, Lake Superior

May 26, 1993

Ted and Eero, two of my best friends, kept me company the whole day. It felt so good to be with them that I began to feel homesick in advance. Eero had finished his Ph.D. six months before and taken a professorship at the University of Pennsylvania. I was happy for him, but MIT seemed much bleaker without his companionship. Eero was just up for graduation and the hooding ceremony.

"Falcons and new Ph.D.s are the only creatures to be hooded," Eero observed.

May 27

Eero and I ran around the house looking for things that might conceivably be useful and threw them all into my minivan until there was no room for a passenger. A brand-new forest green Dodge Grand Caravan doesn't make much of a fashion statement, but it will hold seven cameras, a filing cabinet, Rollerblades, a mountain bike, clothing for four seasons, 50 books, hundreds of audiobooks, lectures on tape, and camping gear.

Every hour further knotted my stomach, accelerated my breathing, and killed my desire to go. After looking forward to this trip in the back of my mind for six years and thinking about nothing else for a month, all the wonderful things I could do with a summer in Boston paraded themselves before my eyes:

- "I could find a Ph.D. thesis topic."
- "I'm never going to make real friends or find a wife if I don't stay in one place for more than a few months. I could probably really get to know some nice people on weekends at the beach."
- "I could write some software and earn thousands of dollars."
- "This would be worth doing with a companion, but where is the glory in wandering around aimlessly alone, like the drifter in *The Postman Always Rings Twice?*"
- "I'm not a loner; why am I running away from the community of friends I've spent 15 years building?"

Memories of butterflies in my stomach before previous trips stiffened my resolve. I joined the evening rush hour exodus from Boston on I-93 North.

After an hour, traffic thinned to the point that I often could see no car in front of me. Virtually the entire trip could have been characterized as "sunset," and it was lovely to see both the scenery and the light change at 65 mph. My doubts about the trip faded with the light, and by the time I entered Vermont, it was hard to imagine why I'd gotten so worked up. A sumptuous dinner and warm reception from some family friends awaited me in Burlington.

May 28

Downtown Burlington has some quaint brick buildings, but the cold rain falling on the gray waters of Lake Champlain didn't inspire me to get out and sample the lakeshore bike path. By 9:15 I was on the Interstate speeding north through beautiful rolling hills, accompanied by a fine selection of classical music on the radio.

"You'll know you are in Canada when it gets ugly," said my friends in Burlington.

They weren't wrong.

God blighted Quebec by scraping a glacier over it until it became nearly as flat as the most boring parts of the Midwest. Vermont's beautiful mountains stop just at the border and are replaced by overworked-looking fields. The divided four-lane highway becomes a dangerous undivided three-lane demolition derby. Bucolic rural towns with lovingly made and maintained buildings melt into cheap, aggressive developments of thrown-together and ugly structures. Rest stops with free coffee and cookies disappear. Most of the radio stations are still pop, but the lyrics and announcements change over to French. In fact, more of the songs are in French than in France itself.

Montreal stands out from the rest of Quebec like a diamond in a plate of mashed potatoes. Gleaming office buildings tower over bustling streets and intimate old neighborhoods. Every part of the city teems with streetlife and the pedestrian rules. The youth hostel is an old townhouse in a particularly nice section of downtown. I checked into a 16-person mixed-sex room, then drove straight to Old Montreal, which was curiously dead. A few tourists shuffled about at a lugubrious pace.

Along with every other tourist, my first stop was Notre Dame with its famous chancel and lovely modern stained glass. If you'd come straight from Paris's Notre Dame, you'd be struck by the small scale, the lack of ambition, and the crudeness of the artwork. However, sitting down to a couscous at a nearby café immediately conjured up memories of Paris. Well-dressed women, tall and lean in their trench coats, hunched together in conversation before stepping outside for a cigarette. Trim men in fashionable sport jackets read neatly folded newspapers. I read the *Mirror,* Montreal's alternative/arts newspaper . . . correction, Montreal's *Anglophone* alternative newspaper: Canadian customs officials are seizing large shipments of American small press books at the border searching for books on homosexual themes; the *Mirror* was banned from a public library in a nearby suburb because of an explicit AIDS prevention article.

Personal ads in the *Mirror* are distressing. Five times as many men are looking for women as vice versa. There is an implicit assumption in all of the ads that only Anglophones need apply (one or two said a French speaker would be OK). Subtlety is out. A "professional black woman is interested in developing a long-term relationship with a single white lawyer." Nobody blushes at explicit sexual and financial requirements.

One woman attempts to raise the tone: "Wild SW artsy fartsy redhead sks (20–40) to enjoy films, muzik, SNL reruns & won't run from the occasional theological chat."

A man rejoins in another ad: "Once my Manuel enters your artsy-fartsy and knocks you out about and thoroughly spermeates U, fini la theological chats."

Despite the "post op transsexual lesbian 33 wait don't faint I'm happy, employed with many interests seeks gay woman for relationship," I tired of the newspaper. After a tour of the waterfront, I sampled the fabled Underground Montreal, essentially shopping malls clustered around metro stations. A movie theater inside shows movies only in French—no English subtitles, not even for a Branagh *Much Ado about Nothing* that had been dubbed. I protested, "In Paris you can see English movies with French subtitles and even French movies with English subtitles." An usher apologetically said, "There are theaters for Anglophones and tourists on St. Catherine Street."

It struck me then that two cities of the mind share one physical city. With separate newspapers, TV stations, movie theaters, neighborhoods, and personal ads, it is amazing to me that an Anglophone and a Francophone can even hold a conversation because they've so little common ground ("Did you see that great article in the newspaper yesterday . . . oops, I forgot that you don't read my newspaper.") Ontario and Vermont have bilingual highway signs, but here even the Byzantine parking regulations are laid out only in French. It feels like lunacy, but Francophones claim it is the only way they can preserve their culture in the midst of 270 million Anglophones.

As an American nursing his junior high school French, I was treated as a neutral in the Anglophone/Francophone war and was able to enjoy the carefully tended exotic culture here. Only French style and high-tech could have produced the shockingly hip Musée de Rire (Museum of Humor), which had opened on April Fool's Day. Automatic elevators and doors unfold the history of humor before visitors wearing infrared audio receivers. Sound bites in the appropriate language are broadcast from invisible transmitters at various locations. Claire, a trench-coated 25-year-old who held herself like the most sophisticated Parisienne, was just behind me in every room.

How did she feel about sharing her city with the Anglophones?

"For me, it isn't a big deal. I've lived all my life in a quiet French-speaking suburb, and I only meet Anglophones when I come downtown to work in a hotel. All the same, I don't think Montreal is so segregated by language. I'm very open-minded."

Does she have any Anglophone friends?

"Actually, no."

Did she feel a strong tie to France?

"I've never been to Europe. I take all my vacations in Florida and the Caribbean. I want to be warm."

I retired to the youth hostel to relax with Samantha, my Macintosh computer. Computers had helped me earn my crust of bread for 20 years, but I'd never been given to anthropomorphizing them. My PowerBook 170 laptop changed the way I looked at machines, however. It was the first machine that liberated me from rather than chained me to my desk. I brought it on a group bike tour in New Zealand. Most of the other cyclists were young German women. Every night I would pull out the PowerBook to write my diary, and they began to joke about it.

"It must be your girlfriend since you insist on spending every night with it. What's her name?"

"It's just a machine."

"She has to have a name!" they demanded.

"Well, I've always wanted a girlfriend named Samantha," I replied. The name stuck.

Samantha was going to keep me from being lonely on this trip by fetching electronic mail from friends around the world. I wouldn't be alone; I'd be sharing my trip with a hundred friends by exchanging personal messages and sending everyone a trip report each week. After ripping apart the hostel's phone system and connecting to the network, I found only a few pieces of mail. I decided that I had to send in order to receive, so I sent messages to a dozen friends and retired to my crowded, poorly ventilated dormitory.

May 29

Despite Gore-Tex weather, I decided to be a megatourist. My first stop was that quintessential British institution, the Botanical Gardens. These are allegedly the second best in the world (after London's Kew Gardens). The Chinese garden was primo, but the Zen Garden in the Japanese section was nothing compared with the Huntington Library's in Pasadena. I walked across the street to the 1976 Olympic complex, which frightens with its vast concrete wastelands and inhuman scale. It contains a small zoo masquerading in the best politically correct style as an environmentalist "BioDome." More interesting was the ride to the top of the "world's tallest leaning tower," which was delayed by Quebeçois labor disputes until 1987. This tower holds steel tethers for the Kevlar "convertible top" to the stadium. It is a darn impressive piece of engineering that enables the stadium roof to be reeled in.

The sun came out, so I biked up to the top of Mount Royal, the source of the name "Montreal." That this 800′ peak gets the title "mountain" should tell you a lot about Quebec topography. My rad L. L. Bean mountain bike drew Patrick and his brother Danny into conversation with me.

"We're French but we think the Frenchification of Quebec is stupid, especially the separatist movement. Young guys like us just want jobs."

We admired the views of the St. Lawrence and downtown, and then I descended for a heavenly *éclair au café*—"French food; American prices." I cycled around the ritzy Anglo Westmount area and back through downtown. So many people were out at 5:00 PM on a Saturday that it reminded me of Italy during the *passeggiata*.

International youth finally appeared at the youth hostel. An Australian couple, an English girl, and two German girls were sitting out on the front stoop discussing America.

"America has the worst racists in the world, and the press covers it up," noted the English girl. "Just read Noam Chomsky."

"I don't know," said an Australian. "I've lived there for a year and found that a black guy with a college degree and a middle-class car is treated like a middle-class person; someone of any race who looks and speaks like a member of the underclass is treated badly."

"Well, that's even worse then, isn't it? They only evaluate people on the basis of how much money they have," retorted the English girl with a triumphant expression.

"I don't know why U.S. newspapers always report on neo-Nazis in Germany but never on all the neo-Nazis in the U.S.," said one of the German girls.

I'd just returned from several weeks in Germany, so I had a cogent explanation for this. "You probably hate your sister more than any minority, but you don't suggest putting her into a concentration camp. Why not? Because much as you might hate her, you don't deny that she is part of your family. U.S. bigots might dislike blacks, but they don't say that blacks aren't American—they can't really imagine a U.S. without all the minorities, and thus there aren't many true neo-Nazis. Germans by contrast have a very clear idea of who is and who isn't German. Dark-skinned people aren't German, even if they've lived in Germany for a few generations. German bigots have a very vivid image of what Germany would be like without the minorities."

"We aren't prejudiced!" exclaimed the German girls. "We don't like foreigners living in Germany who don't work—they just live off taxpayers like us and our parents. But neither we nor the rest of the German people dislike Turks, most of whom work hard." (The front page of the next day's newspaper carried a story from Germany: neo-Nazis burned five Turks to death.)

My friend Klaus told me later that most of these people are refugees and can't legally work because they are supposed to be repatriated to Yugoslavia or wherever once it is safe.

I showered, changed, and ran down to the Place des Arts to L'Ópera de Montreal's *Die Fledermaus*. The 90% Quebeçois/10% American cast was first rate, and the pit orchestra was the full Montreal Symphony Orchestra. The hall seats 2500, about the same capacity as Boston's Symphony Hall, built in 1900. However, the modern Place des Arts was constructed to give each patron much more room, and hence the result is a concrete monstrosity with approximately the same size and acoustics as an American basketball stadium; the singers had to be amplified for the recitatives. Trying to understand the (mostly) German singing and read both French and English supertitles was enough of a challenge to make the evening interesting.

I collected my email just before going to sleep, but nobody had replied to the messages I sent the day before. My friends had forgotten me.

Sunday, May 30

After fortifying myself with a coffee éclair and a bowl of café au lait, I hit the Trans-Canada Highway for the two-hour drive to Ottawa. The road was four-lane divided but a bit uneven and completely devoid of either rest stops or McDonald's! Canadians don't put their money into highways—the Trans-Canada wasn't even completed coast-to-coast until 1962. Rolling hills were the scenic highlight of the trip.

Ottawa comes up out of nowhere, and it is hard to find the center of this sprawling complex of undistinguished modern government buildings. Imagine if Washington's L'Enfant Plaza had been hit by a tornado and all the buildings were set down intact but in a random arrangement. You'll get a surface parking lot next to some fairly nice three-story structures next to a horrifying concrete-and-glass bureaucracy palace next to the new Moshe Safdie-designed art museum. Canada has 1/10th the population of the U.S., and Ottawa is only 1/10th the size of D.C.—about 300,000 people. Queen Victoria was ridiculed for picking this backwater as the Dominion's capital back around 1850, and her critics may have had a point.

Moshe's creation, the National Gallery of Canada, was my first stop. Even before going in, there were many things to note. First, in Washington the art gallery is just "*The* National Gallery," as though it is absurd to contemplate any other. Here they've a more outward-looking perspective and almost apologetically note that it is only "of Canada." Despite some good Lawren Harris paintings, the Canadian collection was ultimately a disappointment. I remembered better Canadian paintings in Toronto and kept thinking that the whole category betrayed a lack of inspiration. Styles were clearly derived from first Europe and then the U.S. There was no coherent way of looking at the landscape, as developed in the Hudson River

School. In fact, oftentimes the landscape appeared confusing or threatening. Canadian artists must not have had the unqualified love affair with their land that American artists had.

Next stop was the Museum of Canadian Photography, which is in plush digs but had only two small shows to present and no permanent collection. Vainly trying to turn a Cirrus card or MasterCard into some cash, I combed the big downtown mall for cash machines. We think that we have the ultimate mall culture, but the Canadians have us beat. Savage weather has led them to mall up their downtowns on an unprecedented scale. Malls aren't out in the suburbs, but smack in the middle of downtown where you'd expect to find individual shops and little streets.

One museum and one mall over quota for my flat feet, I grabbed my bike and I started around downtown, across the bridge to Hull (a French town in Quebec) and then back around the Parliament buildings, which pointed up another big contrast with Washington: the Parliament buildings don't have the same kind of antitank fortifications that our Capitol Hill has. I started up the riverside bike path, but got stuck after six miles. Just as I needed to ask directions, a 21-year-old Chinese girl appeared. She was named Maple by her parents who immigrated here 25 years ago and developed a tremendous streak of Canadian patriotism. In terms of appearance, seriousness, and decidedness of personal philosophy, Maple was the very image of Lily, the first woman I ever loved.

"I'm not happy with our Canadian welfare state. How can people be content to live on government handouts? Why don't they work to have more freedom and live a better life?"

Had she ever traveled to a country where incompetence and lassitude are the norms?

"No. I've only been to Florida."

I recommended she visit Egypt, and that got Maple started about tourism.

"Why would you even want to come to Canada? It is so expensive."

That Americans will promote their hometown, no matter how dreary, I'd always taken to be a sign of idiocy. When Maple wrote off her whole country, I realized that it is just a matter of love. When one loves something, be it rusting car, bulldog, or pot-bellied balding man, it becomes beautiful in one's eyes (that doesn't stop the neighbors from laughing, unfortunately). That love makes the ugly beautiful is a cliché, of course, but that love explains an otherwise intelligent person's faulty opinion of a place is something I hadn't realized. Americans by and large still have that Puritan notion that the land is a gift from God; their bayou might smell like a swamp to you, but they love it.

After parting from Maple, I biked another 12 miles or so up the Rideau Canal to Hog's Back Falls. Towards sunset, there were clouds of insects that it actually hurt to encounter at 15 mph. All the other cyclists were apparently having the same problem, for they rode with their mouths clamped tightly shut and those without glasses winced painfully as they squinted with their heads down.

My teachers in public school unanimously predicted that I would come to a bad end, but even they would probably have been surprised to find me at the Ottawa City Jail. In fact, this has been converted into a youth hostel, and the cells are quite cozy. Everyone there directed me toward the Peel Pub's US$0.70 spaghetti plate. Two 20-year-old French girls from across the river in Hull took an interest in Samantha, and we started to chat. We talked long enough that I learned about their French heritage, which would not have been evident from their unaccented English. It turns out that the Quebeçois in Hull are truly bilingual and fairly well integrated with the Anglophones, in stark contrast to the Montrealers.

Monday, May 31

Nothing but driving. Appallingly bleak scenery obscured by relentless rain for the first six hours. By the time Lake Huron came into sight, the landscape got a bit more interesting, particularly as some of the trees had yellow and red leaves. If there had been more sun, it would have looked like Vermont in the autumn.

What could not have been confused with Vermont was the pitiful state of Ontario farmers. Without U.S.D.A. farm subsidies, they are reduced to shabbiness if not actual poverty. Farmers have to make money on the free market, and they do it by driving ancient trucks and using dilapidated facilities. I couldn't help thinking what a miserable life these people have out here. The landscape is terribly boring, the weather is bad most of the year, there is nothing manmade of any distinction, and there are no people around. If not for their cable TV, I'll bet that people in these 1500-person towns would go stark raving mad. It is no wonder that most are so anxious to up and leave for the cities.

I took one decent photo the whole day: a strip mall with a Canadian Bible Society shop next to an "Adult Entertainment Parlour."

It was just about 9:30 when I checked into the Algonquin Hotel in downtown Sault Ste. Marie, the junction of Lakes Superior, Huron, and Michigan. Prices and elegance level are about 1/10th that of the hotel's namesake in Times Square.

June 1

Determined to make it back to the good ol' US of A, I went straight down Main Street to the impressive, if absurdly named, "International Bridge." One gets a much bigger welcome to the U.S. and Michigan than one gets in Quebec. There are free maps, tourist guides, and friendly chatter. My first stop was a small truck stop for poached eggs and toast. My waitress was a plump healthy bleached blonde.

What was there to see in "the Soo"?

"Pretty much nothing."

Didn't she want to move away?

"Yes, but I'm not old enough. I'm only 16."

She looked tired enough to be 20.

The landscape is a bit on the flat side at first, but the trees were pleasingly multicolored considering the season, and numerous little lakes break up the monotony. Lake Superior is jewel-like, although with the water at 40 degrees and the air at 46, I wasn't tempted to swim. I stopped at the famous Tahquamenon Falls, second largest East of the Mississippi and exactly 1/1000th as impressive as Niagara.

Lunch was in the ore-mining town of Marquette. I settled into the old-fashioned Vierling Saloon for a lemonade, soup, and Cajun chicken salad from the "Heartwise" portion of the menu; yuppie eating has gotten this far at least. I'd been feeling a bit lonely through Canada so I tried to retrieve my electronic mail while waiting for my food.

It should have been a two-minute operation with the Vierling's staff kindly lending me their credit card processor line, but computers somehow never live up to their promises. Friends send email to me at MIT through the Internet, which started

out in the 1960s linking computer scientists doing research for the U.S. Department of Defense. Internet today is a worldwide network linking over 10 million computer users (and doubling every year) from Australia, Japan, Russia, Senegal, South Africa, Israel, Italy, Ireland, Canada, and everywhere in between. The most basic Internet service is email, where a collection of digital information is sent from one user to another. I could mail a chapter of this book, for example, from MIT to a friend in New Zealand in about 30 seconds. Unlike a fax, the actual characters are sent so that transmission is error-free—a piece of email can be forwarded 100 times from one user to another without the little corruptions that would occur in a fax or photocopy. Best of all, the service is free to most users!

Rather than make a long-distance phone call to MIT every time I wanted to read my mail, I signed up with America OnLine, a commercial network with local phone numbers through the U.S. and Canada. For $10/month, I could receive and send an unlimited amount of electronic mail through their Internet gateway, a computer hooked up both to America OnLine and Internet. I simply instructed my computer at MIT to forward a copy of each message to my account at America OnLine, and my friends didn't even have to learn a new email address for me.

America OnLine had a local phone number in Marquette, but somehow Samantha couldn't establish a connection. I was thus forced to assuage my loneliness by conversing with strangers.

Scott, John, Mary, and I talked about life in Marquette. They'd all visited California and John had even lived there, but none would trade the beautiful scenery and weather for their peaceful Upper Peninsula life.

"I'm a mechanic at an ore mine," said Scott in a gentle but almost incomprehensibly thick Upper Peninsula accent, "and John welds at the mine next door. Together the mines employ about 2000 people, and that's the basis of the whole economy for this 50,000-person town."

Scott bought me a drink and asked me to tell him whether his daughter was making the right choice in studying mechanical engineering, specifically human limb replacement.

"She turned down U. of Michigan to go to Michigan Technical University here in the U.P. I work 70 or 80 hours a week so that she can concentrate on making something of herself."

What did he do with his leisure time?

"There isn't much, between working, lifting weights, and riding my big Yamaha."

Mary, the bright-eyed bartender, fielded calls from her 10-year-old son and told me about her life in between. She married a carpenter at 20 and divorced at 24. She had a bachelor's in psychology and was about to go back to school to study nursing.

"My son wants to be a surgeon. He says he's going to support me once he gets his first job. He'd like to have kids, but he hates girls. He talks about us two adopting."

Did she think about remarrying?

"It is difficult to find a suitable man here."

It hit me then: for a guy in Marquette, a surefire pickup line has got to be "I don't work in an ore mine, I don't own a motorcycle, and I don't shoot animals."

Old U.S. Highway 2 runs nearly straight from Marquette to Duluth, connecting the main streets of a dozen reasonable-size towns, mostly stretched along the shores of Lake Superior. An open sky hosted several large cloud banks, with occasional rain and a bone-chilling cold. Towards sunset I began to appreciate the beauty of the Midwest: the separation of earth and sky and the reflections of the evening sky in numerous lakes. Capturing it would require a patient photographer who didn't mind either freezing or being bitten by black flies (or both). I didn't stop to try.

How big is Lake Superior? Thirty-two thousand square miles. Thirty-two times the size of Rhode Island. Four times the size of Israel and New Jersey. Twice the size of Holland and Switzerland. As big as Maine and Ireland. That much I knew, but I wasn't impressed until I drove for an entire day at 60 mph and just barely made it from one end to the other.

3

Minnesota, Sinclair Lewis, and Jewish Bikers

Duluth! The word fell upon my ear with a peculiar and indescribable charm, like the gentle murmur of a low fountain stealing forth in the midst of roses; or the soft, sweet accents of an angel's whisper in the bright, joyous dream of sleeping innocence.

—James Proctor Knott, in the House of Representatives, 1871

Wednesday, June 2

You might have toured Venice in a gondola, trekked the Himalayas, and slept in the Louvre, but you haven't lived until you've been on a cruise around Duluth's harbor. Here is the magnificent industrial face of America that is so often hidden from Easterners. Duluth's industry is storing stuff that comes in by rail from the Heartland and loading it onto boats for shipment to the Great Lakes region, the East, and the World. Massive grain elevators and iron ore docks are numerous, but the city's pride is a new mountain of coal emptied by a $200 million German-built conveyor system that won the Civil Engineering Award, previously given to the Hoover Dam and the Golden Gate Bridge.

Kirk, a good-looking Scandinavian-American college kid, filled me in on life in his hometown.

"Lake Superior is 400 miles long. Even now the water isn't above 37 degrees. When the wind comes off that water, you get a wind-chill of −100 degrees.

The economy is dead flat due to the collapse in iron ore mining. Once I finish my manufacturing management degree, I'm moving to Colorado."

Why Colorado?

"I lived there for one year in high school, and it beats Hell out of Duluth."

Town Babbitts are not giving up without a fight. They spent $20 million to build a container handling terminal; it was used once for a demonstration 10 years ago. They spent $15 million for a fine convention center; it is in Duluth. They turned a brewery on the lake into a Ghiradelli Square upscale shopping mall clone; it was empty.

You won't begrudge the Feds those gas tax dollars if you get back on an Interstate highway after a few days of hard travel on two-lanes. I-35S to Minneapolis makes for lovely driving, if a bit dull due to the lack of towns, hills, lakes, or color in the trees. The only thing that breaks up the monotony are the occasional casinos! That's right, the Indians are sovereign and, with partners from Las Vegas, operate huge casinos for Minnesotans. The result is Vegas without the high-rises and Mafia feel.

The Twin Cities rise up like Oz out of the flat landscape, "divided by the Mississippi River and united by the belief that the inhabitants of the other side of the river are inferior" (Trevor Fishlock, *Americans and Nothing Else,* 1980).

Minneapolis went whole hog for mirrored-glass megaliths, which isn't so bad; Mies van der Rohe looks a lot better after staring at trees for 15 hours. Everything works here to an appalling degree. The bus shelters are beautiful glass gazebos with piped-in classical music (nice Mozart and Chopin; no angst-inducing Mahler here). Buses run on time. People would be shocked to pay a crushing tax burden and receive nothing in return.

This is an UnCity in many ways. A fundamental difference between village life and city life is that primary relationships are replaced with functional relationships. In the village you buy your food from Bob, whom you've known since childhood, who happens to be working in the supermarket. In the city you buy your food from a supermarket clerk whom you could see every day and never learn his name. Minneapolitans haven't understood this. When you walk into a store or a restaurant, people say hello to you, unlike in Boston, where they'd wait for you to approach them and attempt to transact business. Here you relate as people first, as consumer and vendor second.

Moll Flanders would have had a delightful time here: natives are woefully unprepared for the sort of malevolent self-invention that is possible in cities. At a touring performance of *Aspects of Love,* I sat next to a local family. One of the daughters had lived her whole life in Minneapolis; she invited me to come visit the next day and go sailing. Her sister, though so clear of eye and smooth of skin that it would be difficult to believe that anything bad had ever happened to her, had been schooled in suspicion and human evil at Harvard Law School. She remembered an intangible obligation for the benefit of her naive sister and nixed the invitation.

Oh yes, even if you don't care for Andrew Lloyd-Webber, try to see Aspects of Love. *It is more than your average love pentalateral with incest.*

To the extent that anonymity and functional relationships are beginning to prevail here, it distresses people as much as it might have an 18th-century Londoner. I walked into a Vietnamese restaurant in artsy Uptown. The only other customers were Eric and Laurel, who looked a bit like movie actors. Eric had short blond hair over a trim but solid Midwestern build. Laurel had leggy delicate features and a sideways baseball cap over long blond hair. They cooked gourmet food for a bed-and-breakfast in a Wisconsin town an hour from Minneapolis. Although they looked quite happy with each others' company, Laurel immediately greeted me with a friendly "hello," and we started to chat about their life in a community of 175 versus their old life in the city.

Didn't they miss the potential for human contact in the city?

"I lived here for three years, and I think it is much harder to meet people in a city," noted Eric. "Everyone knows everyone else in our village, and people park with the keys in the ignition."

"It isn't as backward as you might think. We have intellectuals in our town who live semicommunally and home-school their children," Laurel added.

How was it working out?

"We were skeptical at first, thinking that kids needed to be socialized with each other, but the home-schooled children seem so much happier, better adjusted, and better educated than factory-schooled children."

I parted from Laurel and Eric with an invitation to drop in anytime they had a spare room.

I thought that the Canadians had us beat in mall culture, but that was before I drove 20 minutes south to the Mall of America, formerly a baseball stadium, where over 12,000 people work and 100,000 shoppers can roam in comfort. The central courtyard comfortably accommodates a Snoopy theme park with roller coaster, and stores have street addresses. It was a disappointment, however. Instead of 10 times as much variety, the mall just has 10 near-clones of each type of store. There are plenty of things that one can't buy in the mall—even Berlin's KaDeWe department store has a broader range of goods.

Friday, June 4

I breakfasted with Al, an attorney originally from Brookline, Massachusetts.

"I came out here to work for the attorney general for a summer and then decided to settle here. What shocked me about Minneapolis was that people had faith in the system. No assumptions were made about the kinds of people who were arrested. It wasn't just the prosecutor's office or the judicial system. People believe in the government school system here.

"Life here is working out for me. My main problem now is that I'm upset with myself. I spent a lot of my life pushing race-based affirmative action, and now I'm beginning to think it is a mistake. I don't think Clinton is making a good choice in nominating a civil rights attorney general."

Al was referring to a vigorous public debate of which I'd been blissfully unaware. My increasing habit of ignoring newspapers was catching up with me. After breakfast, I drove out to St. Paul's Cathedral, a reasonably faithful copy of Rome's St. Peter's. Four mosaics under the dome celebrate cardinal Midwestern virtues: Justice, Fortitude, Temperance, and Prudence. Any Italian will tell you that one of the most important things about St. Peter's is that there are no paintings; it is decorated with more impressive stone carvings, sculptures, and mosaics. Yet somebody incongruously stuck a single oil painting on one of the cathedral walls here.

A quick ride downhill to downtown St. Paul was enough to convince me that St. Paul is Minneapolis's plain sister. The few nice towers are separated by horribly ugly 1950s and '60s concrete monsters. Although St. Paul is the state capital, the taste mavens at the Federal Reserve Bank chose to locate their magnificent modern palace in downtown Minneapolis, upstream on the other side of the Mississippi, 15 minutes away by Interstate. About St. Paul, one might fairly say that there is no "there" there.

Heading northwest on I-94 listening to Minnesota Public Radio's noontime classical program, the rolling hills unfolded before me under patchy clouds and 65 degrees. I ate lunch in Sauk Centre, population 4000, with Wendy and Angie, two recent high school graduates. Solid German-American girls born and raised in this agricultural village, they hated having all of their secrets known and believed. They were ready to move away to college and cosmetology school, but not ready for anything as big and far away as the Twin Cities.

"Life here is really boring. School is boring and really easy. A lot of people drink and smoke dope."

"What about all those 'DARE to keep kids off drugs' T-shirts everyone here seems to wear?" I asked.

"Well, probably more than half of our high school class has tried marijuana."

So they thought Sauk Centre was losing the War on Drugs?"

"I wouldn't say that. I bet we'll be the last generation of dope smokers."

It is usually easy to forget America's Calvinist heritage, but Sauk Centre will shove it in your face. Calvinists take seriously the notion that ultimate judgment is reserved for God. We might be convinced that we are right, but there is always a trace of doubt. This kept anyone from being beheaded in the American Revolution (contrast that with the revolution in humanist France). On the other hand, sometimes showing both sides of the coin leads to bizarre results. In Germany, I'd sometimes asked why there weren't any Nazi museums and people said, "Don't be ridiculous; why would we promote something we should be ashamed of?" Folks in Sauk Centre just wouldn't understand this.

Any town might be proud of a son who won the 1930 Nobel Prize for literature, the first American to do so. But what if he won that prize by writing *Main Street,* a book about how venal and narrow-minded the townspeople of "Gopher Prairie" are? Sinclair Lewis was born here in 1885 and left to go to Yale, travel the world, and settle in New York. His boyhood home is now on Sinclair Lewis Avenue. Main Street has been renamed "Original Main Street." There are banners all up and down this inspiration for Lewis proclaiming its status as such. Weirdest of the weird was visiting the Chamber of Commerce Sinclair Lewis Interpretive Center.

"I thought Sinclair Lewis had particular scorn for the kinds of boosters who formed the Chamber of Commerce. How come they built this nice highway rest stop for their most vicious satirist?" I asked the woman running a biographical video.

"I don't know. I haven't read any of his books."

My AAA TripTik® lavishly praises most of the country through which I'd roamed, but about western Minnesota and eastern North Dakota, the only thing nice they could find to say was that the highway has "good alignment and grade" (i.e., it is ruler straight and pancake flat). It is true that eastern North Dakota is flat enough that radio stations could mount their antennae on the roof of an old Chevy. But there is real beauty in the open grasslands, numerous grass-filled ponds, and extensive sky.

Tonight was my first night camping. There is nothing like a full moon overhead, prairie grass underneath, 20 miles of separation from the nearest houses, and . . . the sound of 2000 Harley-Davidsons. Yes, I was at a motorcycle rally where the free spirits of North Dakota convene, leather-clad and helmetless.

"You can park your cage over there," waved a young woman.

"What's a 'cage'?" I asked.

Everyone broke into uproarious laughter and passed the joke through the local crowd. It turned out that any kind of car is a "cage"—thus did I augment my previous store of biker wisdom and lingo, which had been limited to the aphorism, "Better your sister in a whorehouse than your brother on a Honda."

SINCLAIR LEWIS
INTERPRETIVE
CENTER
CHAMBER
OF
COMMERCE
INFORMATION
OPEN
WELCOME
REST AREA

GOPHER
PRAIRIE
MAGIC KEY
INNS
MOTEL
VACANCY

With assistance from the first passerby, I pitched my tent in the Caravan's headlights. It was after 11:00 PM when I strolled around the main portion of the rally, where people were getting tattoos and dancing to a live band. Free beer lubricated social intercourse.

"Are neo-Nazi groups as popular out here as the media would have us believe?" I started a conversation with a young woman.

"I've never seen any except on television," she replied while sipping a Coke. "Our lives are centered around children, church, movies, and riding our Harleys whenever we can. My husband works as a welder, I stay home with the kids, and we live in a community of 100. It's a very quiet existence."

Has she thought about moving?

"I've lived a lot of places, but North Dakota is the best. A few people say they are tired of it here and talk about leaving, but they *never* do. We don't have the kind of crime and craziness that you see in big cities. People stick together and have a real sense of community."

Determined to stir the pot, I pointed out that Bismarck, the state capital, has only 1/200th the population of Los Angeles or New York and therefore it wasn't surprising that there were fewer and less interesting crimes. My interlocutor wasn't offended, though. Despite their often formidable appearance, North Dakota bikers are a gentle group. Only once was I ever afraid of any of the rally participants.

He was a 6′ 3″, 240 lb. guy with a black beard and a beer gut poking out from under his black Harley T-shirt. At about 7:30 AM, he roughly shook a nearby camper awake and demanded, "Are you a Jew?" The sleeper said, "No," and the big guy moved to the next tent, asking the same question. By the time he got to me, I was concerned, but I nervously answered, "Yes." He said, "Great! We need a tenth for a minyan."

WLA-45

4

Yellowstone

Saturday, June 5

William Bradford described Massachusetts as a "howling wilderness," but that is only because he hadn't visited the Dakotas or eastern Montana. The weather forecast described the 20–30 mph winds as "light." If anyone wants to spend our tax dollars to build a few mountain ranges between the Dakotas and Canada, they'll get no argument from me.

Downtown Bismarck is a compact affair of low-rise functional buildings and one-way streets. I found the YMCA open but the swimming pool closed, so I exercised the desk clerk in finding me a phone jack with which I could connect to America OnLine. There was precious little email, and people whom I'd contacted by telephone said they'd never received the messages I sent. It seemed incredible that a commercial network, equipped with the very latest in hardware and software, could be less reliable than the 25-year-old Internet, which I'd used for 15 years without problems. Furthermore, America OnLine denied that there had ever been anything wrong with their service. Nonetheless, I was becoming convinced that messages were being dropped, vanishing into thin air, something that was theoretically impossible with modern networking protocols. My screams of frustration attracted Steve, a local Lutheran pastor.

"What I can't believe is how America can't engineer a better snack machine," Steve noted, pointing to a massive screw-drive machine in the corner.

"Would you expect better given the paltry salaries engineers are paid?" I asked. "Why would an intelligent person choose to be an engineer rather than a doctor, lawyer, or MBA?" This attracted a few teenage Y employees.

"I can't have any sympathy for people who make $50,000/year," Steve said. "Show me someone else who has a master's degree and earns $12,000/year."

I raised my hand.

After swimming a mile, I strolled out past a couple of little girls alone in the lobby. They said goodbye to me and it stunned me. I'd never had to learn to talk with children because East Coast families so carefully school their kids not to talk with strangers.

I was just getting to like Bismarck when it was time to leave to follow the trail of Lewis and Clark (1806) up the Missouri River's mini-canyon on the Great Plains. With the right light, the grasslands and hills are haunting, and even passing coal mines and power plants were surprisingly clean and appealing. The Missouri is the boundary between the flat eastern half of the state and the hilly western half. Bob, a weathered Pentecostal auctioneer, explained this to me: "The Wisconsin Ice scraped over only the eastern half of North Dakota. The Missouri River was actually formed by water melting off the top of the glacier and hence gives a good indication of the extent of the ice sheet."

Despite torrential rain, I breezed west on I-94 to Theodore Roosevelt National Park in the North Dakota Badlands, which are similar to but much less touristed than their South Dakota cousins. The interplay of clouds and solid rays of fading sunlight at the Painted Canyon overlook was the stuff of photographers' dreams. By the time I hauled out my 50 lb. medium format camera and tripod, the clouds achieved ascendancy and banished the magic.

I camped in the national park, which was rather quiet compared with the biker convention the night before. A car pulled up next to me, and a 16-year-old girl got out of the car clutching a doll. She stared straight at me, and I jokingly said, "Nice doll." The words had barely escaped my mouth before I realized that she was not fully developed mentally and there is a virtue in keeping one's mouth shut. I spent the evening talking with Amber and her parents.

"She loves *Little House on the Prairie* and reads it over and over again. We drove here from Michigan and stopped in Minnesota to visit the actual house.

Amber is just a delight to travel with; she's never had a mean thought about anyone."

I'd never understood what parents meant when they said they were just as happy with their handicapped children as with their normal children. Why weren't they angry with God for burdening them? Amber was the first mentally handicapped child I'd spent any time with, and the evening made it obvious that one could very easily love such a child just as much, if not more.

SUNDAY, JUNE 6

After a quick tour round the national park under the cloudy skies that had dogged me since Vermont, I drove west to Billings, Montana. Montana is where General Custer made his ill-fated 1876 last stand against Cheyenne Indians brazen enough to insist on their treaty rights. Two clerks at the downtown Sheraton, which soars an incongruous 23 stories above the flat town, gave me an education on modern white/Indian dynamics.

"I grew up speaking only English because even my parents can't speak Cheyenne. They went to a Catholic school growing up and would get beaten if caught speaking it. The priests didn't want students talking behind their backs," said the Indian desk clerk. "I went to a much better school than they did. It was massively funded by the federal government, and we had equipment that most schools couldn't even imagine. The only problem was that it was an hour and a half bus ride each way."

How could he think if he spent three hours a day on a noisy school bus?

"Noisy? You don't understand. This was the nicest coach you've ever seen. Big, quiet, with TVs and radios behind all the seats."

Rand McNally calls Route 212 the most scenic road in America. On the map it is the most direct route from Billings to Yellowstone, but crossing 11,000′ high Beartooth Pass complicates matters.

I stopped at a gas station convenience store in Red Lodge, the last town before the pass.

"You'd better call the sheriff's department to find out if the pass is open. It was closed earlier in the day, and it is already 6:30. You don't want to be caught up there overnight, believe me," said the cashier.

Although there was a pay phone just outside and I hadn't bought anything, when I asked for the number she dialed it for me and handed me the phone. The prognosis was iffy, so I pressed on up the mountain under gray skies shedding a slight rain.

The road quickly became tortuously twisty, and the shoulder disappeared to be replaced by jagged, threatening, overhanging rock. Then the real fun started: I arrived in the clouds at about 7000′ and ducked in and out of the mist, passing 8′ snow drifts and enormous frozen lakes (remember this is *June*). After about an hour I began to appreciate the desolate moonscape of pine trees sticking out from the snow, but the strain of driving three hours under these conditions made me happy to arrive at Roosevelt Lodge in the northeast corner of the park.

JUNE 7

Cold torrential rain poured down, and the power failed during breakfast. I curled up with Samantha next to the lodge's fireplace and wrote some Common Lisp code for a research project at MIT. After a couple of hours, it was still raining, but my Puritan work ethic had dissipated; I pulled out *The Joy Luck Club* and listened to Randy, a rugged flannel-shirt-and-boots guy, play Joplin rags on the upright.

"I came here 14 years ago and fell in love with Yellowstone. I didn't go to college so that I could be a reservations agent for TW Services [they manage the park's lodges], but I never want to leave."

What did his family think of his choice?

"They can't understand why anyone would choose poverty and isolation. My brother, whom I'd not seen for eight years, and his wife and kid came to visit me not long ago. They could only find enough activities to interest them for a day and a half."

What about women?

"Nothing going. I'm kind of a loner."

I drove over to Mammoth Hot Springs and walked among the fabulous terraces, residues of various minerals bubbling up with the water. Each terrace forms the rim of a limpid blue hot pool. My memory of them was gleaming white with occasional streaks of bright blues, yellows, and reds, but everything today looked about as gray as the sky. The rain restrained itself while I had a long conversation with an elegant Parisian couple who spoke virtually no English. Madame peppered me with questions about the best way to see the foliage of New England while Monsieur urged her to slow down her rapid-fire French.

TUESDAY, JUNE 8

Morning broke a little less miserable than yesterday, and I was grateful that it wasn't raining or bitter cold. I drove out to Tower Falls with Hiromi, a girl from Tokyo who'd been going to college in Colorado for a couple of years. Thomas Moran made Tower Falls famous on several canvases during his 1874 commission from the U.S. Congress. In the modern world of TV documentaries, Interstate highways, and frequent flyer miles, it was a strain to imagine a time when hiring an oil painter was an essential aid to determining whether the land was worth making our first national park.

Hiromi was about 5′ tall and looked like a sprite tripping down the trail into the canyon, especially by comparison with my 6′ 190 lb. carcass lumbering down into the canyon after her, propelled by the 50 lbs. of photography gear strapped to my back. When we got to the bottom, we were entranced by the noise and spectacle of the snowmelt-engorged torrent plunging 500′ off the side of Yellowstone Canyon. Careful to avoid getting too much spray on my $15,000 Rollei 6008 camera system, I set up my tripod and carefully exposed a few 6 × 6 cm pictures. My career as a Thomas Moran wanna-be ground to a halt when the camera battery died and my spare proved to be discharged as well.

> I looked into a gulf 1700′ deep, with eagles and fish-hawks circling far below. And the sides of that gulf were one wild welter of colour—crimson,

> emerald, cobalt, ochre, amber, honey splashed with port wine, snow-white, vermilion, lemon, and silver-grey, in wide washes. The sides did not fall sheer, but were graven by time and water and air into monstrous heads of kings, dead chiefs, men and women of the old time. So far below that no sound of its strife could reach us, the Yellowstone River ran—a finger-wide strip of jade-green. The sunlight took those wondrous walls and gave fresh hues to those that nature had already laid there. Once I saw dawn break over a lake in Rajputana and the sun set over the Oodey Sagar amid a circle of Holman Hunt hills. This time I was watching both performances going on below me—upside down, you understand—and the colours were real! The canyon was burning like Troy town; but it would burn forever, and thank goodness, neither pen nor brush could ever portray its splendours adequately.
>
> —Rudyard Kipling, 1889

> It is my opinion that we enclose and celebrate the freaks of our nation and of our civilization. Yellowstone National Park is no more representative of America than is Disneyland.
>
> —John Steinbeck, *Travels with Charley,* 1962

We continued upstream on the rim of Yellowstone Canyon until we came to the magnificent pair of waterfalls at its front. On my first trip to the West, I'd found this canyon much more beautiful than the Grand Canyon and would have described it as Kipling did. Under gray skies, it was still beautiful, but the magic was gone.

Driving back, we encountered a herd of parked cars. Ten elk dotted both sides of the highway, and 15 tourists exchanged theories.

"It's a female moose."

"Es ist ein Hirsch." (It is a deer.)

"They're elk!"

Conversation halted when I pulled out my friend Henry's 300/2.8 lens. This baby comes in its own Nikon suitcase and costs and weighs about as much as a good used car. With the massive sunshade attached, it looks like a bazooka. The bull elks' antlers were covered with fine fuzz that glowed white when backlit by the afternoon

sun. Fujichrome Velvia was pumping through the camera at a prodigious rate when I remembered Galen Rowell's comment that "there are 100,000 images of elk in the files of stock agencies worldwide."

Yellowstone is enormous. Hiromi and I had driven about 100 miles yet seen barely a corner of the park. Stefan, a blond German youth with an absurdly loaded bicycle, was nearly keeping up with us as we stopped at successive turnouts.

"I flew into Los Angeles a month ago, so I'm quite used to the mountains and the extra weight by now. The rain has been a problem, though, and I've had to seek shelter day after day. Fortunately, Americans have been very kind, and I've found a free place to sleep almost every night."

What was the part of the trip he liked least?

"I don't like watching news about Germany on television here. A few days ago I saw something about five Turks being burned. Why can't they concentrate on positive aspects of Germany?"

Keeping in mind that networks have only 22 minutes for the news, exactly what everyday German scene did he expect would be as compelling as Nazis burning people alive?

"I think your media has an anti-German bias."

June 9

Pleasant though the lodge was, my cabin at Roosevelt was freezing and smelled like mildew. I decided to move to a nearby campground. As I was throwing all my yuppie toys into the minivan—the fruit of years of living purely for myself—Carl, a 37-year-old Mormon engineer from northern Utah, was packing up his five obedient children and solicitous wife. Their procession into a Ford Taurus wagon taught me what it means to be a real man. Carl looked a bit weathered but was confident that he'd lived his life well. He told me about the two years he took off college to proselytize for the church, something that only about 20% of Mormons do these days, and estimates he made 20 to 40 converts in two years of knocking on doors in the South.

After returning to Yellowstone Canyon, drawn by a half-kept promise of sunshine, I drove up the Yellowstone River toward Lake Yellowstone. A large collection of white pelicans had gathered on an island in the middle of this 100-yard-wide river. These birds have long orange/yellow bills, but in mating season the top of the bill is crowned with a bizarre flat square sexual appliance. Whatever they do with this is probably illegal in Massachusetts, but I didn't see them use it.

Lake Yellowstone is a large medium-blue lake surrounded by snow-capped peaks—imagine Lake Tahoe with geysers on the beaches. At lunch, I introduced myself to Arleigh, a mysterious Coloradan.

"Be careful with all that silver jewelry around the sulfur fumes. In New Zealand's thermal areas, they say it will tarnish."

"Thanks."

I decided to turn on the charm: "Say, you *are* wearing a lot of silver. If your teeth were black, you could join a primitive tribe."

Arleigh and I swapped "who can get dumped in the cruelest possible manner" stories. I won easily by quoting a German girl who greeted me after an 18-hour international flight: "Philip, there are things about you that I don't like, and I don't love you enough to overlook them. I made up my mind a few weeks ago, but I still wanted you to take time off work and come see me. I didn't want you to be able to say about me that I didn't have the courage to face you."

Arleigh was on a solo photo-safari through the West, trying to figure out whether to attend graduate school.

"My basic problem is that I'm good at too many things and therefore can't choose any *one* thing."

I arrived at Old Faithful just in time for the eruption of the eponymous geyser. Two friendly happy couples waited alongside me and asked me why I was using the Rollei.

"Because the negatives are four times the size of a 35mm negative. Where are you from? Germany?"

"No!!! We're Dutch!" they exclaimed in horror.

"Sorry. How long are you staying in Yellowstone?" I asked, hoping to paper over my faux pas.

"Only one afternoon. We're on a three-week New York to San Francisco bus tour, and we have to get to Salt Lake City tonight. It is our first trip to the U.S., and we want to see everything."

"That's absurd! You can't even see California in three weeks."

"Americans see Europe in three days," they retorted. It sounded vaguely logical at the time, but later I wondered what it would prove even if it were true.

Circling back towards Roosevelt, I came upon a group of bison with two playful calves. As I photographed the two calves nuzzling in the fading light, Arleigh stopped to say, "Hi." We agreed to meet the next night at her campground. Driving on a road cut through high mountains, past waterfalls, and through lovely meadows would ordinarily be enough to ensure human felicity. Yellowstone National Park doesn't stop there, but offers up wildlife with practically every mile of its enormous loop road. I yielded several times to coyote and once to a majestic bull moose.

THURSDAY, JUNE 10

After a day of photography and chatting with tourists, I rolled into Norris campground under a beautiful blue sky to find a campsite just two "doors" down from Arleigh. My next-door neighbors were Tom, a muscular fellow from Maine, his wife Pam, still sporting her thick Boston accent, and their beautiful Samoyed dog Kashi.

"We gave up our apartment in Portland and just hit the road. Pam is a Traveling Nurse and I'm a respiratory therapist, so I can usually pick up day jobs in the same hospital. Whenever we run short on cash, Pam calls up Traveling Nurses and finds out what's available."

Kashi was a real sweetheart, and I played with him for about an hour. The thumping sound made by slapping his powerful chest and the feel of his rough guard hair on my cheek evoked George to the point that I almost cried. I thought about how the trip might have been with George and felt a physical ache.

Yellowstone National Park has one legal mountain bike trail, an old 4WD road just north of Old Faithful. It winds through a beautiful flat valley studded with dead trees standing up amid tall grass and steaming pools. There wasn't a soul in sight, which suited me fine because I was trying out my new "clipless" pedals. These essentially weld the rider to the bike, which is great for maximum pedaling efficiency. Unfortunately, I hadn't figured out how to get out of them. People in Minneapolis had laughed as I screamed and fell halfway over at each red light.

Sixty-degree cold, a gray sky, and a savage headwind made the first six miles hurt a bit, but I forgot my fatigue when I encountered a large herd of bison. They were probably accustomed to cars, but a mountain bike excited their curiosity and they began to follow me. I recalled the Park Service's graphic sign of a person being gored by a bison and remembered the brochure given to every park visitor: "Bison injure more people than any other animal in the park. They can run 30 miles per hour."

I also remembered that my mountain bike's gears allowed me to go only 25 miles per hour. On pavement.

Fortunately, no heroics were necessary to get back to the car—Arleigh informed me later that most bovine creatures are nearsighted and hence tend to approach unfamiliar objects just to get a better look—and an extravagant meal at the Old Faithful Inn felt like Heaven compared with the thunderstorm that had gathered outside.

It was just getting dark when I met Arleigh at the campground. We went across the street to the extensive Norris Geyser Basin, a treeless moonscape of blue, white, and yellow. We sat alone at midnight just a few steps from the Echinus Geyser as it sent water 100′ and steam 500′ into the air for over an hour. Sitting 100′ from Old Faithful in the daytime seemed like a Disneyland attraction compared with this haunting primeval experience of Nature's power.

JUNE 11

Arleigh and I photographed the Porcelain Basin moonscape under overcast skies and then moved out of the park to the west. One elk and some distant bison stopped all of the cars coming into the park, but people leaving the park were jaded and sped by at 50 mph.

Yuppie culture has penetrated deep into the mountains, at least to judge by the hip clientele of the West Yellowstone, Montana, bookstore/espresso bar. Arleigh didn't want to spend big bucks at the yuppie pizzeria, so we ducked into a white trash café. My sandwich came drenched in mayonnaise, which nauseates me. I apologized to the waitress for not specifying "no mayonnaise," and she took it back to the kitchen shaking her head just a bit.

"I can't *believe* you forgot to ask for no mayonnaise!" exclaimed Arleigh contemptuously. "If you don't like mayonnaise, how could you possibly forget?"

A bit later, Arleigh proposed that we travel together for awhile.

"To tell you the truth, Arleigh, I like to nurse the illusion that women find me attractive. It depresses me to spend too much time with a woman who I'm sure turns up her nose at me, even if I'm not that interested in her. Usually women don't say anything that punctures my little balloon of desirability, and I can be happy thinking they find me attractive while they are perhaps thinking the opposite—this could go on for years with some women. However, the contempt you expressed for me over the mayonnaise incident forced me to realize that you wouldn't find me attractive even if I were the last man on Earth."

"You are the most insecure man I've ever met."

A fairly scenic drive, studded with a bull moose and thundershowers, brought me to Butte, Montana. Once one of the richest towns in America, the population has been shrinking since the copper mines closed. Downtown bears the mark of easy fortunes and is strewn with once-fancy shops and magnificent bank buildings. At the Berkeley Pit overlook a tape-recorded voice told me about the tons of copper (plus 700 million oz. of silver and 3 million oz. of gold) that had been taken out of this 1800′ deep hole. The pit is now filling up with water, reversing the effects of years of drainage and threatening to turn half the town back into a swamp. Furthermore, the tailings contain enough arsenic and cyanide to make this one of the most notorious Superfund sites. A livable house in town costs between $6000 and $18,000. All of the town's museums are free, everyone is helpful and nice, and it would have been lovely if I hadn't gotten the impression that people were almost desperate to attract visitors and new residents.

I ate an inexpensive Mexican dinner consumed amidst the faded splendor of what was once a marble bank lobby. I talked to a 30ish guy who was living modestly in Butte working 50 hours/week at WalMart.

"You wouldn't see that in Boston," I remarked. "You'd have to work 80 hours/week at a job like that to have even a chance of living decently. It would hardly be worth your while to slave away just so that you could live as well as people on welfare."

"That's why we don't have homeless people in Butte," he concluded.

Listening to an AM station from San Francisco, I pressed on to a youth hostel in Missoula. The program seemed to fulfill every Easterner's stereotype about San Francisco; it was an interview with a bartender who'd written a book about how to meet women. The best line he'd overheard was this:

"You look just like my first wife."

"Really? How many wives have you had?"

"None. You're the first."

SATURDAY, JUNE 12

Missoula is a bizarre cross between Western misfit loner culture and Cambridge/Berkeley granola culture. The University of Montana dominates the town's mountainside and sets a tone different from that of Billings or Butte. It is tough to say why, but Missoula beguiles and traps people despite one local's observation that it was an "easy place to get by, but a hard place to get ahead." I planned to stay one night and ended up staying three. Missoula helped me understand John Steinbeck: "Montana seems to me to be what a small boy would think Texas is like from hearing Texans."

The owner of the film lab was a grizzled Canadian who came here in '68. He does E6 in two hours and dispenses philosophy at the same time.

"I've lived just about all over the U.S. and don't have any interest in the landscape anymore. I don't understand why people spend so much time and effort photographing it. In fact, even the local scenery doesn't do much for me. I'd be just as happy if I never saw a picture of Yellowstone or Glacier."

How come he stayed?

"Well, it beats living in the East. All I can say is that people in New York are obviously easily amused if they were willing to pay $50 for a shallow Broadway show and then spend three hours discussing its fine points."

Not all the natives are blind to the charms of the local landscape. Lynn, raised in Kentucky, came here for a summer photo workshop and stayed to pursue dual careers as a massage therapist and fine-art photographer.

"It is a great place for immigrants because the locals are so lacking in skills. A lot of the people doing massage here don't have any formal training at all. Unfortunately, a lot of folks here, especially men, are prone to excessive drinking. Social customs are pretty different from what I was used to in Kentucky also. People here don't seem to invite each other over for dinners or whatever."

Walking into the local espresso/fresh-squeezed juice bar, I attempted to hold the door for a 25ish woman and she utterly refused to precede me, giving me a look rather akin to what Clarence Thomas might expect walking into the lesbian/feminist bookstore in Cambridge. Fortunately, people inside were friendlier, and I hadn't looked at the full tables for more than 10 seconds before Dawn, a wistful 22-year-old super-Midwesterner-but-dying-to-live-the-adventurous-Western-life, invited me to join her.

Dawn had dropped out of Indiana University and moved to Cleveland because her ex-boyfriend wanted to kill her (Credentialist Society footnote: her Mom was much more upset that she might not finish school than she was concerned about her safety). Dawn was the kind of beauty that men build worlds around with the assumption that they can bend her to their will. When they discover that she has a will of her own, their world falls to pieces and hence she is a natural heartbreaker.

"I just hated the Midwest because it was so boring. I freaked my family out by moving here with no job in sight. My boyfriend and I just drove out here one day. He gets on my nerves now—we're sharing a two-bedroom apartment but not as boyfriend/girlfriend anymore."

Why didn't she move out? Wasn't it a bit painful for both of them?

"We still have nearly a year to go on the lease."

In the evening I drove out to the national forest to camp by a stream. No fee, no people, no noise but the gurgling of the stream.

SUNDAY, JUNE 13

A perfect blue sky and reasonably warm day! After a long drive up a winding narrow dirt road that passes through beautiful high mountains, I reached the ghost town of Garnet. This was a gold mining town inhabited periodically between 1860 and 1940. The few tourists were greeted by Frank Fitzgerald, who was born here in 1912.

"My father owned one of Garnet's 13 saloons. The saloon and a lot of the rest of the town burned down, though, and everyone moved away. I went into the Navy for four years during World War II. What I really loved were books, so I studied English Literature at University of Montana under the G. I. Bill."

Was that good for a job back in those days?

"Oh sure. I taught high school English for years in Idaho and eventually became a librarian. That was the most fun."

What about now?

"I live up here in the ghost town during the summers and down in a village 10 miles from here in the winter. I've got a telephone there."

I told Frank about my plans to visit Alaska.

"I always wanted to go there but never managed it somehow. You're really doing it the right way. I'd never go except by ship or car; you just can't see anything from an airplane."

JUNE 14

Anxious to make the most of Nice Day #3 of this trip, I went mountain biking in the distressingly named Rattlesnake Wilderness area, which starts just a few miles from downtown Missoula. I saw a few snakes, but wasn't too worried because I figured they were more likely to bite the bike than me. I rode about 16 miles up a stream into a valley surrounded by steep forested mountains. At a charming waterfall, I stopped to chat with Lea, a Utah native who'd moved here from Atlantic City.

"I just felt at home in the West. A lot of Easterners have trouble adapting socially here because they don't understand the subtleties of our culture. There is also

SIZES
34-36
38-40
42-44
46-48

some discrimination against immigrants from other parts of the country. One of my best friends is a short Italian-American woman from Boston. She hardly has any friends and feels that her coworkers discriminate against her."

What brought Lea to the woods?

"Stories. I work in a bookstore and think about stories when I hike. When I get to a nice place to stop, I sit down and write for awhile."

I met Dawn again at a funky riverside coffeehouse in downtown Missoula. She scanned the paper for organizations looking for volunteer work.

"I'd like to do something to help other women. Maybe an abortion counseling or advocacy group."

She told me the real story of her crazy obsessed lover back in Indiana. She'd been with him not because she liked him but because of his money and friends, especially his connections with a local rock star. When even his appurtenances weren't enough to hold her any longer, he kidnapped her and imprisoned her in an out-of-town motel room.

"He'd bugged my apartment and played me a bunch of tapes, demanding to know who were the people talking. The sound was so bad, I couldn't even figure out what they were saying. He was paranoid and kept drinking. 'Go to sleep if you want,' he'd say, 'I won't touch you.' 'Yeah, right,' I said.

"The odd thing was that he was most suspicious of Bill, who lived upstairs from me. Bill was just a friend at the time, but he's the guy I came out here with.

"I managed to escape once, but he chased after me and caught me. I was screaming, but nobody came to help me. Then, after 12 hours, he just drove me home with no explanation."

5

Marriage, Montana, Mountains

June 15

I discovered why the season in Glacier National Park doesn't start for another month. Rain, rain, rain. I hid from the rain at breakfast, sitting next to an extended Western family.

"It is kind of funny how incompetent all of our sons are at math," said a mother.

"Well, I guess it doesn't matter. It's a shame they need to get through trigonometry to get into a four-year college," a relative replied and everyone nodded agreement. Apparently four years of government by the "Education President" (George Bush) wasn't enough.

I hid from the rain at midday, hunkering down in a lodge with a biography of John von Neumann, developer of modern computer architecture, game theory, and important portions of atomic bomb theory and practice. The book had been thrown together by Norman Macrae, former editor of *The Economist*, and the writing was ponderous, but the vitality of turn-of-the-century Budapest intrigued me. To hear Macrae tell it, nearly all of America's cultural and scientific achievements post-1930 may be attributed to Hungarian Jews fleeing from Germany's expanding shadow.

Macrae's book also shattered one of my misconceptions about Einstein and the Manhattan Project, which I'd thought he'd instigated. It turns out that Einstein's letter to Roosevelt in 1939 was delegated to a do-nothing committee. It wasn't until Vannevar Bush, who made his reputation as an MIT professor, went to Roosevelt in late 1941 that Roosevelt authorized the project.

When the rain slowed to a drizzle, I ventured out into The Cedars, a forest carpeted with impossibly green glistening ferns. The truly dedicated photographer wasn't discouraged by this weather, but I used my scuba diving camera. Lassitude overtook me after an hour, and I returned to the lodge to read, eat, and sulk before retiring to my wet tent. I hadn't found anyone to talk to, and this was one of the lowest days of the trip.

June 16

I drove over the Logan Pass on Going to the Sun Road, named after one of the tallest nearby peaks. The "Going to the Sun" name dated back to Indian times but in view of the heavy cloud cover I felt that the name had been chosen as a personal torment for me. Heavy snow had kept the road closed until just a few days before, when it was opened by dynamiting a 60′ snowdrift (so don't complain the next time you have to shovel the driveway).

Glacier is remarkable for the skinniness of its mountains. A tall ridge here was scraped out on both sides by thick glaciers during the ice age, thus leaving the mountains fit and trim with near-vertical walls. It is a testament to human arrogance that someone decided to build a road right up the side of one of these vertical walls.

I rolled into the East Glacier youth hostel and was quickly swept up into a social whirl. Joe, a combination mountain man and 1960s throwback, appeared with his two angelic sons and invited us all to his campsite on Two Medicine Lake for a bonfire. It was amazing that someone so bearded and unkempt could have such neat children, but the kids mostly live with their mother and we never got a look at her. Joe was probably most interested in the company of Ali and Michelle, two Australian

22-year-olds, but he graciously included me, Sky, a divorced Christian drifter, and Ronen, recently released from the Israel Defense Forces.

Ali and Michelle cooked me dinner, and we headed out to the bonfire together, where Ronen charmed everyone with his engaging smile, remarkably good English, and vast repertoire of Beatles and Paul Simon songs. We all sang while Ronen strummed his guitar and Joe accompanied on fiddle. The atmosphere of conviviality seemed surreal after the loneliness and despair of the day before.

Ali and Michelle crystallized a few thoughts I'd had about Australia. A bartender in Cairns told me that Australians together in his bar talk cooperatively but that Americans together all try to talk "on top of each other." Ali and Michelle certainly exemplified the openness and lack of snobbery that is refreshing in Australians, but they also illustrated some of what repels me about the culture.

First, Ali and Michelle put absolutely no stock in education. They'd just as soon be with someone ignorant as learned. When I compare them to women I've met who are insistent on finding Harvard-educated husbands, I find the lack of credentialism salutary. However, I can't shake my conviction that people are obliged to develop their minds.

Second, I had the car radio tuned to a classical station, and Ali just blurted out, "I don't like classical music." Most Americans would hesitate to admit that or would express a desire to learn more about a taste that is allegedly refined. I gave Ali credit for candor, but her lack of striving went against an American tradition of self-improvement that goes back at least as far as Ben Franklin. Shouldn't people always strive for better educations for their kids and even for their adult selves?

THURSDAY, JUNE 17

Ronen and I hit the road. We had plenty to talk about while traversing Going to the Sun Road under a brilliant blue sky. Ronen had just separated from Laura, a beautiful non-Jewish American girl he'd met in the San Francisco youth hostel. They'd been instantly attracted to one another and had a great time together for some weeks. Nonetheless, she thought she couldn't live in Israel based on what she'd heard; he thought he couldn't live in the States.

"I think I could succeed here and probably make a lot more money than in Israel. But I'd miss my friends, Israeli humor, and my extended family. Also, I think Americans are shallow and insincere."

Just because "I'd love to, when I have some time" means "Maybe when Hell freezes over"?

"No. It is deeper than that. I love Laura, but I've seen her kiss hello to women and later tell me how much she hated them. Anyway, international romance is tough."

I contributed my theory that international romance is easier than intranational romance in some respects. Two Americans might be compatible in deep ways but won't date each other unless they are sure they match up in dozens of extraneous categories. For example, a Cambridge liberal might categorically refuse to date anyone who hadn't voted for Bill Clinton, an Ivy Leaguer might look only at other Ivy Leaguers, or a Connecticut WASP might restrict himself to Daughters of the American Revolution. A foreigner, however, isn't going to care for whom an American voted, might not be sure what schools are in the Ivy League, and probably wouldn't understand our cultural subtleties enough to distinguish "the right sort of people."

Under a perfect blue sky, Going to the Sun Road took one's breath away. There is a drama to this landscape that is comparable to that of Yosemite Valley. After a hike to a high mountain lake, we drove back to the Logan Pass (top of Going to the Sun), and I hopped on my bike to ride down 3000′ in 12 miles, averaging 25 mph without pedaling. Ronen drove the van down to the bottom, and I greeted him with a grin that took hours to fade.

"How can you go back to Israel after seeing this?" I demanded.

"Now you sound like the million Russians who've come to Israel in the last two years. They don't want to serve in the army, claiming to be 'immigrants' who will move to America as soon as they can somehow manage rather than 'olim' who have chosen Israel for spiritual reasons."

"Maybe they miss the 'big country' feeling. Russia may be an untenable place to live, but it can point to a lot of achievements in science, literature, art, and architecture," I offered.

"That's possible, but we give them $7000 per person the minute they arrive. A family of four would get about half the price of a nice condominium. Instead of being grateful, they just complain about how nasty and difficult everything in Israel is."

Ronen hitched a ride back to the youth hostel, and I went back over Going to the Sun once more. Sunset's reddish glow and shadows lent some poetry to what had been stunning but inhumanly stark. With company from a gentle mountain goat, I took some photographs before heading down to my campsite.

June 18

A crisp clear morning. Kirk, a divorced father, and his 12-year-old daughter Amy were sitting down to breakfast at the next campsite and immediately invited me over for some delicious pancakes. It was distressing to see the pain of a broken marriage and a kid being batted back and forth between two houses. Kirk and Amy live in Indiana, where Kirk is a machinist for the Navy. Kirk reinforced my belief that Americans aren't content to let themselves go intellectually and live the easy life: "I don't have a television because it is too addictive and would keep me from doing other things."

Once back at Logan Pass, I hiked through a blinding white landscape on a slippery packed snow trail to Hidden Lake. I shared the view of the frozen lake (this was mid-June!) with mountain goats and two Berliners, Wolfgang and Angela. They'd rented a motorhome in Los Angeles, stopped in a supermarket, and the cashier was the last American they'd talked to at any length. Though university-educated, their knowledge of American history and culture had a few gaps.

"One thing I've been wondering for weeks," asked Angela, "why do Indians need reservations? Would they be killed if they left them? What about white people, are they ever allowed on reservations?"

I moved over to the Many Glacier region of the park for the night. It is indeed possible to see many glaciers in this area. When the park was created, there were 100 glaciers, but 50 have subsequently melted away. It turns out that there was a mini ice age about 3000 years ago and that all the glaciers of Glacier National Park will likely be gone in another 100 years.

SATURDAY, JUNE 19

While taking the tourist cruise boat around Josephine Lake, I spotted a large tan form moving among the green trees. It was headed up a hiking trail after a couple and their two young children. I tapped our captain on the shoulder and asked him what it might be.

"There's a bear behind you. There is a bear behind you," our captain hollered at the oblivious hikers. They turned their heads back for a moment and then started to move along at a brisker pace. The 400 lb. black bear just loped along the trail and then up the mountainside a bit to eat berries or whatever. It was my first time spotting a bear in the wild, although Kleanthes, a friend back at MIT, had predicted the scene almost perfectly weeks before my trip:

"Daddy, shouldn't we be carrying a gun in case of bear attack?" asks a worried child.

"Oh no, son. The wilderness is our friend. Bears are shy and gentle," explains the father, a nice liberal Sierra Club member.

"Yeah, right," growls the bear as it devours both child and father.

I drove back to East Glacier and dropped into a counter seat at PJ's Diner. I shared the counter with Joseph, a leather-faced Blackfoot Indian wearing a Stetson hat. He was proud of his tribe's aggressive heritage, noting that most of the tribe was of mixed blood because they kept stealing other tribes' women. In fact, I recalled that Sacajawea, the 16-year-old Shoshone who accompanied Lewis and Clark, had been previously separated from her tribe by the Blackfoot.

Joseph was pretty well versed in Massachusetts politics, and we swapped Ted Kennedy jokes:

> Woman interviews for a job with Kennedy.
> Kennedy: "You realize that you'll have to travel a lot."

Woman: "That's OK."
Kennedy: "And that to save money we'll have to share a hotel room."
Woman: "OK."
Kennedy: "And on some nights we will be having sex."
Woman: "That's all right."
Kennedy: "Do you have any questions?"
Woman: "Well, if we are having sex, I might get pregnant and I wonder what arrangements you've made for obstetrics insurance, maternity leave, etc."
Kennedy: "Don't worry; we'll cross that bridge when we come to it."

Heather, the waitress, was another young woman whose face appeared to have nothing written on it. Yet her unscarred face belied another horrific story. One of four whites in a high school of 400, she married an Indian at age 19 and was now 21 and getting a divorce.

"I didn't realize it, but my husband had a violent temper. Spouse abuse is quite common in the tribe, both by men against women and even vice versa. I'm going back to college now. My father gave me a taste for reading, and I was a star in high school before marriage derailed everything."

As I left, I noticed a sign by the counter: "Expecting the world to treat you fairly because you are good is like expecting the bull not to charge because you are a vegetarian."

6

Freezing to Death in the Canadian Rockies

Saturday, June 19 (continued)

"Do you have any guns?" asked the officer at the Canadian border, and then I was into Alberta. Some of Montana's friendliness evaporated as every gas station sprouted an enormous "washrooms for customer use only" sign. The landscape was completely flat, but I'd seen so much of the Rockies that being able to set the cruise control on 60 and relax was a relief.

Approaching Calgary from the vast emptiness of Alberta, one enters into the kind of capitalist cornucopia that Americans so badly wanted to show the average Russian back in the Cold War days. One mall after another hits the traveler with a relentless intensity, and some of the stores are overgrown to an absurd degree—supermarkets are four times the size of Boston's largest, for example.

It was rather hard to even see the city at first, so obscured was it by an enormous cloud of pollen whipped up by the wind. Closer up it reminded me of Minneapolis: big glass skyscrapers climbing from nowhere and rapid reversion to flatness. There is one unmistakably Canadian feature, however, a tall cylindrical tower with radio antennae and a tourist restaurant. It must say something about Canadian psychology that they've built special round towers in Montreal, Toronto, Calgary, and

Vancouver when most U.S. cities manage nicely with ordinary square office buildings. What would Freud have said?

Calgary's youth hostel was full of the usual Germans and Australians, plus a few surprises. Hauling out Samantha earned me the company of a couple of delightful Japanese girls, Keiko and Kazuyo. My position on the couch later earned me the company of Judy and John, an unlikely pair of Northern Irish and plain-old-Irish. Having spent a whole life reading newspaper accounts of troubles between the English and Irish without having actually visited Ireland, I was surprised to see them so friendly with each other and even the English travelers.

"Is Judy Protestant or Catholic?" I asked John.

"I've never asked," he replied. "The fights that you read about in the newspaper are carried on by poor uneducated scum. It isn't relevant to our lives."

Late in the evening, I chatted with Yvonne, who had prepared for her trip in the best British tradition. I told her that I'd been confused by a highway sign an hour south of Calgary: "Head-Smashed-In Buffalo Jump."

"Oh. I read all about that back in London. There are two cliffs over which Indians used to drive bison. One Indian would play a dead calf and one would play a live calf and blend in with the herd. At some point, they'd both jump up and start shouting, and the confused buffalo would just jump off the cliff. The place gets its name from a warrior who wanted to see the jump from the bottom and, predictably, got his head smashed in by the 500 falling buffalo."

Sunday, June 20

I biked about 20 miles around Calgary today. My first stop was the modern and scrubbed Chinatown. The people looked an odd combination between corn-fed Iowan and typical slim Chinese. They were definitely thicker than your average Chinese-American. I took some dim sum to Prince's Island Park and ate on the grass before heading out to bike up the Bow River.

Calgary is a knot of slick modern urbanity that disintegrates after just a few blocks. One is abruptly swept from soaring 30-story glass tower to one-story auto repair shop. Riding back through a nasty 20 mph headwind, I stopped at the downtown interconnected multistory shopping mall complex (is there any Canadian downtown that lacks one?) and bought a few trinkets. I finished my tour in Kensington, Calgary's equivalent of Greenwich Village. It lacks only sizable bookstores or really pleasant cafés to be a contender. In fact, many parts of it look rather like suburban U.S. strip malls.

It is a beautiful hour's drive from Calgary, the shopping mall amidst the plains, to Banff, where the young, beautiful, rich, and Japanese shop till they drop. One approaches the Rockies first indistinctly and then, before one realizes it, one is in a river valley with mountains all around. I arrived in Banff around 7:00 PM and, with plenty of daylight in front of me, headed straight down a mountain on my bike. The trail was terrifyingly steep, especially for a man surgically attached to his bike with Shimano SPD pedals (into which one clips special cleated shoes akin to ski-boot bindings). The river flats were populated with beavers, take-no-prisoners mosquitoes, elk, and pleasant Swiss-Germans. One of the first differences between the U.S. and Canada is that elk here are regarded as a major hazard. In Yellowstone, one is presented with dramatic imagery of bison launching tourists into orbit with their horns, but elk are painted as being fairly benign. Here the park service has gone so far as to close certain trails because during calving season the elk are allegedly out for blood.

Monday, June 21

I met Keiko and Kazuyo again and gave them a ride down to the mirror-flat Vermillion Lakes. Just five minutes from the town's shopping malls, we saw elk, a diving osprey catch a fish and lose it, and a bald eagle calmly perched in a tree. As we drove up the main highway toward Lake Louise, it occurred to me how very sharp the peaks are here, in many ways more dramatic than most of the American Rockies or the Sierras. A lot of mountain enthusiasts prefer the look of the landscape here, although rock climbers don't appreciate the unsafe sedimentary rock.

As we wound our way up the mountain to Moraine Lake, I recalled a German encyclopedia's first photograph under the entry for the United States: "USA. Morain Lake im Banff National Park in den Rocky Mountains." Wherever you stand on the

controversy of which country owns the lake, it glows with an eerie turquoise light, reminiscent of Poe's poem "The City in the Sea." This glow persists even on a gray day like today and is caused by light bouncing off fine rock dust in the water. The dust is scraped off mountainsides by the glaciers that feed the lake.

On the lakeside path, we talked with aristocratic Mexicans who said they'd traveled a lot in both Canada and the U.S. and were treated better in Canada. Keiko thought the 35-year-old graying man and 20-year-old woman were father and daughter, but in fact they turned out to be boyfriend and girlfriend—apparently there's hope for all of us overaged bachelors south of the border.

We drove through a hard rain to Lake Louise and soon came upon the magnificent Chateau Lake Louise, built in stages starting 100 years ago by the Canadian Pacific Railroad. Like everything else in the deluxe tourist trade here, it now caters mainly to the Japanese. I had a nice chat in the chocolate shop with Brian, a ski/mountain bike bum who'd come here for the bohemian life seven years ago and had grown by imperceptible steps into a *petit bourgeois* merchant. I bought a couple of Lindt liqueur chocolate bars, but they later proved to be emasculated alcohol-free versions of the slices of Heaven one gets in Switzerland.

Lake Louise itself is a green jewel backed by a glacier-covered mountain, and we had a nice walk around the shore before moving on to a riverside campground. We pitched the tent and ate a picnic while killing enormous mosquitoes whose heavyweight carcasses presented a disposal problem once they'd been crushed. Toward the end of a pleasant after-dinner stroll in the fading 10:45 PM light, I stopped to talk to a couple of scruffy hitchhiking guys. Keiko and Kazuyo looked a bit scared and retreated 50 yards or so down the road. They said they'd avoided taking a package tour because they wanted to drink in the local culture during their 10 days in Canada. I wondered how they could do that if they were afraid of the local people.

I stripped naked and crawled into my sleeping bag while my companions were in the bathroom. When they returned, Keiko wryly noted that I was "shirtless."

"Only animals sleep in their clothes," I responded.

Keiko and Kazuyo got into their sleeping bags fully clothed.

June 22

Even after 24 hours together I never felt that I achieved any real understanding of Keiko and Kazuyo's motivations or aspirations. Their English was pretty good and they were about my age, yet a huge gulf yawned between us. What did they hope to accomplish in their lives? Where did they want to be in five years? What was fundamentally important to them? I couldn't have begun to say.

After shaking off the cold and damp of the campground, K, K, and I shared a breakfast table in the youth hostel café with the radiant blond blue-eyed Thomas, a Dane at the end of an 11-month round-the-world odyssey. Despite the 50-degree drear, Thomas was all set to rent a mountain bike and hit the hardest trails in the area. I was still trying to read *Main Street,* having acquired it at the Sinclair Lewis home in Minnesota, I was exactly three states and one province behind in my reading. I would have been happy to sit out the day reading, but Thomas shamed me into activity. Leaving the Japanese girls to make their way north to Jasper, we donned our cycling gear and sallied forth. I wore a Gore-Tex jacket over a cycling jersey, cycling pants, Lycra leg warmers, and SPD shoes. Thomas wore longish Eurostyle drawstring pants, a sweatshirt, a plastic jacket, and loafers (!). I lent him some extra biking gloves and a fanny pack for his camera.

Thomas and I started up the trail, he with the natural vitality of youth, me with seasoned wisdom, some biking conditioning, and technique. I got up all the hills, albeit not without some bitching and moaning as we climbed 600′ in a raw wind. My ears hurt from the 50-degree cold and the 20 mph headwind, and I lost sensation in my exposed fingers after just 30 minutes. Thomas had no such complaints, but he was standing up in the saddle and trying to overpower the slippery slopes. By applying power in bursts, he just threw gravel all over the place and didn't move his bike forward. I spun my cranks smoothly, swiftly, and relentlessly, staying on the saddle, and didn't have to suffer the indignity of walking.

While gazing at the quiet forest and occasional river valley vistas and ducking hailstones, we shared some interesting conversation. Thomas is 19 and has just finished the Danish equivalent of German *Realschule* (a kind of high school that is a more practical alternative to gymnasium). He's going to do military service, one of an unlucky 25% or so who lost a lottery, and then go on to university (still free) in Denmark.

A few months before, I'd met a Czech émigré architect in Prague who was just returning after eight years in Denmark. He'd described the Danes as unwilling to accept immigrants in their social lives or even in the first rank of jobs.

"Your friend is right. Danes aren't accepting at all, especially of Turks who stubbornly cling to Islam. After one or two generations they should convert to Christianity. That's the religion of their new home," replied Thomas, who added that he himself was not a religious believer.

"There aren't even many Danes who feel genuine sympathy for the Turks being killed by neo-Nazis in Germany. We don't like the idea of Germany invading Denmark again, but most Danes think it understandable that Germans are irritated by an alien presence in their midst. I've got some Turkish friends and am probably more open-minded than the average Dane."

I'd never before realized how unusual the U.S. and Canada are in not having an official religion.

Lake Louise is probably the world's nicest youth hostel, and the lounge is superplush. Relaxed after the ride, I chatted with Ralph, a schoolteacher from Prince George, B.C. Ralph teaches correspondence school for 40 fourth through seventh graders. Some live in the middle of Nowhere, B.C., but quite a few live in reasonable-size towns and have simply exercised their option to learn at home.

"Disciplined students need about three hours/day to get through the standard curriculum. They send me papers by mail. I used to teach in a traditional public school, and correspondence school is better when a child has reasonable parents."

Ralph was playing Risk with his German cousins, and I was struck by how different Canadian and German cultures are. Despite having similar genes, their mannerisms and even their facial expressions were completely different. Ralph looked rather contemplative, questioning, and studious, his cousins stolid and self-satisfied. I would never have guessed that they were related.

Thomas and I had planned an afternoon ride, up 1200′ to Lake Moraine. I felt rested, but the 30 mph wind driving a cold rain made me think twice about riding up an exposed ridge. Thomas saved me from having to wimp out: "I'm dead tired from this morning's ride. I can't go."

I spent the rest of the day exploring the various commercial offerings of Lake Louise, letting Thomas cook me a pasta dinner, and chatting with folks in the hostel lounge. One doesn't meet too many bona fide English émigrés in the U.S. anymore, and therefore it was interesting to speak with Jean, a 61-year-old woman born in Liverpool. At age 19 she'd refused to marry a nice Jewish guy of 31, not because of his ethnicity but because he was too old. She has spent the rest of her life regretting this decision, for the English army officer that she did marry proved to have an upper lip that was just a bit *too* stiff.

"My sister was a war bride living in Vancouver, and she convinced me to come over with my 6-year-old son Malcolm. I had to leave an older daughter in England with my husband. He was so angry with me for emigrating that he cut me and Malcolm off entirely."

Was her sister able to support her?

"Oh, we started to fight after three months so I moved to my own apartment and got a job as a secretary. Malcolm was a precocious chap. When he was only 7, he gave a dramatic lecture on Rommel's North African campaign during show-and-tell. The teacher called me up to say that he'd inspired her to undertake her own study of WWII desert combat."

At the age of 40, Jean married a man in the construction business, and they quickly had a daughter, Alisa. Her husband worked himself into an early grave, and Jean and Alisa were left on their own once again. They aren't close for a variety of reasons, one of which is that her mother can't abide Alisa's academic lassitude.

"Alisa is very beautiful. That's the basic problem. Why should a girl study if men are sending her flowers all the time? Now Alisa's fat charmless friend Dawn . . . *there's* a great student."

Ralph and I talked until 1:30 AM. Ralph told me about the year he took off from U.B.C. to study at a fundamentalist bible college in California. Education had

been poisonous to his faith as he failed to reconcile the idea that the New Testament was divinely inspired with the dramatic inconsistencies in the accounts by different apostles. A deeper feeling that the Jewish/Christian god might not be such a great one had been inspired by his reflection upon all the violence that had been allegedly authorized by this god. Ralph went all the way back to God's instructions to the Jews to wipe out the Canaanites after the Exodus from Egypt. Moving forward, he looked at all of the wars allegedly authorized by God, e. g., against the Muslims, the Jews, various heretical sects and pagans, etc. A god that was right at home in the violent ancient world looked a little out of place in the modern love-in of British Columbia.

Ralph switched gears and ran down the Israelis for their intolerance in refusing to give citizenship to Jews for Jesus.

"You expect better of them because of your implicit assumption that Israel is somehow controlled by people like yourself, i.e., with good English middle-class values. Remember that a good chunk of the population stems from the 500,000 Jews kicked out of Arab countries after Israel won the 1948 war. They came from the bottom strata of poor Arab societies such as Iraq and Morocco and spoke no European languages and hardly even any Hebrew. They might be Jews in name, but they were Arabs in culture. How tolerant do you expect Saddam Hussein or any other product of Arab culture to be?"

"Well, not very," Ralph admitted.

"Since a large proportion of Israeli voters are either bona fide Arabs or Jews from Arab countries, you should in fact be surprised that Israel is any more tolerant than Iraq," I said. "Bruce and I took a cruise down the Nile with two German sisters. Rita said, 'Why don't these stupid people learn how to serve soup? Every day they spill the soup in the same way, even though we actually went over once and showed them the proper way to do it.' I said, 'Rita-baby, look around at the people carrying sugarcane on donkeys. Does this look like Germany? If everyone here tried to find a better way to do his job, Egypt would be as developed as Germany.' Even when evidence to the contrary is staring them in the face, people have a hard time shaking the assumption that everyone else thinks as they do."

One of the things about Ralph that surprised me the most was his sentiment against Asian immigrants: "Canada shouldn't admit Cambodians and Vietnamese because they haven't the language or job skills required to succeed here. They've no choice but to turn to violence and gangs."

"That's one nice thing about the U.S.," I responded. "We may be dependent upon Asians to engineer our cars and produce our consumer electronics, but we are able to home-grow most of our criminals."

We parted on the subject of women. Ralph is 39 and in conflict: "I'm drawn to Christian women and simultaneously repelled by their anti-intellectualism and inability to think."

JUNE 23

Back in the town of Banff I was struck by the preponderance of Japanese. In America, our reputation for violence keeps scenic areas from becoming Japanese colonies. Another thing that draws Japanese to the Canadian national parks is their policy of limited laissez-faire rather than monopoly. For example, a wealthy Japanese tourist on a rainy day in Banff National Park is able to visit a Polo shop and dozens of similar enterprises; in Yellowstone he or she would be sitting in a 100-year-old lodge lobby listening to Stephen Foster songs. It struck me that there is really no part of the U.S. where one feels a stranger in one's own land. Chinatown is exotic, but most of the customers in a restaurant are Chinese-Americans rather than tourists from China. Even in places that have no industry other than tourism, there are just too many intra-U. S. tourists for foreigners to ever constitute a majority.

A government worker expressed the prevailing local sentiment: "It is eerie going into a shop where the salespeople don't speak English. There's good sport to be had imitating the more ridiculous Japanese and Germans, but I prefer to live 20 miles from here in a little village that is 'more Canadian.'"

At 7:00 I ducked into *Jurassic Park* at the town's quad movie theater. I'd spent a good part of the day fighting with America OnLine. They were acting in the best tradition of Corporate America: deny everything; obfuscate; treat the consumer with bland indifference—we have lawyers and he doesn't. Nonetheless, I had finally proved that the problem lay with their system, the shining product of hundreds of millions of dollars of investment and the latest crop of 22-year-old C hackers. Just as I was trying to think of a way to save America's children from turning into the kind of pathetic drones who write C code for companies such as America OnLine and Microsoft, Steven Spielberg came to my rescue.

Spielberg paints the definitive portrait of the early 90s industrial computer programmer: fat, bitter, underpaid, and unsatisfied. His job security comes from a nasty collection of 2 million lines of C code that nobody will ever understand or get to work properly. He won't get the steaming pile of offal to function correctly, but by continuous intervention he can keep his employer living in hope and forking out $50,000/year.

June 24

I hit the road intending to go straight toward Jasper, but quickly picked up a hitchhiker who convinced me to explore adjacent Yoho National Park first. Takakkaw Falls, though puny by Yosemite standards at a mere 1000′, is one of Canada's highest and most easily accessible. On the way there, I got a great view of the back half of a train going into a mountainside and the front half coming out going the opposite direction. This spiral railway tunnel is part of Canada's coast-to-coast rail link.

Lunching in Field, where the tourism industry is confined to the postcard rack at the general store/café, I met Steve, a long-haired lean outdoorsman. Steve came here in 1970 from California and stayed to make his living skiing. Not for Steve the life of saying "bend ze knees, five dollars pleez" to the coltish daughters of the elite. This loner prefers mountain solitude and makes his living climbing up into the high passes on special skis in the winter, looking for potential avalanches. When Nature threatens highway or railroad, she is given a little push by a 105 mm howitzer antipersonnel round. Several thousand of these $600 babies are often expended in a season around Banff/Jasper.

Steve will be 50 soon and has some slight regrets about being left out of the materialism party, but he feels younger and more vital every day thanks to eating strange ancient Chinese herbal foods and absorbing the philosophy of Deepak Chopra. Ironically enough, Chopra is an endocrinologist who used to work at New England Memorial Hospital, about one mile from my house in Melrose, Massachusetts. We listened to one of Chopra's lectures integrating psychological and immunological research, insights from the trances of ancient Vedic seers, and the Maharishi's Grand Unified Theory.

Chopra goes back to the Hubel and Weisel experiment exposing kittens to only horizontal or vertical lines; they ended up able to see only the kinds of lines they'd been exposed to. We function with a neural system that functions only to reinforce what we were exposed to in the first place ("premature cognitive commitment"). We commit ourselves to a certain reality, and then literally our nervous system serves to reinforce conceptual boundaries we've established whether or not the world really looks that way. Without acknowledging Bishop Berkeley, he offers many of the same criticisms of the "superstition of materialism," i.e., that since all we have available to us are sensory experiences we can't know what the world is really like. Chopra claims that technological developments will overthrow the superstition, although he doesn't say how.

Chopra claims that there are receptors to neurotransmitters not only in the brain but also in cells throughout the body. "T-cells, lymphocytes, etc. eavesdrop on what we are thinking!" Also these cells make the same chemicals as the brain when it thinks. It is tough to tell the difference between the immune system and nervous system. Even stomach cells have this property of sensitivity to and production of brain chemicals. "So people who talk about a 'gut feeling' or 'heart ache' are in fact speaking literally. It is wrong to confine the mind to the brain."

Chopra cites a recent study that concluded that the two most important risk factors for death from coronary artery disease are self-happiness rating and job satisfaction. More people die of heart disease at 9:00 AM on Monday than at any other time. Chopra cites a study using medical students during exam periods that found stress depresses Interleukin-2 levels and even DNA cell activity. If you feel exhilarated, Interleukin-2 levels go up. Since one anticancer treatment with this drug costs $40,000, a ride on a roller coaster can produce millions of dollars of Interleukin-2.

Space and time themselves are artifacts of sensory experience. In India, there were tribes where people just got to be better athletes with age, doing better at 30, 50, 60! Guys plateaued rather than deteriorated. Blood pressure got lower and heart rate slower. Lungs became higher capacity. (At this point I became rather skeptical; all the older Indians I'd seen in photographs looked to be in pretty sorry condition.)

It was nearly 4:00 PM by the time I extricated myself from Steve's hospitality and Chopra's lilting exhortation to drift off into a "field of information." With six hours of daylight ahead, I poked my way up the fantastic Icefields Parkway, stopping every now and then for a little hike, a turquoise lake, a look at the jagged peaks, and once to watch a good-size black bear and her two cubs mosey through the woods.

My most interesting roadside conversation was with another Philip. He works for the Canadian parliament's foreign affairs committee and observed that a principal difference between Americans and Canadians is that racist Americans will openly admit their prejudices whereas racist Canadians will try to disguise themselves.

"Well, at least you guys made a real contribution to the politically correct lexicon. I saw a newspaper article referring to immigrants as 'New Canadians.' It made me think that somebody regards anti-immigrant sentiment as a serious problem," I noted.

"We let in proportionately far more immigrants than the U.S. I think that explains some of the animosity. We also have a lot of social disruption right now. The Atlantic provinces [New Brunswick, Newfoundland, Nova Scotia, PEI] are going to empty out because there just aren't any jobs. Russians and Portuguese routinely defy the 200-mile limit and have depleted the fish stocks so much that the Canadian government imposed a ban on all fishing. It destroyed a whole way of life."

I spent the night at the Columbia Icefield Pass, where I chatted with a bunch of Canadian environmentalist painters. Pam, who's lived all around North America, is upset that Canada lags the U.S. in terms of environmentalism. "People still have the attitude that the country is big enough that they can use up part of it and move on. What upsets me the most is that we sell huge forests to the Japanese and then they clear-cut them."

FRIDAY, JUNE 25

Occasional patches of blue poked through the low clouds, and a raw wind made me happy to be inside a "Snocoach" on the Athabasca Glacier, just one of the rivers of ice that flow out of the enormous "lake of ice" that is the Columbia Icefield. One rides in a $480,000 vehicle with six 6′-diameter tires over the four-mile-long, half-mile-wide, 100′-thick glacier, which is surrounded by 11,000′ peaks with their own little glaciers. We got out of the Snocoach for 20 minutes at the top of the glacier but were cautioned not to walk too far due to the large crevasses.

Next stop was the viciously overpriced café at Sunwapta Falls. Laissez-faire within Canada's parks leads to great values where there is competition and shameless ripoffs where there isn't. Leif and Darryl, two 26-year-olds, proved that one need not be from California or have gone to college in order to be "rotated 45 degrees into the complex plane." Despite their prosaic highway department day jobs, they were so New Age that Los Angeles seems positively Old World by comparison. It is not important to work for success; the important thing is to get it. One gets what one wants by having a pure true desire. Any failure is explained after the fact by the statement, "He didn't really want it."

"So the Tacoma Narrows Bridge blew down because its engineers didn't have a pure desire to see it stand? And the George Washington Bridge remains because its engineers did have a pure desire?" I asked.

"Now you are getting it," Darryl encouraged me.

Luck has nothing to do with anything. I couldn't poke holes in their theory with any of my questions. Bill Gates is rich because he had a purer desire than the other folks hawking 1950s-style operating systems back in 1982, not because he was lucky enough to be picked by IBM. Poland suffered not because it was unlucky in being in between Russia and Germany but because people there all have subconsciously chosen to be oppressed.

"Most of the Poles are probably there because they made some bad choices in a previous life," Leif noted. "You can't escape karma."

Modern medicine is a complete fraud. People make themselves sick by suppressing anger and can heal even advanced cancer by thinking appropriate thoughts. Psychic healers can pass their hands over your ruptured appendix and bad stuff is magically replaced by good stuff. Sinclair Lewis showed that broad prairies don't breed broad minds, but after all of these New Age conversations I was beginning to think that high mountains breed high, i.e., "stoned" minds.

Feeling a little stoned myself, I drove north toward Jasper, stopping to look at waterfalls, a herd of mountain goats with two tiny lambs, and a large grizzly bear. Mr. Grizzly was impassively surveying the highway from the edge of the woods (maybe 75′ back from the road), perhaps thinking about crossing. The five or six cars that quickly gathered to gape presumably changed his mind, and he just turned around back into the woods.

Jasper itself is less a Japanese colony than Banff and more a traditional center of mountain hedonism. The public swimming center here not only has a fine workout pool, but also a great Jacuzzi and a huge waterslide! I swam one kilometer and then rested my bones in the Jacuzzi with two guys from Frankfurt. If I'd thought Germans who tour the U.S. parks in their hermetically sealed motor homes had little affinity for American culture, that was because I hadn't met those visiting Canada. These two are spending five weeks in Canada, but are scrupulously avoiding the U.S. because, as they cheerfully averred, Americans are all slobs.

I spent the rest of the evening reading *Main Street* (432 pages) and writing a few postcards for the Internet-challenged. Canadian stamps are a bit larger than their U.S. counterparts, graphically more complex, bilingual, and in relatively understated colors. One might infer that Canadians are used to more space, are attuned to subtler distinctions, and are more understated. Unfortunately, they also appear to be inefficient as postage is 50–100% more than in the U.S. and Canadian stamp packaging is much more wasteful. One wouldn't think it possible, but Canadians actually have a lower opinion of their post office than we do. They complain that the workers are unionized and absurdly overpaid, that mail is delivered at a glacial pace, and that much mail is actually lost.

I encouraged them to look on the bright side: "You hardly ever have a post office shooting spree here."

Saturday, June 26

The morning broke clear and blue-skied, and I rode up the Whistler Mountain gondola to a fabulous view. I walked around a bit up there and finished *Main Street*. There was a 15-minute wait to get back down on the gondola, and I chatted with a family from Arkansas. I told them how surprised I was at the number of New Agers in the Canadian Rockies.

"Too many people call themselves New Age who haven't adequately studied. I've been looking at it for two years; there's a lot of truth to it," responded the husband, a churchgoer and video rental mogul.

What about Bill and Hillary?

"Just wait until the end of his term; the public will love Hillary then," he gushed. "The only people in Arkansas who haven't met Clinton are those that didn't want to."

Later in the day, I biked out to the Valley of the Five Lakes, taking advantage of the Canadian national park system's liberal attitude toward mountain biking.

"Only three mountain bikers in Jasper can get up all of the hills on that trail," cautioned the Lycra-clad animal in the bike shop.

Just as I was thinking that the ride wasn't nearly as tough as advertised, the Mother of All Hills appeared out of nowhere. It was probably 70′ high and rose at a 20-degree angle; rocks and roots made it especially gnarly. I snapped out of my SPDs about one quarter of the way up and huffed up the rest. After about two miles I came down a hill, and a group of four young hikers jumped two feet into the air.

"We thought you were a bear! We saw two bears half an hour ago."

I climbed up about 600′ with frequent small depressions through fairly closed-in woods before coming to the first of the five lakes. A very impressive little sign with distances to various lakes and the highway convinced me that I couldn't get lost on this trip. Each lake was a dark green little treasure, and the ridge trail afforded views over each lake to the big mountains around Jasper. I'd kind of lost count unfortunately and continued along the shore of the fifth lake when I should have turned. The trail became an obstacle course of huge logs, rocks out the wazoo, and eventually impossibly steep slopes filled with trees. I backtracked and fought my way out the usual route, which was no picnic either.

I finished the 16-mile ride past swimming beavers and grazing elk.

Sunday, June 27

Under drizzly skies I packed the soaking wet tent and went over to HavaJava for breakfast. The front page of the Edmonton Sunday paper carried two stories most prominently, one on securing a child seat in an automobile, one on a recent U.S. missile attack on Iraqi intelligence headquarters. The 20-year-old tragically hip U. B. C.

student behind the counter was upset about how the poor Iraqi-in-the-street would see this attack.

"Why didn't the U.S. ask permission from the U.N. before doing this?" she asked.

Perhaps because of the U.N. committee that has spent the last 25 years trying to define "aggression"?

"Americans are so much more aggressive than Canadians. I don't know any Canadians who think violence is justified, and I've hardly met any Americans who are as progressive," she observed.

"If 99% of the Americans you've met are traveling in motor homes, I'm not surprised," I responded. "You should visit the People's Republics of either Berkeley or Cambridge if you want to find kindred spirits."

"I'm studying political science, and I keep coming back to one question: Why are there still people in the world building the atomic bomb?"

I don't think she'll be able to use my response in her bachelor's thesis: "Perhaps it was because the last people to use it won a war?"

After a brief rainy hike through Maligne Canyon, I had a long soak in Miette Hot Springs. I chatted there with a couple from nearby Edson. He works processing sulfur beads for industry and voiced very similar political views to what I'd heard across the U.S. In particular, he feels more like an inhabitant than a citizen.

"All the political power is in Ontario and Quebec. It doesn't make any difference for whom one votes. We've not had a real choice for 20 years; both parties are the same."

You are now Entering
WORLD FAMOUS
ALASKA HIGHWAY
ALBERTA
POOL
ELEVATORS LTD
DAWSON CREEK
FARMERS MARKET

7

EDMONTON TO THE ALCAN

MONDAY, JUNE 28

After being tortured by America OnLine, the finest flower of 1990s corporate computer technology, it was a joy to use Internet, the bastard child of the spare hours of underfed computer science graduate students. Because Internet is free, people tend to be generous with network hospitality and the University of Alberta computer science department was no exception.

I settled into a machine vision laboratory with a couple of young women from mainland China. Dozens of messages were waiting for me at MIT that America OnLine had lost! My friends hadn't forgotten me after all. I spent the whole day responding to friends, posting questions on bulletin boards, refining chapters of this book, and printing.

The fabled West Edmonton Mall was but a pale shadow of the Mall of America. Built in three phases, it is more a haphazardly connected group of unrelated buildings than one coherent structure. Just being inside was disorienting even when one's local surroundings were pleasant and familiar. It is allegedly slightly bigger than Mall of America, with 16,000 employees and a quarter of a million shoppers on a peak day.

There are three nonstandard attractions in the mall. The first is a theme park with a frightening rollercoaster. It looks much more violent than Space Mountain and throws people through standard and twisting loops multiple times. The second attraction is an intricately tangled collection of waterslides. The third is a submarine ride complete with a Kodak-funded replica of the Santa Maria. The variety of shops seems a bit greater than in Mall of America; I managed to buy Plato's *Symposium* dialogue, which had eluded me in bookstores spread across 2000 miles.

"May I please have a $3.50 frozen yogurt and an ice water?" I asked a taciturn middle-aged woman. She gave me the yogurt, took my money, then refused to give me the ice water.

"You have to buy an Evian. Two dollars," she grunted.

I wanted to throttle her, but I reflected that it would have confirmed the American reputation for violence.

Edmonton was an easy place to leave—"Houston without the charm" is how I took to describing it. Laissez-faire zoning plants skyscraper next to vacant lot next to two-story shabby hotel next to four-story Canadian downtown mall. Calgary is definitely Alberta's class act. Edmonton is so ugly that people are apparently discouraged from taking photographs: despite having roughly the same population, Edmonton does not have the high quality photolabs that Calgary has.

Perhaps people, when confronted by ugliness for long enough, eventually learn to close their eyes. They avoid being horrified but are forever after blind to beauty as well. Thus an art historian from Edmonton can't appreciate a Vermeer as well as an accountant from Paris. Just walking around the streets of Paris for a lifetime has built up in the accountant a capacity for aesthetics.

I hit the road at 10:00 PM for an eerie drive northwest through the prairie. Even at 2:00 AM the northern part of the sky never really got dark. When I was finally ready to sleep, I just pitched my tent by the edge of desolate Sturgeon Lake and collapsed.

Tuesday, June 29

Grande Prairie's Leisure Center was nearly a clone of the lovely aquatic center at Jasper: big Jacuzzi, water slide, and warmish training pool. The coin-operated lockers were exactly the same design as in every other swimming pool in Canada, and I began to get some of the same "small country" feeling that I'd had in New Zealand. In the U.S. there is such a plethora of products that one never gets used to any one design.

In *Main Street,* prosperous farmers and merchants in Gopher Prairie, Minnesota, often up and move to Alberta to build a life exactly like the one they'd left behind. That was in 1912. Lewis might have been on to something:

> Grande Prairie has Tremendous Potential—slick 1993 visitor's guide
>
> Watch Gopher Prairie Grow—opening slogan for James Blasseur's "boosting" campaign in *Main Street*

Grande Prairie's indifferent architecture and city planning would have outraged and depressed Carol Kennicott. The two downtown streets have been made one-way so that cars might better roar through. "Downtown" is a collection of one-story shacks housing nondescript shops. The one building that stands out is an absurdly huge 14-story black glass monolith whose owners were too embarrassed even to stick their name on the top.

Even if all the residents of Grande Prairie have had their aesthetic senses assaulted, their hospitality remains intact. Shelly, a young mother, noticed my Massachusetts plates and stopped her truck to chat. She'd just been laid off from her job at Safeway and was delighted to be collecting Canadian unemployment while her husband worked. She'd never been to Alaska herself and spoke a bit regretfully about the reduction in free time imposed by her two daughters. Shelly encouraged me to pursue my dreams and live life a little differently: "Too many people get stuck in a rut and never do anything interesting."

At Mike's Lube & Clean, where I had the Caravan's oil changed (6800 miles), a burly mechanic suggested I go to the Pepperpot Café where I could get a "nice quiche and salad." I'd listened to the occasional Canadian try to distinguish Canadian culture from American, but kept thinking that both countries are the product of English middle-class culture spread out into a vast wilderness. Even if the U.S. and Canada had been established on separate planets and there were no cross-border influences, they might look similar to an outsider.

Kameel Nasr's *The World Up Close* provided lunchtime reading and a perspective on this issue. Nasr chronicles his adventures as a lone cyclist in places that are truly different from North America: Tanzania, where people would rather wade through mud for a lifetime than spend an afternoon throwing together a dock; Morocco, where hashish merchants formed human chains across the road to force Nasr to stop and buy their wares.

Nasr's list of good countries to visit: the U.S. because you can get a free bed and dinner every night just by asking nice; France because, well, it's France; Italy because of the bike racing culture; Nicaragua under the Sandanistas because it is a utopian paradise despite U.S. oppression and the only Latin American country where officials don't demand bribes; Algeria because it feels damned peaceful after one has been assaulted by merchants in Morocco; Egypt because of the Bedouin hospitality and despite drivers' bizarre habit of blowing their horns nonstop.

Countries to skip: the U.S. because it has too many mountains; Germany because 12-year-old boys will yell at you for breaches of etiquette; Israel because people are rude to everyone and suspicious in particular of a Palestinian-American cyclist/author; Yugoslavia because people there make Israelis look positively polite; India because it is too hot and disease-ridden; non-Nicaraguan Latin America because people have been turned into bribe-taking impoverished despairing malcontents by U.S. oppression; China because it is easy to get lost using a Mandarin phrase book to tour Canton.

The road from Grande Prairie to Dawson Creek, Mile 0 on the Alaska Highway, rolled through fields of brilliant yellow blossoming canola seed (née *rape seed* but renamed *CANada OiL* seed by some advertising genius). Once in Dawson Creek, I joined the fleet of motor homes at the Alaska Highway Museum and absorbed the story of the highway from an old film.

Work on the highway began just four months after the Japanese attacked Pearl Harbor. Pentagon strategists decided that the next logical Japanese move would be to invade Alaska: "Whoever controls the Aleutians controls the Pacific." Before obtaining Canadian consent, the project was announced in Washington and troops were sent to Canada. Two weeks later, the Canadian prime minister announced his government's approval of the project without alluding to the Americans jumping the gun.

> At this spot in the spring of 1942 at the height of WWII, the U.S. Army engineers began the construction of the overland route to Alaska. Nine months

> later at the cost of over $140,000,000 the road was completed. This is a road construction feat unsurpassed in modern times. 11,000 troops and 16,000 civilians were employed in this project.
>
> There are 133 briges [sic] & 8000 culverts embodied in the 1523 miles of gravel highway. The rattle and roar of the mighty bulldozer was a source of amazement to both the local white man and the northern Indian.
>
> Over this lifeline to the Northwest, thousands of troops, food & war supplies have been transported. In more recent times, the mighty H-bomb was known to travel this route. It was maintained by the Canadian Army until April, 1964. Maintenance was then taken over by the Dept. of Public Works, Ottawa.
>
> — sign in front of Alaska Highway Museum

Now we could move men and materiel up to defend Alaska should the need arise (or evacuate the defeated and terrorized populace in case things didn't go our way). According to the film, two hundred people died building the road but urban geeks learned to fish and hand-feed bears, so it wasn't all for naught.

Six months after Pearl Harbor, the Japanese in fact invaded the Aleutian Islands, hoping to establish a supply/staging base there. Thanks to valiant American/Canadian resistance, the Japanese were repulsed and we were able instead to use the Aleutians as an air base for the first bombing attacks on Tokyo (ultimately bombed so badly that proponents of dropping the first A-bomb there were forced to concede that it wouldn't do much additional damage).

Throughout the War, the highway was continuously improved although never paved. American salesmanship convinced the Canadian Army to buy the road in 1946 for $77 million. Tired of maintaining the gravel road, the army tried to give it away to the province but they wouldn't take it until 1962. By the 1970s enough motor homes were making the run that somebody got the brilliant idea of paving the road, and now it is mostly paved.

Fortified with information and snapshots of the Mile 0 milepost, I struck out through farms and then some of the most boring scenery of the trip so far, vaguely reminiscent of northern Minnesota. Although distant mountains are sometimes visible, the forest on both sides of the road has been brutally clear-cut and indifferently replanted. One gets a palpable feeling of the rape of the wilderness.

A few hours on the Highway is sufficient to see that the local economy is based on delivery of three services: windshield repair, tire repair, and (most worrisome) welding. I expected to need the first, doubted I'd need the second, and prayed I wouldn't need the third. Most of the first 300 miles is pretty well surfaced. What is paved is in better condition than most Cambridge streets; only a few short sections of gravel surface have punishing potholes.

Once in the "town" of Fort Nelson, I hung out with Samantha at Dan's Neighbourhood Pub. It is strange at night to walk from the bright light of the outdoors into a dim bar. One usually associates civilization with light, but in the summer here darkness is an exclusive product of civilization. Marcy, the bartender, was a lifelong Fort Nelson resident who'd been away only to study biology at Vancouver's U.B.C. Marcy planned on graduate school, although not at MIT. Why not? She'd never heard of MIT. I'd expected the "people of the Alaska Highway" to be solid hardy pioneers, but Marcy was very delicately constructed with a slight build, dark hair, and pale skin.

Kelly, a compact 28-year-old with an open face and a shock of brown hair, born and raised in Grande Prairie, looked over my shoulder as I wrote a rather vicious account of his hometown. This drummer/miner/Pepsi-merchandiser had lived in Vancouver for five years and supported himself as a freelance drummer.

"I shared an apartment with a cute blonde older girlfriend until I introduced her to her husband. Breaking up with Breean didn't drive me out of the city; I moved when it became 'Hongcouver.'"

Kelly invited me to join him in his Pepsi-funded motel room in town and I did, acquiring my very own double bed for the first time since East Glacier. Paradoxically, I didn't sleep all that well. Kelly and I stayed up talking until 2:00 AM. He spoke about sharing a house in Grande Prairie (only $65,000 Cdn!) with his girlfriend of six years and of the struggle to remain faithful to her in spite of temptation.

"Women just throw themselves at me after concerts. They don't care if a guy has a bad character as long as he is a musician. I don't have too much trouble resisting, though. Sex for the sake of sex isn't as important to me as when I was 17."

We were about to drift off when Kelly asked a disarming question.

"Why would anyone call himself 'Jewish' and not 'Christian.'"

Mechanically, I said that I supposed it was because there were people who accepted the Hebrew Bible but not the New Testament, nor that the Messiah was Jesus, nor any of the 50-odd other "would-be Messiahs" of the last 2500 years.

"Oh," said Kelly, with a look indicating he shared my belief that this wasn't much of an answer. "I've never met any Jews before. It seems kind of odd that someone would accept only half of the Bible. I'm not much of a churchgoer myself, but I was raised Baptist in Grande Prairie."

Kelly talked about how the choices one makes early in life inexorably determine one's position at retirement. He estimates only about 3% of folks are able to reach Paradiso, i.e., "cruising up the highway in a motor home with plenty of money for gas."

Kelly's Inferno?

"Sharing a bus with 60 other smelly people."

JUNE 30

Kelly left early in the morning, and I found myself unable to sleep but also unable to face the gray rain. I lay in bed and read *The Symposium* from start to finish. I won't presume to summarize Socrates and friends, but the part that I like best is Aristophanes explaining homosexuality versus heterosexuality. Originally, people did not go about singly, but were physically joined together with another person. There were male-male, female-female, and male-female combinations. You had four legs, four arms, two faces, etc., and when you wanted to move fast you did it by cartwheeling. The Gods became angry with Man at one point and split all of these couples up, taking the extra skin and making belly buttons. People now wandered around desperately lonely looking for their old partners.

If you are a woman seeking women, you were originally intended to be part of a female-female pair; if you seek someone of the opposite sex, you were originally intended to be part of a male-female pair; if you are a man seeking a man (the most praiseworthy kind of person), you must have originally been intended to be part of a male-male pair. People who find the exact person for whom they were originally intended happily remain with that person for a lifetime; people who don't, continue to search. Aristophanes cautions us to worship the gods carefully; if they get angry again they'll split us all in half and we'll have to hop about on one leg.

My shower fogged up the mirror enough to reveal a message in soap: "It was fun to meet you, Philip. Have a great trip, Your friend, Kelly."

After filling the car for a shocking $40 Cdn., I continued north. The highway quickly disintegrated into long gravel sections littered with potholes. Oncoming vehicles were few, but most materialized out of the rain as huge trucks spraying gravel at my windshield. For three hours, I passed more clearcut forests, climbed over a small mountain range, and spent a long time next to a river meandering through fields of rock left behind from the time a mighty glacier had flowed in the valley. Large collections of trees ripped out upstream littered the sides of all the channels.

At Liard Hot Springs, I soaked in the 104–109 degree mildly sulfurous water. Most of the soakers were stereotypical Canadian motor home drivers, retired guys with pale skin and big guts hanging over their swimsuits. I chatted with Sallie, a young Coloradan mother and her perfect 10-year-old son Ben. Seeing the mountains of the North has been her dream for years, but this is the first time she has managed to get away from her word-processing job. She has left her second husband behind painting houses while she and Ben roam.

Sallie invited me to a turkey hotdog roast at her campsite. Proving Rousseau's point that civilized man is inferior to the American Indian, we couldn't get a proper fire started even though we sacrificed *both* the Alberta campground guide and the Montana lodging guides. Seeing Sallie and Ben together made me think how much fun it would be to have a child along on this trip. On the other hand, I was probably romanticizing the experience of showing a child the wonders of the world; most of the *actual* parents I'd met on the trip were a touch shell-shocked.

At about 8:30 I pressed on up the highway, continuing until 11:15 when I felt dead tired. I camped next to a creek and rushed to put up my tent before the mosquitoes ate me alive. After 6000 mosquito-free miles, they'd suddenly come out with a vengeance.

Thursday, July 1 (Canada Day)

Trying to drive and kill the 15 mosquitoes that had entered the van at the same time was a challenge, but I managed somehow and spent an uneventful hour and a half driving under gray skies.

> Park the vehicle on a firm and level surface.
>
> —Dodge Caravan Owner's Manual

The last place that fit this description was 400 miles back in Dawson Creek. My inspiration for reading started at 60 mph with a peculiar sound and a pronounced desire on the part of my minivan to exit the highway to the right. I managed to keep the car on the road and braked lightly to a stop with the car 25% off the road.

My right front tire was completely flat. The shoulder, as along so much of the Alaska Highway, consisted of a 20-foot-deep ditch. Traffic was pretty light, but mostly huge motor homes, tandem semi-trailers, and flatbeds hauling oversized mobile homes. Hills front and back prevented anyone from seeing me.

I'd no alternative but to drive on the rim until a better tire-changing spot could be found. I drove about one quarter mile to a spot with a wider shoulder and better views for traffic, but still was only able to get the car 50% off the road.

Task #1: get the spare tire out from under the car.

It was easy enough to winch down from the chassis, but there was no way to slide it out from under the car. The spare was hemmed in on all sides by the rear tires, the exhaust system, and the trailer hitch. I considered jacking up the driver's rear side of the car, but didn't relish operating a scissors jack smack in the middle of the Alaska Highway. At this point I congratulated myself on having made my will just before leaving Boston. Taking all 500 lb. of junk out of the car lifted the trailer hitch enough that I was able to drag the spare out.

Task #2: figure out if it would be possible to jack the car.

The highway here is dramatically crowned, and the shoulder drops down at a 10 degree angle at least. The only way to level the car would in fact be to park it directly over the yellow centerline, so "level" was out of the question. "Firm" was not an adjective that one would normally apply to the dirt-and-gravel shoulder, but I didn't think towing the car 30 miles to the nearest gas station was an option.

Keeping first the spare and then the flat tire under the rocker panel—in case the car fell off the jack, it would theoretically come to rest on the spare wheel rather than on the brake rotor—I managed to jack the car with a minimum of trepidation.

> And I will cast abominable filth upon thee, and make thee vile, and will set thee as a gazingstock.
>
> —Nahum 3:6

By the time I'd finished changing the tire, I was covered in black or brown filth from head to toe. As the exterior of the car was so encrusted in mud that the license plate was no longer readable, it should have come as no surprise that the stored-under-the-car spare was thoroughly filthy. Nonetheless, I couldn't believe the sorry state of my clothing and the dirt under my fingernails.

Changing the tire wasn't the best hour of my trip, but I did get something positive out of it: the knowledge that, Kitty Genovese notwithstanding, Real North Americans won't abandon their fellow human being to his fate. At least half of the passersby stopped to offer assistance, including two women traveling with two babies in car seats (being a true gentleman, I naturally didn't deprive them of the opportunity to get some "hands-on" experience with a lug wrench). A pyramidally corpulent Maine couple stopped in their motor home, and we had a pleasant time recalling our last meeting in a North Dakota gas station. Even during long intervals between trucks, I wasn't lonely; crowds of mosquitoes and a few wasps gathered to observe and assist.

When I got to Watson Lake, I managed to get what looked like a nail hole in the tread fixed for a mere $13 Cdn. but was disappointed to find the swimming pool closed for Canada Day. I showered at a gas station/laundromat/café/showers (a very common combination up here) and was never so glad to be clean again. Watson Lake is the first town in the Yukon Territory, a region the size of California with a population of 30,000. Canadian territories have as much power to make their own laws as provinces. The principal difference is that territories aren't required to fund their own operations to the same extent as provinces.

Canada Day is yet another distinction without a difference. They could have picked July 4 to celebrate their independence but, instead, in 1867 Canadians picked July 1. It makes cross-border travel gratuitously confusing. Whatever the date, the celebration is the same as in the U.S.: barbecuing mysterious parts of dead animals, inane diversions for children, hiding from thundershowers under tarps at picnics, and drunk driving. I crashed the town's mass picnic and gulped down a hot dog under a tarp but didn't manage to strike up any conversations with the distracted parents and soaked adolescents in attendance.

EAGLE RI
Meißen
Bezirk Dresden
(GREATFUL)DEAD OR BUST
EUGENE OREGON
WALDO
LUMSDEN SASK
Tanzschule Rohde
Rheinbach / Bonn
West-Germany
363-CPA
537-TOY
ROSES ARE RED
HIPPIES ARE HAIRY
WE FOLLOW THE DEAD
TO SEE OUR
NELSON
NELSON
LOCKPORT
ILL.
PAUL
&
ATIANA
MARSH
PURDY ROAD
Pernegg
Schwäbisch Ha
Clover Tours
GO BIG ORANGE
HI-CREST AUTO
Hartenholm
Kreis Segeberg
WALKERTON
STEFANO Rd
Municipalité Lac Supérieur
BOB & MARJIE WARREN
SEBASTIAN FL.
1992
JAMES JORRITSMA
NEER LANDIA, ALBERTA
Box 203 T0G 1R0
YOMING RIDE
KET

Three hours of driving through sometimes torrential rain brought me to a café just east of Teslin, Yukon. After driving past one rat shack gas station/café/motel after another, it was a relief to see some warm and tasteful natural wood architecture. Dave and Carolyn preside over this oasis. Dave has lived here for 20 years, spending the winters teaching all grades (7–9), all subjects, and all twenty students in Teslin Junior Hall.

"They are mostly Native and unfortunately more inclined to alcohol than academics," Dave sighed as I ate superb baked-fresh-by-Carolyn rhubarb pie and ice cream. I was much more upset by his next bit of information.

"This is the worst summer for mosquitoes in history, all over the Yukon and Alaska. Getting out of a vehicle in Denali National Park right now is tantamount to suicide."

8

Alaska at Last

July 2

The booming metropolis of Whitehorse (pop. 22,000) is capital of the Yukon. Here one finds an assortment of loud smoky bars, cheesy tourist traps, riverboats old and new, and the pleasant Loose Moose café, where I took to diarizing. Whitehorse is rich in history due to the vital role played by the Yukon River in the settlement of the Klondike. This river flows out of the mountains just to the south and then arcs northwest through Dawson City and eventually straight through Alaska to empty into the Bering Sea near Nome. Before roads were built, flat-bottomed paddlewheel steamers used to transport miners and supplies all through the region. After touring the SS *Klondike,* conveniently beached in downtown Whitehorse, I stopped to picnic by the river.

The Duke family was parked next to me. For two to four months each year, the Dukes close their frame shop in Surrey and fly to North America, usually to Florida, then drive cross-country and back. "We've done this 14 years in a row now, although we've only been to Alaska three times so far," they allowed; it hit me how little I'll know this great land even after this trip.

One mile from downtown, I parked at the hydroelectric dam's fish ladder and was disappointed to find that the salmon don't come back here until late July (it *is* rather far from the ocean after all). Just as I hauled out my mountain bike, Kaarin appeared with Grizz, her dog, who looked unbearlike despite his name. Kaarin is an

Anglophone Montrealer who gave up on McGill after she couldn't learn any more Arctic biology. She's going to spend next year at the University of Alaska, Fairbanks, where they've an entire building devoted to the subject. Alaska, incredibly enough, gives resident tuition rates to residents of the Yukon and Northwest Territories. Kaarin has been living out of her old Chevy hatchback and camping "wherever."

Kaarin directed me down a dirt road toward Miles Canyon and eventually off onto some ski trails. I was beginning to get comfortable with my SPD pedals, but the trail became very technical at times with as many as three logs to hop over in one foot of trail. Under a resplendent blue sky, I zoomed through the woods, trees to my left, the dark green waters of the Yukon to my right. The last bit of the trail drops about 50′ down the side of a steep slope. A flat trail notched into the hillside would have been nice, but this was essentially a sideways line on the slope. About halfway down, my back wheel started to slide over the edge. I thought I was finished. Somehow I managed to modulate the brakes and balance to keep it together. I wouldn't want to try it again.

Miles Canyon looked magnificent. The afternoon sun shone on 120,000 gallons of water a minute rushing through a narrow granite gap. Red rock and deep jade water make a striking contrast. I rode over a bridge to the other side of the Yukon and up to a paved road looking over the Yukon behind the hydroelectric dam with mountains in the background.

After a swim in the Lions Club pool and dinner, I met Kaarin downtown where she is house-sitting. The house had been recently condemned by the city, and a quick glance was enough to understand why. "In Canada, as long as tenants are living in a condemned structure, they can continue to occupy it," Kaarin explained.

We read the *Yukon News* personals, which are remarkably *truly personal!* Anonymous meetings simply aren't possible in this town of 20,000. Don't bother placing a standard ad, e.g., "Tired of superficiality? 30ish woman of fine character and discernment wanted by thoughtful man for elegant dinners, philosophical discussions, and serious commitment. Must measure 38D or larger." You already know all the single women in town, and if you don't get on with them you have the following options: move or get cable. Kaarin's friends had placed a typical *Yukon News* personal: "Kaarin, The Queen of Carnage, coming soon to a town near you. Adipose present [she'd had a job hacking adipose fins off fish], work experience absent, maybe shave legs! Love and peace; the gang at 304."

Grizz's provenance was interesting.

"Rick left his wife, his child, and his dog, but I could only take his dog." It turned out that Rick put his wife's head through a wall before leaving as well, which made me wonder aloud why women couldn't find better men.

"They don't want better men," Kaarin responded. "At least that's what a friend of mine says. He wears his hair in dreadlocks even though he's pretty conservative. He claims that women only like men who are bad for them or at least appear to be so. I think he's right because all the nice guys I know are permasingle."

Permasingle? Is that like permafrost?

"That's what I call anyone who hasn't had a steady girlfriend or boyfriend for years."

Kaarin is doing her share to make sure that the nice guys of the world stay single. Her last boyfriend and she were together five days a week in a lakeside cabin; on weekends, he went to the Big House to pay his debt to Yukon society.

"My family back in Montreal was fond of referring to him as 'The Convict.'"

Saturday, July 3

I lunched at the Talisman Café with Lloyd, a heavy equipment operator who moved here a year ago, and his girlfriend Ruth from Ontario. Lloyd was trying to convince Ruth to move out here also. Lloyd is straightening the Alaska Highway about 300 miles east of here, mostly with Caterpillar D9 bulldozers. He looked remarkably fresh for a guy in his mid-40s who works construction 55 hours/week.

"I love my job. I'm going to be knocking over trees and pushing dirt around until I'm 65. Do these look like the hands of someone who has worked construction for 30 years?" Lloyd asked as he turned up his smooth palms. "I work in air-conditioned or heated comfort. Mechanics grease and clean the machines."

Lloyd's mother was a schoolteacher, but she didn't object to his being pulled out of school at age 15 to work on the farm. Lloyd wants better for his children, but they thwart his desire by indulgence in alcohol and by working moronic low-paying jobs.

"I've tried to get them into heavy equipment operation, but they can't be bothered to try and double their pay. They're lazy because they've been living with their mother, whom I divorced some years ago."

He seems to be doing better with Ruth, a vivacious fortysomething blonde who is just a touch careworn from divorce and too many years tending bar.

"I don't know if I can move to Whitehorse. I've been having fun this weekend, but I'm used to a variety of people," Ruth wondered.

"I'd expected the women of the Yukon to be built like me [6′, 190 lb.] and the men to be built like grizzly bears [9′, 900 lb.]. Who was it that said, 'You won't find any Canadians in the North; only mad dogs and Scotsmen'? But actually the spectrum of people I've met here has been pretty broad," I noted.

"Best of all, Whitehorse is swimming in beautiful women," Lloyd interjected with a gleam in his eye.

Our waitress came over just then to underscore the issue. Erika, a stunning, dark, tall 25-year-old Hungarian fashion plate, came here five years ago chasing after her boyfriend, whom she ultimately married. If she lived in New York, she'd be a haughty fashion model or a pampered East Side trophy wife. Life in Whitehorse is different; her husband one night put a gun to her head and those of their two toddlers. She's been on her own for two years working seven days a week at three jobs (waitress, flower arranger, and dog trainer). She sees her children about five hours a day and makes the equation balance by only sleeping five or six hours a night.

"I was raised in Miskolc, a town of 600,000 next to Budapest. I was surrounded by ambitious architecture and urban sophistication. Whitehorse has beautiful people, but is too boring, untasteful, and full of junk."

Has she found romance here?

"I'm dating a 23-year-old. He's sensitive; he's a writer. But we don't get along so well because he feels guilty about not wanting to settle down and make a lifetime commitment. I don't pressure him to do anything, but he pushes himself."

Erika was remarkably sunny, cheerful, and active for a single mother with three jobs. She told me of her plans to drive 12 hours round-trip in a weekend to attend the Dawson City music festival. Even that isn't a rich enough life for her taste.

"I don't live the way I want to live. I'm just going to keep trying until I get my way."

Two hours of beautiful driving brought me to Haines Junction. Every mile of the road revealed a photo opportunity with wildflowers in the foreground, a stream in the midground, and dramatic peaks in the background. Six miles past the junction, I turned off onto the Alsek Road, which is a ribbon of dirt heading straight for the highest mountains in Canada. A deep creek across the road made further travel by minivan inadvisable. I hauled out the mountain bike and tightened my SPD pedals to weld me a little more firmly to the bike. I was, on the one hand, afraid of falling over and pulling the bike down on top of me, but, on the other, was even more afraid of popping out of the SPDs just when I needed power to keep me going through a rocky or muddy bottom.

The creek turned out to be far worse than it looked. It flowed fast over a sandy bottom and was nearly two feet deep. Thus were my shoes and socks soaked through in the first 100 yards of the ride. The temperature was about 65 degrees but a 25–40 mph wind made it feel much colder. Going directly into this wind was agony. I crawled along at a few miles per hour while my ears hurt from the cold air rushing past. The trail was so rocky or creek-strewn that I couldn't keep my eyes on the scenery. I returned to the car ready to buy the next suspension mountain bike that crossed my path.

As the edges of clouds began to tinge with color, I drove along the shores of Kluane Lake, whose shimmering blue-green waters were once home to the world's record trout (70 lb.). For an hour, I had Kluane Lake on my right and the Icefield Mountains in the distance on my left. Rising up to about 20,000′, these mountains are also home to the world's largest nonpolar icefield. I was tempted to stop and take a scenic flight, but my desire to reach Alaska was a bit feverish. I drove until 11:00 PM and camped by the Donjek River.

July 4

As I passed Canadian customs, I reflected on the appropriateness of re-entering the United States on Independence Day. My joy was postponed, however, because a combination of road construction and 22 more miles of Canadian territory delayed my homecoming. If you can survive in this wilderness, a flat forested valley, you are apparently welcome to enjoy a 22-mile strip of Canada without having to declare yourself. Until recently, the U.S. left nearly 100 miles of border land open in this manner, but customs and immigration were recently moved to within half a mile from the boundary.

> This unfortified boundary line between the Dominion of Canada and the United States of America should quicken the remembrance of the more than a century old friendship between these countries, a lesson of peace to all nations.
>
> — stone monument erected by the Kiwanis International in 1982

Whatever other kind of example it serves, the border is a great example of tree cutting. Marking the border, the 141st meridian from the Arctic Ocean to Mt. Saint Elias (600 miles) has been denuded of trees in a 20-foot-wide swath.

A mustache and paunch in uniform waved me into the U.S. without asking more than "Did you buy any alcohol or other things in Canada?" My first real American encounter was a few miles up the road at the Texaco. Paying $1.39/gallon for gasoline would have made me apoplectic just a couple of weeks ago, but after the US$2/gallon prices in Canada, it was a relief. Rhonda, the cashier, is a schoolteacher in Oklahoma nine months of the year.

"I'm thinking of moving up here. The average Alaskan schoolteacher makes well over $40,000 [the nationwide average was about $37,000], and they can retire with full pension after 20 years. I'm not sure if I can handle the long dark winter though."

Noting her naked ring finger, I pointed out that Alaska might be a good place to meet men, who tend to predominate in such wilderness areas.

"That's what I came up here to avoid," she plaintively responded.

I arrived in Tok, Alaska, a rat shack town of 1000, at about 4:00 PM and promptly parked myself at the famous Gateway Salmon Bake, where one can simultaneously satisfy cravings for barbecued salmon and reindeer sausage. Walter Holland was clearing tables, and he exemplified what I was to later learn about Alaskans. All one has to do to hear an interesting story is ask someone how he got here.

"Oh, I walked up here from Mexico with a Malamute. It took me four years to get this far, and I'm going to start walking/snowshoeing to Siberia when the trails freeze over in October."

Was it a tough walk?

cf. Frederick Law Olmsted's A Journey through Texas *(1857): "It is our misfortune that all the towns of the Republic are alike, or differ in scarcely anything else than in natural position and wealth."*

"Well, I walked from Connecticut to Oregon a few years ago. That took me three years, but now I can pick up some cash anytime I want speaking about my walks in public schools. My biggest problem is that the Malamute likes to attack porcupines. I have to carry knock-out serum and a syringe so I can pull the quills out."

What wisdom had he gained from his years on the road?

"Most towns are the same."

Driving the 200 miles from Tok to Fairbanks, I couldn't help noticing how crowded Alaska felt. Despite a population density 1/300th that of New York State, it still seems much more settled and less free than the Yukon Territory. There are at least 10 times as many side roads, most of which go into land owned by one of the native corporations established by Congress in the '70s. The Indians used to regard their songs as private and the land as common. Times have changed and "no trespassing" signs abound; one can't just throw down a tent on any old spot as in the Yukon.

My perspective on Alaska had been largely formed by my first Alaskan friends, whom I met in Amsterdam back in 1984. At one museum after another, I kept running into Rick, a rugged bearded state prosecutor from Juneau, and Kathy, a statuesque law student. We decided to accept Fate and team up.

"Alaska attracts people who are just too socially maladapted to live in the Lower 48. It is theoretically the last place in the U.S. where people can nurse their idiosyncrasies far from the intrusions of government and community," Rick observed. "We used to catch people all the time with oversized weapons, such as 50 cal. machine guns. Their defense was always the same: 'Well, a couple of years ago I was charged by a grizzly. I shot him with my rifle, and the bullet just bounced off his forehead.'"

My favorite Rick and Kathy story starts with us touring Amsterdam's Red Light District. We stopped to talk to one of the barkers, a guy who pulls people in from the street to attend a sex show. Rick asked the barker where most of his customers were from. He told us that Japanese and Germans were his best customers, but that people came from all over the world. I then asked if he didn't have to speak several languages in order to do his job. Of course, he said, "I speak English, Dutch, German, Japanese, French, and one word of Hebrew." "Oh," I inquired, "what's that, 'Shalom'?" "No, it's mumphulumphul..ble," he responded. "What does that mean?" we all asked. "It means 'live fucking on stage.'"

Shortly after crossing the Trans-Alaska Pipeline, which looks depressingly insignificant for something that cost 8 billion 1977 dollars, I rolled into Delta Junction, where the Alaska Highway ends. Right next to Milepost 1422, there is a horrifying yellow sign with black schematic figures. A huge bison is crashing into the front of a light truck, whose driver is being ejected from the vehicle through the windshield. One of the truck's tires flies off toward the right. I counted myself lucky that in six days on the Alaska Highway I'd suffered only a flat tire while getting a real feeling for the size of the continent, meeting a lot of interesting people, and not having to pay a dime for shelter.

Reflecting on this last point, it occurred to me that civilized man may indeed have gone overboard in the shelter department. Thoreau thought that single men should live in plywood coffins so that they'd not have to spend their days working to pay rent. Today virtually all of us own steel-and-glass coffins-on-wheels that, when supplemented by a tent, would seem to Thoreau like luxury. Yet, despite the fact that we are already protected from inclement weather, we insist on building ever more elaborate monuments to impress other human beings. I was a few minutes into this thought when a country-western song came on the radio: "My parents think I'm doing swell. I tell them that I'm staying in Beverly Hills, sleepin' in the Hotel Coupe DeVille . . ." ("Hotel Coupe DeVille" by Al Anderson and Craig Wiseman).

I rolled past Calvary's Northern Lights Mission in the town of North Pole. KJNP, "your 50,000 watt Arctic voice of the Gospel," took me right back to medieval times and Thomas Aquinas's divine hierarchy with their 4th of July prayer: "Thank you God for giving us this great land where all may worship in tolerance. We know that all authority is established by you." I wondered how the "tolerance" theme would have struck David Koresh.

David Koresh, born Vernon Wayne Howell, led a fundamentalist Christian community in Waco, Texas, that had stockpiled guns. The Federal Bureau of Alcohol Tobacco and Firearms laid siege to the compound for two months during early 1993. Janet Reno authorized a military assault on the compound in order to "protect the children inside." During the 6-hour assault on April 19, 1993, 400 CS gas canisters were fired into the building, and tanks breached its walls. An ensuing fire and collapsing walls killed 75 of the 84 people inside the compound, including 25 children. The government prosecuted the survivors on a variety of charges but failed to obtain convictions on the more serious ones.

Monday, July 5 (a holiday still)

Fairbanks is Rat Shack Writ Large, but the University of Alaska's museum is one of the world's most interesting per square foot. They've excellent exhibits on the geography, wildlife, and history of each part of the state. There were also some good films about the aurora borealis, which the bright sky keeps one from seeing until September. After an hour there, I stopped at the nearby Pizza Hut to write my diary. I'd just told the waitress, Lisa, a college kid from Pennsylvania, how anonymous and frightening I found Fairbanks (pop. 77,000) after the Yukon. Marcia and Tony leaned over from the booth next door and explained that the pipeline project ruined Fairbanks.

"We used to have bumper stickers that said, 'Happiness is 10,000 Okies heading south with a Texan under each arm.' Prostitution and all other kinds of crime came with the pipeline. Door locks on houses used to be unheard of, but now one has to lock the house; everyone used to stop to help stranded motorists, now one doesn't dare."

Marcia moved up here when her first husband started at the University of Alaska. The Army sent Tony here rather than back for another tour of duty in Vietnam because his brother was also in 'Nam. Tony stayed to work construction. Tony made me feel like a girlie-man driver with his tale of his most recent trip up the AlCan. In order to save $6500, he bought his Chrysler minivan "Outside." He left Tacoma, Washington, at 2:30 on a Tuesday afternoon and arrived here Thursday at 10:30 PM. It was December, and he had unstudded, unchained, all-weather radials.

"Driving is easier in the winter on the AlCan because all of the bumps are filled in with snow and ice. I just set the cruise control on 80."

After poking around the tourist information offices and the mushing museum, which are semi-interesting, I stopped in at a tour office and chatted with the staff. When I noted that Fairbanks would not win any prizes for architecture, the fellow there said that I should "think of Alaska as one big park and the cities are just campgrounds." My next stop was Alaskaland, where admission is free and the attitude is low-key. One of the most interesting portions is the aviation museum, which highlights U.S./Soviet cooperation. I never knew that we sent 8000 fighters, bombers, and cargo planes via Alaska to the Russians during WWII! I'd spent so much time reading magazine articles about Japanese superefficiency that I'd forgotten our strengths. The United States in the 20th century had a staggering amount of leftover energy and capital. We tipped the stalemated scales of WWI. We rebuilt Germany in the '20s, by pumping in millions of dollars to stabilize the mark after the hyperinflation of 1923. During WWII, we supplied the Red Army and the British, used massive amounts of materiel to save American lives while defeating both the Germans and the Japanese, and did 20 years of physics in two years to build the A-bomb—a project the Brits gave up as too costly. We rebuilt postwar Germany and Japan. Then we fought a Cold War with Russia and hot wars in Korea, Vietnam, and Iraq without crimping the civilian economy too badly.

Anxious to see a genuine tourist trap, I decamped to Marcia and Tony's hometown hamlet of Ester and the Malamute Saloon. The show was nearly sold out from bus tours, and it dawned on me that touring Alaska without reservations or a place in an organized tour is a dicey proposition in the summer. All tourism here is crammed into June, July, and August. Many activities are therefore simultaneously shockingly priced and sold out. Furthermore, this ain't Paris, where you can walk across the street and do something else if you can't get into the opera; the next attraction may be 300 miles down the road.

One of my tablemates was a power engineer who was seduced into working on the pipeline for 12 years, living one week up in Prudhoe Bay and then having a week off down here. I noted that I'd been tempted to fly up past the Arctic Circle to see the oil fields and Eskimo villages. Like most people I'd spoken to, Larry had never developed much affection for the North Country.

"Imagine Kansas with millions of mosquitoes and more wind."

KODAK TX 6043
TX 11
TX 12
TX 13
TX 14
TX 15
TX 16
TX 17
TX 18
TX 19

KODAK TX 6043
TX▷2
TX▷3
TX▷4
TX▷5
TX▷6
TX▷7
TX▷8
TX▷9
TX▷10

While we rubbed our feet in sawdust, four versatile actors told the story of life in the original Alaskan mining towns in song and dance. They also recited the Robert Service poem "The Cremation of Sam McGee" that I'd already heard twice, such a staple is it of Alaskan tourism. In typically American fashion, this English-Canadian poet has been appropriated without mention of the fact that he rarely left the Yukon Territory.

> There are strange things done in the midnight sun
> By the men who moil for gold;
> The Arctic trails have their secret tales
> That would make your blood run cold;
> The Northern Lights have seen queer sights,
> But the queerest they ever did see
> Was that night on the marge of Lake Lebarge
> I cremated Sam McGee.

One Alaskan commented that "it is our misfortune to have had a Robert Service rather than a Robert Frost."

After the show, I rung up Tony, who came down the hill to fetch me in his minivan. We drove up unmarked, unsigned, unmailboxed streets to his house on the hill and went inside. Tony told me that he'd built this house himself for Marcia and their family. Although its architecture was more functional than decorative, it looked remarkably square and solid.

Remarkably, rather than bloat up the bureaucracy to absorb excess oil revenue, the state distributes $1000/year directly to each Alaskan as long as he or she remains in the state or is a full-time university student.

Tony complained about the outrageous property tax rates in Alaska (about 2% of assessed value, or slightly lower than in Massachusetts). I pointed out that with no sales tax, no income tax, and $4000/year in Permanent Fund checks (one for Marcia, Tony, and each of their children still technically living at home), they were in fact making a profit of about $2000/year by virtue of living here.

The interior was comfortably furnished, although dogs, a cat, and aquariums inevitably created some disarray. I hadn't been inside more than a few minutes before Marcia set before me two huge delicious made-from-scratch brownies topped with four scoops of vanilla ice cream.

Don't come to Alaska if you don't want to eat hearty, son.

We talked until nearly 2. Tony told of his days as a Med-Evac team leader on a helicopter in Vietnam. Wasn't it incredibly dangerous?

"We were under fire sometimes, but most of the time we were protected by helicopter gunships."

So your helicopter never got hit?

"Oh we got hit all the time. The worst was one trip where the pilot was killed by a machine gun shell through the chest. The Huey had hydraulic controls so it remained stable, but the co-pilot had been wounded also and he froze up. I had to help him fly the helicopter back to base. We'd been trained for that; it wasn't a big deal."

Tony thinks the Vietnam veterans who complain of flashbacks and war trauma are contemptible. Not only were so many people sent to Vietnam that one would expect a fair number to have gone crazy afterwards, but the streets there were littered with hallucinogens for sale, both synthetic and natural. Tony is more of the "I did my job in the Army as best I could" ex-military guy as opposed to the super-patriotic gung-ho Rambo type. He didn't even bother voting in the last presidential election: "Bush conceded well before the polls closed here."

Marcia talked about how, as head teller in her bank, it was difficult to train and motivate bank tellers. They only get paid $6/hour, though, and it seems that they can't realistically hope to ever make enough to support a family properly. Marcia spoke of the trials and tribulations of raising her adopted children with her ex-husband. She'd always thought that parents were to blame for children who dyed their hair orange or green, but changed her mind after coming home to find half of her daughter's hair shaved away. "You can't be with kids 24 hours/day."

Tuesday, July 6

I wasn't up and showered until after 10, and by then Tony had come back from his construction site because the required materials hadn't arrived. Marcia fixed us all prodigious quantities of sourdough waffles, and we chatted some more while looking at the Fairbanks paper. The top stories concerned a local boy who'd been burned by an aerosol can in a campfire and a British Columbia man who'd bulldozed his ex-girlfriend's house.

I wasn't allowed to leave without more of Marcia's home baking: a mammoth banana bread. I went back to Fairbanks to look up a friend who'd given me incomplete directions. I was reduced to flagging down a red Thunderbird driven by a young-looking fellow with an attractive blonde companion. He filled in the missing details and invited me to come to his house up the road if I couldn't find it or needed the phone.

My friend wasn't home, so I went to the "Thunderbird house." As I drove up the driveway, I was shocked to find that it was an architecturally tasteful stone-faced quasi-mansion. This was really the nicest building, public or private, that I'd seen since maybe Whitehorse or even Edmonton. Randy ushered me in and introduced me to his wife, Cathy. They looked so young that I initially thought it must be their parents' house.

Randy defends doctors in malpractice suits. The beautiful 32-year-old Cathy was his second wife, and the young-looking Randy turned out to have two daughters just out of college! East Coast attorneys his age wear the grime of 20 years of recirculated skyscraper air around their sagging middle.

Randy and Cathy were delighted to find out that I knew Marion, daughter of Bernard Kelly, one of Alaska's foremost plaintiff's attorneys. Cathy had worked for a big medical malpractice insurer, which is how she and Randy met, and they'd squared off in court with Kelly on several occasions. In the history of the state of Alaska, only three or four doctors have ever been found liable for medical malpractice; one of those cases Randy lost to Kelly.

We had a wide-ranging conversation for several hours, during which Cathy offered me all kinds of ice cream and beverages. Cathy had moved here a year ago from Lincoln Park (Chicago's equivalent of the Upper West Side) and was surprised to find out how much civilization existed in the wilderness. She'd initially labeled Randy Geographically Undesirable, but now found that even the winter darkness wasn't so bad.

"In Chicago it was a bit dark when I'd go to work in the morning and thoroughly dark by the time I got home at night. I don't really feel that I'd ever had a significant amount of daylight to be robbed of."

Randy was raised in Arizona and likes the Western culture out here.

"People are always willing to open their hearts and their homes to strangers. Alaska felt like home from the minute I landed here," Randy remembered. "Nobody here in Fairbanks would move to Anchorage. Sure, it is a lot warmer there, but it is so damp that it feels colder."

In response to my questions about how they'd met, Cathy spoke of her years dating in Chicago. She couldn't understand why men weren't content to have a good time night after night on dates without sleeping together. She didn't think that the fact that men were paying for several dozen dinners, symphonies, etc., entitled them to sex.

"No matter how irrational the belief, men have to maintain the fantasy that they are the one person who is really attractive to a woman. It is ultimately no fun spending time with a woman who isn't attracted to me," Randy noted. "Men are romantics. Male suicides outnumber female suicides by an order of magnitude. Women think about raising children and are naturally more practical minded. They don't look for soulmates but hunt practically for men who meet fixed criteria, matching guys up against big checklists."

"Oh, that's completely false!" Cathy exclaimed. "Although, of course I wouldn't date anyone who didn't have a postgraduate degree. And naturally he'd have to have the proper sort of job. Well, and one couldn't really expect anything lasting if one partner were neat and the other sloppy. . . ."

General observation I about Alaskans: They divide the year into light and dark almost as much as warm and cold. Daylight here is precious, and people are very conscious about losing it. Every weather report contains the length of the day and, right now, how many minutes shorter it is than yesterday. Six minutes may not seem like much to you or me, but several times I heard Alaskans lament their imminent loss of the sun.

General observation II about Alaskans: The southern senators who objected to Alaska's statehood in 1959 may have had a point. People here aren't all that bound to the rest of the country. Alaskans speak of the Lower 48 as "The States," and it sounds just as far away to them as it does to Americans I'd met who were working in Cairo. People here feel themselves to be a breed apart with a distinct culture and distinct capabilities. I wouldn't call them unpatriotic, but I get the impression sometimes that if the Lower 48 were to sink into the ocean tomorrow, it would make the front page of the *Daily News-Miner* for a day and then life would go back to normal.

Reflections on finally reaching Alaska: How did I feel about finally reaching my destination? Lucky to have driven 7000 relatively crash-free miles. Awed by the size and variety of our continent—this just has to be the best piece of real estate on the planet. Warmed by the good hearts of my fellow North Americans. Daunted by the prospect of touring a state one-fifth the size of the Lower 48 in just four weeks (three on land and one by ferry down the coast).

9

Denali

July 7

A huge rainbow directly in front of me lured me south to Denali. The two-lane highway follows a ridge with lake-filled valleys on both sides. It looks like wilderness, but there is some sign of land use, either an unmarked dirt road or a mailbox or a business at least once every five or ten miles. I was reminded of how much more settled Alaska is with 500,000 people than the Yukon Territory with 30,000.

Denali means “the great one” or “the big one” in the local native tongue. Denali National Park is slightly larger than Massachusetts, contains one gravel road, and no trails. If you have the constitution and wilderness survival skills of a grizzly bear, it is a very pleasant place to spend a summer. I arrived there at midnight to find the north sky dappled with yellow and orange clouds; the south sky was a soft blue. I drove about 14 miles into the park, as far as one can with a private vehicle, and imagined that I saw 20,320′ Mt. McKinley from the highway, something that is possible only on 30% of summer days.

At 1:00 AM, I pitched my tent in Morino Campground, a walk-in campground only a 10-minute walk from the Denali Park Hotel parking lot. All the other campgrounds were full of motor homes.

Thursday, July 8

A business-like rain made the morning dreary, but the weather improved enough by 11:00 AM that I embarked upon a four-hour voyage with McKinley Rafts down the Nenana River. This is a swift gray current of 37-degree water that cuts its way through a reasonably dramatic canyon. Six months before, I'd gone through Class V rapids ("risk of death") in Australia, so I asked if the Class III rapids wouldn't seem tame by comparison.

"It's true that we don't have too many rafts tipping over or people falling out, but when they do, hypothermia sets in within three minutes," the sales clerk said with a cheerful smile.

Our trip consisted of me, two yuppie women friends in designer shades, and 27 U.S. Army soldiers and wives being led by Jim, their Baptist chaplain. I ended up in the back of a raft with a silent black soldier, Jim, and Darleen, an enlisted Army bus driver. We donned rain gear and life jackets, then set out on flat fast water occasionally roiled into waves by invisible rocks. Jim told me that he didn't have problems with his Army flock abusing alcohol.

"Alaskans are a bunch of fat misfits who spend the winter in a drunken stupor. In the Army, if you have a drinking problem, you get help, and if it recurs, you get out. Today's Army doesn't tolerate overweight or alcoholic soldiers."

Jim said that not too many folks in either Alaska or the military are fond of Bill Clinton. "For one thing, his position on gays in the military hasn't made him too popular. Homosexuals exaggerate their prominence in the population to get more attention." No sooner had I said that I'd only met a handful in my life than Darleen piped up, "I'm getting a divorce from my husband because he's gay." Jim wanted to help homosexuals change their "deviant, learned behavior." I asked him if that wasn't asking quite a lot given that people had such a hard time shedding simpler habits such as smoking and, closer to home, knuckle cracking. Shouldn't he "walk a mile in their shoes" by trying to give up his desire for women? Apparently not.

Jim likes to hunt moose and is upset that the local wolves, none of which he's ever seen, are killing some too (popular bumper sticker: "Eat Moose; 5000 Wolves Can't be Wrong"). Along with many other Fairbanks hunters, Jim would like to start hunting wolves in earnest. I opined that perhaps the North American continent was big enough for wolves and that they might be left alone with their families to their harsh existence (wolves only live to an average age of 4 in the wild, as opposed to 13 or so in zoos).

"Extinction is good. If God had meant wolves to live, he wouldn't have created humans with guns."

When we got out of the river for lunch, I was chilled to the bone. When the sun was out, it was tolerably warm on the river, but sitting and doing nothing with one's feet in 37-degree water was a mite nippy. Unlike previous rafting trips I'd taken, where everyone paddles, it was deemed too hazardous in these hypothermia-inducing waters to have anyone lean out of the boat and paddle. The guide rowed from the center with a big set of oars. Our raft was self-bailing, but there was still some frigid water collecting in the bottom of the boat.

I'd only brought a couple of snacks, but Real Americans won't let their fellows go hungry. Gentle mooching yielded a tuna sandwich, cookies, and Whoppers. We got back into the river for some more serious rapids, but I was a bit too cold to enjoy them. This was Darleen's first whitewater trip, though, and the whoops of joy of this heretofore soft-spoken woman were infectious.

I hurried back to the plush McKinley Chalet Resort to warm up in the hot tub with Mark and Woody. Mark, a long-haired writer, and I talked about his three years here in Alaska. He came here with a master's in social work to accept a lucrative job with the state. Mark was based in Anchorage but frequently flew out to see his clients, Aleuts (pronounced "alley'oots"), on various Aleutian islands.

"I quit because, much as I despise conservative politics, I couldn't help feeling that they were on to something when they said, 'Give a man a fish and you feed him for a day; teach a man to fish and you feed him for a lifetime.'"

A bona fide dropout like Woody made Mark look positively timid. Woody was the product of a redneck father and a hippie mother and grew up in Barnes, Wyoming (pop. 50). One grandfather was a minister and had to watch Woody's aunt convert to Judaism. On the other side, Woody's uncle went to Israel and changed from Fundamentalist Christian to Fundamentalist Islamic Holy Warrior.

Woody clung tenaciously to atheism.

"I was part of a high school graduation class of seven. I was 17 with $1500 and a backpack and decided that I could just as easily flip burgers in Hawaii as in Barnes. After 18 months in Hawaii, I went back to U. of Wyoming on a swimming scholarship. One of the first guys I met was Dan Shane, a doctoral student in molecular biology. We teamed up, taking graduate courses for three years. I was doing great, but the department wouldn't give me a bachelor's because I didn't have the prerequisites.

"I left school in 1991 and started backpacking across the U.S. If it didn't fit in the backpack, it didn't fit in my life. Last year, I came up here to work in the canneries and met some Chileans and Argentineans. We hitchhiked across Alaska, caught a plane ride to Seattle, and hitchhiked to Nogales, Mexico. From there, I went with Gonz, the Chilean, for four months in Guatemala, Nicaragua, and Honduras."

Nicaragua didn't appeal to Woody because people there are too accustomed to violence.

"They have rehabilitation camps so guys who've been carrying guns from the age of 8 can learn to shake hands without shooting each other."

Guatemala was nice because people are peaceful.

"Last month Guatemala overthrew their government totally peacefully and nobody even read about it."

Honduras was best, though.

"If you've got the money you can do anything—if you are the right person with the right attitude, you can break laws."

"One thing I learned in Central America is that U.S. poverty isn't squat. People living here on welfare with their decent apartment, bags of food, television, telephone, and clean water have no conception," Woody noted. In fact, he thinks it is absurd that couples in the U.S. will both kill themselves with work in order to have an outrageously materialistic standard of living. "The richest time of my life was when I was dumpster diving; all of my time was my own."

Central America overall appeals to Woody because people there are free about sex and inhibited about violence and death. "I'll never live in the Lower 48 again because people are too blasé about violence and too inhibited about sex. People think machismo is all about power. It isn't. It is about respect. Women have to respect men and if they say 'yes' that means 'yes.' At the same time, men have to respect a woman's 'no.' Thus, women control sex even if it doesn't look that way. In the U.S, women know that 'no' might be interpreted as 'yes' so that they have to be afraid all of the time."

Another reason Woody has sworn off the "States" is that "there are at least twice as many laws down there and you have to obey them. In Alaska, there aren't many laws, and the police don't really care if you obey them. If you get into this mindset where you have to obey the law, pretty soon you have to buy insurance. Then you've got the wife and kids."

Woody told me about a movement called "Buy Back Alaska," started by a mysterious rich guy from Fairbanks who'd disappeared recently. The idea is to buy back all the federally owned land here and then secede from the union. Had I been here in Denali on July 4th, I would have witnessed the most recent skirmish in the state/federal war. Alaskans find it irksome that they are herded onto government-run school buses to see the one road in Denali Park. Fourteen protesters drove through the private-vehicle barrier on July 4th in defiance of the ban. Rangers photographed their license plates but avoided a publicity-generating confrontation.

Marijuana is another subject of controversy. Woody says that a privacy clause in the state constitution makes it impossible for the state to outlaw dope. Until two years ago, one could grow an unlimited amount for personal use.

"Then the religious freaks in Anchorage pushed for a referendum to make it illegal. Nobody in Alaska ever votes anyway so this thing passed with only 15% of the voting age population supporting it. Everyone in the rest of the state was shocked, and now there is going to be a court fight to see if the referendum is constitutional. Meanwhile, we have to buy Matanuska Tundra Fuck. It costs $320 per ounce, but with 24 hours of sunshine it is the best dope in the world."

The new law seems to be that possession of less than one ounce is a noncriminal ticketable offense.

Woody is living out of his 1973 VW camper-van now. It feels like sybaritic luxury compared with living out of a backpack, but he doesn't bother locking it. On the inside of a door is an essay penned by 16-year-old Hunter S. Thompson that asks who is happier, the man who has been tested by life and lived or the man who chose security?

"Woody, when people look at you now they say, 'How wonderful that a 23-year-old is living this adventurous life.' But when you are 50 and your gut is hanging out from under your old tie-dyed shirt, people will say, 'How pathetic that this guy never accomplished anything and is still living out of his VW van,'" I asserted.

"How many guys do you know who are living this way and putting money in the bank?" Woody retorted. "I made $48,000 working January through March on a crab fishing boat in the Aleutians. You can't do that in N.Y."

Can anyone do that?

"Anyone who is tough enough and knows what he is doing with a boat."

I learned from another Alaskan that the job involves hanging over the side of a leaky boat in the dark, 16 hours/day. If you fall into the frigid water, you die rather quickly. Fifty-two people died last year in this industry.

Woody left me with a precious epiphany: "If you want more out of life, give up everything. If you want people to be your friend, give them everything you have. Give them your food, house, companionship, trust, love. When you start hoarding things, that is when the world turns against you."

Friday, July 9

Having gone to bed at 12:40, the sound of my alarm and the sight of gray sky at 6:15 AM was most unwelcome. Nonetheless, I convinced myself that I hadn't come this far to punt, and went over to the bus terminal. At 7:00 AM, I embarked upon The Mother of All Bus Trips: 11 hours over a dirt road in a school bus. Cramped legs, mind-shattering roar, desperate desire to curl up and sleep, and gloomy weather combined to cast a pall over what might be a nice trip. The single road in Denali National Park pushes along a ridge of the Outer Range of mountains, looking across a broad glacial valley to the Alaska Range, highest in North America.

My companions were a singularly typical bunch of American tourists: families with children and some retired couples. Our folksy southern driver asked everyone to shout out where they were from. After a Texan piped up, an Alaskan guy said, "Did you hear that we were thinking about splitting Alaska in half? That would make Texas the third largest state."

We had hardly passed the hotel before we saw a huge moose cow and her calf. She'd sought protection from the bears by bringing her calf around some rangers' living quarters. Smart cookie. Thanks to the presence of some sharp-eyed children, we picked out six bears, numerous caribou, three foxes (one carrying a dead squirrel in her mouth home to the den for her kits), distant Dall sheep, and, most spectacularly, a cagey gray wolf. The wolf magnificently ranged up and down a

hillside about 150 yards from the bus. His dignified face was clearly visible when viewed through a 480 mm lens.

I was thrilled to have seen my first wild wolf, but couldn't help thinking that a TV nature program would have given me a deeper understanding of the animal. Riding the bus was more like the work done by the poor sap who got stuck in a blind for a year with a camera. Watching Nature's outtakes after a full night's sleep, on a sunny day, from the comfort of a quiet Toyota might have been quite pleasant; desperate for sleep and crammed together in Kelly's nightmare of a bus with "a bunch of smelly other people," it seemed unlikely to become the highlight of my trip to Alaska.

The only outcropping of civilization along the entire road is the Eielson Visitor Center. At the bookshop there, I leafed through Kim Heacox's superb book of Denali photos. Heacox spent years here as a park ranger, and his book illustrates most of all the virtue of being in the right place at the right time. He was there when golden light bathed a caribou's rack fringed with red moss. He was there on hundreds of the rare days when Mt. McKinley's summit is visible. He was there when a bear or a moose showed up to turn an otherwise nice landscape composition into a spectacular example of Nature's Glory. The Denali Park of Heacox's book is cruelly different from the Denali Park that any visitor could see, in a way that isn't true for the Grand Canyon, Yosemite, or Yellowstone.

Rangers had embarked upon a short nature walk just before I arrived. However, the appearance of a medium-sized grizzly sent the entire group of 20 scurrying back to the visitors' center. It was pathetic. When in the history of mankind has a bear gone 200 yards out of its way to attack a group of 20 people? I chided them for being cowards.

When we reached our destination, Wonder Lake, we were all sorry to be there. The light was flat overcast. Mt. McKinley was mostly obscured. Mosquitoes by the zillions set upon us. All of the campers who had stayed overnight there were walking around with their Gore-Tex shell hoods up and mosquito nets over their faces. I had planned to come back to Wonder Lake by school bus the next day and camp for the night; my first glimpse of the mosquito nets was enough to convince me to cancel those plans. Seeing so many mosquitoes at once made me realize how

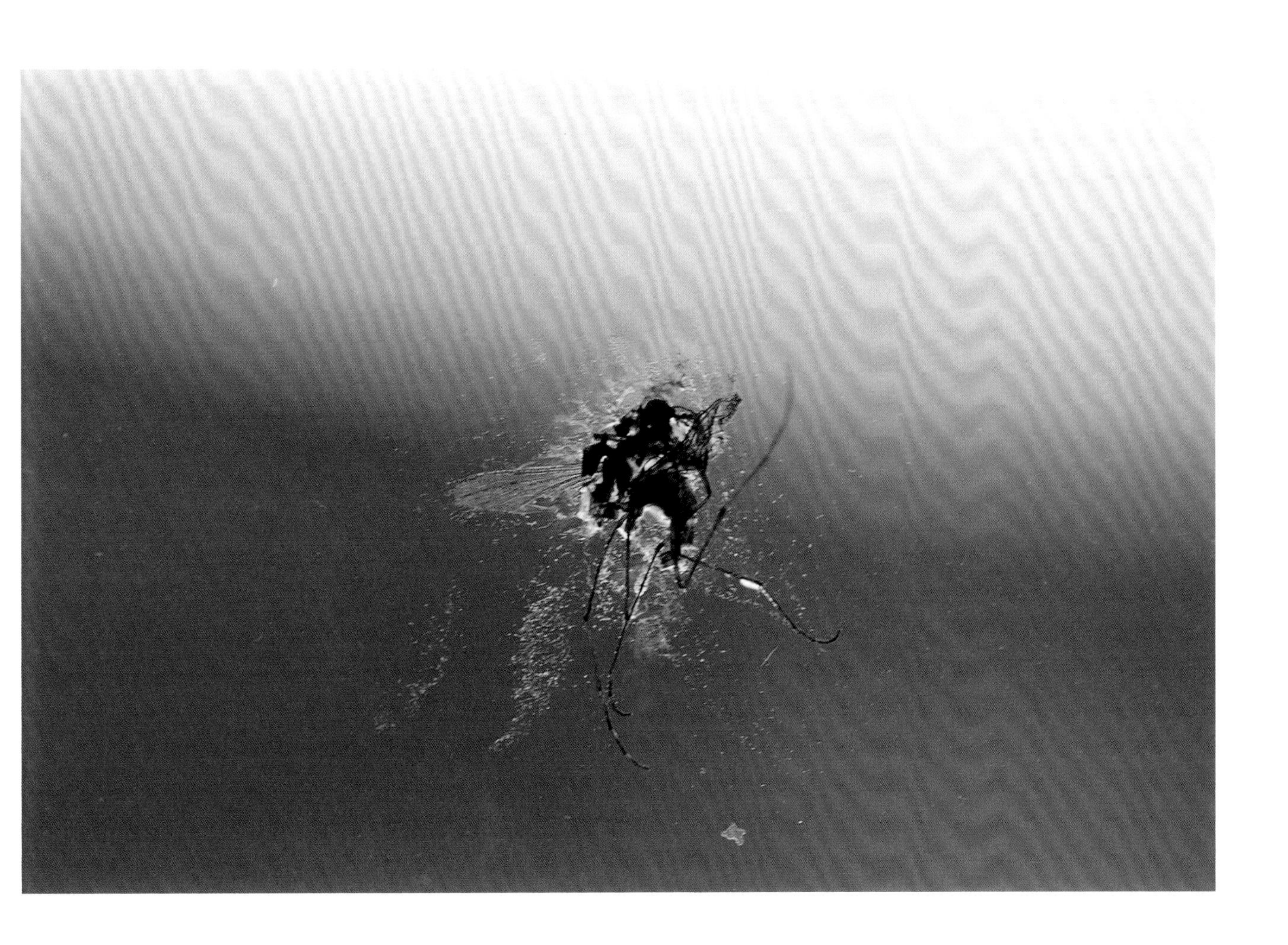

fortunate I'd been so far. Alaska is renowned for mosquitoes, but they have quite a short season and the season is different in each location. For example, at the park entrance, less than 100 miles back, the mosquitoes were mostly out of season and constituted only a minor nuisance.

Two Swiss-German couples hopped on the bus late in the afternoon. Walter, a black-haired 30ish dairy farmer, enjoys dairy subsidies and markets so sweet that he can make a good living with only 14 cows. He has visited 45 of the 50 states, missing only Hawaii, North Dakota, Washington, Maine, and one whose name he'd forgotten. I asked him how he liked Boston and was shocked to learn that he'd spent two weeks with friends in the Berkshires but wasn't interested in seeing Boston because "all big cities look the same." Since he hadn't bothered to see my hometown, I decided to abuse him.

Walter hollered "bear" and made the bus stop for what turned out to be several distant—and already overly familiar—caribou. Afterwards I referred to all the caribou we saw as "Swiss bear." This regrettably started a trend, and rocks became "Connecticut sheep," etc. In perfect idiom he said, "Why is everyone always picking on me?" (Unlike their German neighbors, the Swiss watch American movies in English with subtitles and hence are that much hipper to the lingo.)

Karin, Walter's wife, spoke French, Italian, Portuguese, Spanish, and a truly excellent English. With a sunny and thoughtful disposition, Karin prevented the last hours of the trip from dragging on into days. Karin sells spare parts for Swiss diesel engines, mostly to Latin America. What, you say you don't have a Swiss diesel in your vehicle? Maybe that is because you don't need 20,000 horsepower. Despite their conspicuous lack of coastline, the Swiss have long been one of the world's leading suppliers of big ship engines. The Swiss like to make products that require precision engineering and craftsmanship yet are not so fundamental that they attract the heavy guns of mass-market manufacturers in big countries.

Karin and Walter come to North America nearly every year, and this is already their second trip to Alaska. The only Old World thing they really miss here is "the bread." While delicately trying to spare my East Coast sensitivities, they eventually were willing to state their conclusion that people in the West were much more open and friendly.

"The standard European prejudice against Americans is that you are superficial, but Walter and I have found on the contrary that it was easy to make real friends here. We've tested these friendships over the years and found them as strong as any," Karin observed.

Ask an American what his principal gripe with tourism here is, and chances are he'll say, "All those old fogies in motor homes clogging up the two-lanes by driving 20 mph." Karin said that what she liked best about tourism here is the old fogies.

"In Europe, old people look old. They are old when you talk to them. They feel too old to travel after the age of 50 or so, and after they retire they just wait at home to die. It is wonderful to see old people feeling young and getting out to see things."

Next time I've gotten my Type A personality stuck behind a motor home with a "we're spending our children's inheritance" bumper sticker, I'll try to recall Karin's words.

Both Karin and Walter are distraught over the ethnic tensions fracturing Europe. Karin spoke of the trouble a dark-skinned Swiss girlfriend of hers has just going shopping. Merchants speak to her in broken German on the assumption that she is a foreigner. When her friend tells them she is a "real Swiss," they refuse to believe it. Walter thinks that the industrial economies of Europe have enough troubles of their own and shouldn't have to carry a bunch of lazy foreigners. Karin thinks that people who are comfortably situated shouldn't complain about the resources allotted to the less fortunate, "We have enough and can afford to help others; if there are a lot of freeloaders in Switzerland, it is because our laws encouraged them to come and we should blame ourselves."

I staggered off the bus at 6:00 PM and went straight into the Jacuzzi at the McKinley Chalet. Mark had been there all day chilling out and reading the paper, still recovering from a week in the backcountry where it had rained every day. Joe, a white-haired Irish Philadelphian, settled his ample body into the tub. Joe came from a family of nine, and one of his sisters moved to Anchorage 20 years ago. He and his brothers always talked about coming here to visit but never did.

"Three years ago, one of my younger brothers died of cancer, and it occurred to all of us that we might not live to fulfill our dreams. I immediately flew up here

with another brother, but our wives refused to join us. 'Alaska is too cold; we'll spend the time at Wanamaker's [the big Philadelphia department store].'

"Alaska as the Last Frontier was my dream, and I've returned every year to live it. I'm retired now so I'm spending five months here this time; it's a bit lonely because my wife still won't come."

A reindeer dinner at the chalet proved that *Women Who Run with the Wolves* is a better idea than *Men Who Eat Like the Wolves.*

Saturday, July 10

Acting on a tip from a local photographer, I drove out some gravel roads to an abandoned coal mine and walked into an interesting (and trail-free) canyon. I took a few snapshots and then headed back along the canyon floor/stream bed. What had been firm ground suddenly swallowed my sneakers, and I found myself standing in the mud in my socks. The rest of the hike out was wet, disgusting, and squishy.

After winding down from the hike and lunching at the Chalet, I drove out to the end of the pavement on the park road and pulled the bike out of the car. Bikes are allowed free access to the park road 24 hours/day. The gravel road starts with a 600′ hill, but the beautiful scenery made me tolerant of the climb. I coasted practically all the way to Sanctuary River, which is typical of the rivers on this valley floor. When the park was glaciated, a glacier carved a deep and wide riverbed, then lined it with gravel. The river is just a tiny fraction of the size of the glacier and winds its way back and forth across the huge riverbed. I stopped for a snack by the river around 7:00 PM and felt the benevolence of Nature in the blue sky reflection, in the golden glow of the mountainsides, in the gentle wind that kept mosquitoes from flying, and in the overarching peace. Before you set the preceding words to Beethoven's 6th, I should tell you that I was attacked by a seagull. He kept flying directly at me and then pulling up at the last minute before circling around again. Dumbfounded at first, my caveman instincts came to the rescue eventually, and I conceived the idea of throwing a spray of pebbles in his face. For my first shot, though, I could only find one stone and missed him cleanly. Nonetheless, after the stone went whizzing by, he parked himself on a midriver rock.

My ride back was just as much of a climb but seemed even more enjoyable as the light turned softer and a big rainbow arched over to the Alaska Range, compensating somewhat for the fact that I'd not seen a single mammal. Despite my lack of wildlife spotting, I'd have to say that biking beats the school bus hands down. If I come back, I'll reserve a campground far into the park and take camping gear, especially a water filter, to spend a few nights.

I spent the rest of the day with various Alaskans and summer employees, most notably an 11-year-old boy. Ben's mother was a schoolteacher, and he had just finished a remedial arithmetic course: "I did pretty good. We learned timesing and minusing." All Ben wanted out of life was a television to watch. He couldn't see any value in learning math. I told him about all the wonderful things people at MIT did with mathematics, but he remained unconvinced.

10

Overcharged in Katmai

Seven o'clock and I'm walking back from a waterfall through moss-carpeted forest. There is still plenty of light, but the high clouds and thick forest make the trail a bit mysterious. Following standard procedure in these woods, I am singing a Mozart aria to apprise the bears of my presence. Thirty yards away, a cinnamon-colored form rises up out of the tall grass. The form takes shape as a charging grizzly bear/ music critic. Starting from a dead stop, he closes the 30 yards between us in a few seconds without apparent strain. I raise an arm, say, "Hey, bear" in a normal tone (yes, and pitch) of voice as I move down the steep hillside clutching tree trunks for balance with my free arm. The 350 lb. adolescent stops on the trail 10 feet above me and stares straight into my eyes for five seconds. I could have sworn he was laughing.

July 12–17

Katmai National Park is home to the world's largest grizzly bears, commonly referred to here as the Alaskan Brown Bear. Because of their rich salmon diet, they grow to over 1000 lb. in weight, making them the world's largest land predator. Brooks Camp, where I stayed, is the overnight home of about 150 people and 20 bears, who live in closer contact with each other than anywhere else in the world. Bears are normally solitary animals, but here they've established a wolflike dominance hierarchy. As many as 15 bears congregate around Brooks Falls to grab salmon as they try to jump over the falls to reach spawning grounds upstream.

Wooden viewing platforms over the falls and a marshy area of the Brooks River allow tourists to safely spend an entire day 10-50′ from bears going about their business. Remarkably, most of the bears take little notice of humans and never make eye contact with visitors. The one exception I observed was actually the 4-year-old who charged me. He had been taunted earlier by a German tour group as he paced back and forth across a pontoon bridge. They hollered and jeered at him in German until he came underneath the platform to stare us down. It was chilling to look into his eyes and note his six-inch long claws. As the park gets more visitation, some of the younger bears like this one are losing their fear of humans. The Park Service instructs visitors to always back away from bears so apparently they sometimes learn how much fun it is to run tourists off trails.

Have you ever seen a photograph of a bear standing on top of a four-foot-high waterfall grabbing a salmon out of midair with its mouth? It was taken here. When I arrived in Alaska, I stopped at the first visitors' center and asked where I could find these bears. I was dismayed to learn that they were a $400 flight southwest from Anchorage, that it cost a fortune to stay at the overbooked lodge, that campground reservations had to be made months in advance, and that I might have to stay in the backcountry, at least five miles from Brooks Camp. However, this was why I'd come to Alaska and I wasn't going to miss it.

A 737 jet took me over staggering snowfield-covered mountains that form the Alaska Peninsula, which eventually becomes the Aleutian Islands. King Salmon is a wart in the middle of some smelly tidal flats. Fortunately I only had to spend 30 minutes there before getting in a Twin Otter float plane. I'd read about Twin Otters in books on Antarctic exploration, but seeing the plane was a surprise. With wheels under its floats, the plane is as high off the ground as a 727 even though it only seats about 20. Our pilots were clad in T-shirts and jeans and casually fired up the engines to a roar that would have been deafening if not for the earplugs I'd brought.

After 20 minutes of flying over Naknek Lake, we touched down on its surface in front of Brooks Lodge. Rather than landing with the expected big splash and thud, the plane came down so smoothly that none of us could tell when we'd hit water. Our pilot taxied back into the beach, and we walked on a float over to the sand. Although Katmai is famous for bad weather and biting insects, the skies were blue and the insects mercifully scarce. Our group of eight passengers was met on the beach by Ranger Barbara, a stern woman with close-cropped gray hair. She gave us a lecture on bears, mostly stressing that we weren't to get within 50 yards of a single bear or 100 yards of multiple bears. It was best to avoid wearing insect repellent, and one shouldn't have anything that smells unusual about one's person or tent.

Ranger Barbara dressed me down a bit for having come here without a campground reservation and told me to go immediately to the visitors' center to get on a waiting list. Once I left the beach, bureaucratic ideas about reservations and schedules became ever more indistinct, and each person I spoke with became ever more sympathetic. Ranger Lisa greeted me with a winning smile and radioed the campground hosts, a benevolent retired couple from Albuquerque, to make sure they had room somewhere for my small dome tent. Lisa, Brandeis Class of '81, turned out to be exactly the sort of nice Jewish girl my mother always wanted me to date but whom I could somehow never find in Boston.

I was sharing my site with Hazel and Heather, two diminutive Scottish scholars with lilting accents. Heather is getting a Ph.D. in Scottish Studies, concentrating on potato cultivation around the turn of the century. Hazel won a travel fellowship to Florence last year and another this year to spend three months in Anchorage. They'd just come back from six days in the backcountry. I was delighted that we were only sharing the site and not a tent; even after six days, they didn't want to pay four dollars for a hot shower and towel at the lodge and had decided to wait until they returned to Anchorage.

Before we could even walk to the campsite, three young bears came tumbling along the beach. They were no more than 30 yards away. One went into the water, quickly caught a 15 lb. salmon, and quietly munched it. Another came into the camp and, just as we were told, we got together in a group and clapped our hands and shouted for him to clear off. The Park Service is trying to condition the bears not to roam around the lodge and the camp. However, there are two brothers and a sister that have remained together for three years. They play-fight and generally raise Hell together and have ignored the accumulated wisdom of the rest of the bears. (These bears were to be constantly in my way during the week, bumming around in front of the lodge when I wanted to go in for breakfast and ultimately charging me on the Falls trail.)

I spent the evening eating a buffet dinner at the lodge and relaxing at one of the bear-viewing platforms. The sense of community here is strong. With 60 lodge guests, 60 campers, and about 35 workers, anonymity is simply not an option. Life here is much as it was back in the 1940s when the camp was established. Nature has been subdued with a generator and electric light, the tyranny of the clock has been imposed upon workers (and guests if they want to eat at the lodge), and the roar of the float plane is a common daytime sound, but there are no strangers, no telephones, no RVs, no bus tours, and, until Samantha's arrival, no notebook computers.

Two kinds of people come to Katmai: (1) photographers who can't understand why a grown man would pay $5000 to fly up here and spend two weeks standing up to his hips in icy water in order to catch and release 20 slimy, silver, flopping salmon; and (2) fishermen who can't understand why anyone would lug 50 lb. of equipment one mile and then sit all day taking Pictures #1,437,213 through #1,437,896 of the Katmai bears.

Photographers come here well-equipped. Under ordinary circumstances, the status-conscious might look to see what kind of camera you have. Not here, where all the lenses are so big that even a Nikon F4 looks like a child's toy after it is bolted onto the end of a tripod-mounted lens. Henry's 300/2.8 lens didn't cause any mouths to drop here. Any time I had company on a viewing platform, another photographer had a lens at least as big connected to a $400 Swiss ballhead. The only difference between the pros and the amateurs was that the pros' lenses had scratched barrels and their tripods were much sturdier. I'd never seen anyone old or female carrying a "big lens" before. Well, at Katmai, even the old *and* female carry them.

Famous wildlife photographers Art Gingrich and Mike Lacey happened to be here leading a Van Os luxury photo-safari. Most of their charges were medical doctors toting beautiful $4000 month-old all-white Canon lenses. One of them looked just like Bill Clinton, and he wasn't pleased to hear it. Not only was he a diehard Republican, but Hilary's plan to trim the sails of radiologists such as himself enraged him.

"What business does the government have interfering with the free market in medicine? We should be able to charge whatever we want," he insisted.

Didn't he think that the government's shelling out 50% of the nation's health care dollars through Medicare and Medicaid already made the market less than free?

"That's different."

My favorite photographer at Katmai was Dave, a 78-year-old New Yorker. He'd been here numerous times and thought that it had been ruined by tourists, for whom he had a healthy contempt. Dave had been sent on assignment to Africa about 40 times since 1960. He had trouble with his eyes now and was reduced to using autofocus; he needed me to help him with his Nikon 8008 out on the Brooks Falls platform. Dave never had children of his own but, at age 49, married a woman with five sons. He simply did not love his fellow man and referred contemptuously to our 22-year-old waitresses as "cupcakes." In some ways I wanted to be like Dave. I want to be flying to Africa and Katmai at age 78, carrying my own 300/2.8, Nikon, and video camera. But I think I'd better have some children lest I end up calling even the offspring of bears "brats."

You have to be a moron not to get decent pictures at Brooks. You sit or stand on a platform with an unobstructed view to bears 10-50′ away. Dominant bears occupy prime positions on top of the part of the falls where salmon jump every few seconds. When the salmon are running well, every five minutes a bear will catch a fish in his teeth and hold it firmly enough that blood begins to flow as the fish flops around. If there are plenty of salmon, the bear goes after only the fatty skin, brain, and roe, removing these parts during a gruesome minute or so. The salmon may remain alive for much or all of its consumption. Why do you think they call them animals?

If the salmon aren't so plentiful, a bear will spend a few minutes leisurely chomping away at his catch, bones and all. Big bears eat about 100 lb. of salmon a day to prepare for six months of hibernation. Without ever having an identity crisis, they live for 30 years, sleeping half the year and eating salmon the other half. Why do

humans torture themselves with finding a reason to exist? (If that's too philosophical for you, you'll perhaps admit that the bears' diet casts some doubt on the seriousness of the mercury-in-fish problem.)

A great picture at Brooks is of two bears fighting for a prime spot. They roar at each other with a terrifying force, then bite and hit each other with astonishing speed for 300–1000 lb. animals. Without a motor drive, a lot of film, and some luck, it would have been impossible to get a picture of one bear cuffing another. By the time I saw a bear's arm raised in anger and pressed the shutter release, the arm had already struck the other bear and come back down. Quite a few bears wore substantial reminders of battles past.

A more pastoral great picture would be of a sow and her cubs. Big boars will kill cubs, even their own, so the sow keeps her cubs well away from the falls and the thousand pounders. She protects her cubs aggressively from humans as well as teenager bears. One of my happiest moments was seeing the sow charge the bear that had charged me. The look of terror on his face as he scurried away was well worth the trip to the platform that day.

This was not the limit of my vindictiveness. When the big boars were sated one day and lolling about in the grass, my mischievous friend took a prime place on top of the falls. His inexperience meant that he didn't catch any fish even though many actually hit him in the face. Just call me Captain Ahab, for I waited a full half hour for a big boar to surprise him from behind and send him flying over the falls. When the big boar showed up, though, my antagonist simply scurried off upstream.

You can't expect a lenshound to give you a fair portrait of the fishermen guests, but Roland was one of my favorites. Roland was a solid balding 55-year-old from Sacramento with seven children and 18 grandchildren. He retired from the contracting business because he found state government red tape too intrusive. Now he works for Deseret Industries, an arm of the Mormon church, "rehabilitating bicycles, appliances, and people." County social workers send people who are handicapped, poor immigrants, or down on their luck to Deseret Industries. Newcomers are given a place to stay for a year and a minimum-wage job. People such as Roland supervise and train them in how to be a good cog in the American Economic Machine.

"Social workers try to help them with psychological problems, but we don't make any attempt to convert anyone to the LDS church. We all get paid a moderate wage, but the money doesn't come from the church or the state. We get pretty good raw materials donated by Californians of all faiths, so Deseret Industries is entirely self-sufficient."

After five nights in Brooks Camp, I got to know virtually everyone there, both guests and staff. Given that most of the guests are lords of yuppie society, e.g., doctors and lawyers, the staff contained a surprising number of dropouts who are pushing 30 and lack both the skills and motivation to reenter mainstream yuppie society.

Emma, the most attractive of the "cupcakes" both inside and out, was a 24-year-old Italian-American from Rochester. Upon arrival at the camp, her ambition to learn French over the summer earned her nearly unanimous ridicule. Other staff were afraid that she'd come away with a tangible accomplishment, and they'd have to feel like intellectual bums. Whenever I moved Samantha from her charging perch in the lobby—there are no locks in Brooks Camp and nobody thinks twice about leaving thousands of dollars of equipment lying about in a public place—howls of outrage were raised.

Steve, a bearded 45-year-old hippie/mountain man, was a typical anti-computer protester.

"I'm still recovering from the misfortune of growing up in the Lower 48."

New York?

"Montana."

Is the culture really that different?

"Fences. Fences and welfare-ranching and welfare-farming. The parks there aren't wilderness; they are museums. Even this place is a museum, but the wilderness isn't far away."

What's so bad about bringing a computer into the wilderness anyway?

"A person couldn't possibly be himself with a computer."

But I'd written a 75-page diary since leaving Boston. I could never have done that with a pen.

"I write 75 pages in three days with a pen."

. . . and I grew up in a shoebox in the middle of I-95, worked 30 hours/day, was murdered in cold blood by my father every night, and still managed to write a 2000-page best-selling novel every week in my spare time.

Emma sagely noted that "these guys are really reacting out of fear. They don't have the skills to make it in the yuppie world and are a bit afraid of a peripatetic life of low-paid service jobs in various resorts."

As it happens, I wasn't the only PowerBook addict in camp. Ted Kerasote, a writer for *Sports Afield* and *Outside* magazines, was here writing about bear management. We happened to be sitting next to each other around the lodge fireplace and he'd already heard all about me.

"You must be that guy from Boston."

Ted beautifully illustrated the mellowing effect that living in a Wyoming town of 90 for years can have on someone born on the Lower East Side. In a patient soft voice, Ted summarized his new book *Bloodties,* about animal rights and hunting.

"Hunting in one's bioregion can be ecologically more sound than being a supermarket fossil-fuel vegetarian, i.e., someone who has plugged into America's factory farm system, which has destroyed so many different types of wildlife. Remember that the wheat field used to be a buffalo range, pesticides kill animals, and combines kill all kinds of small animals. Exploration for the oil that powers the combines and makes the pesticides displaces and kills animals."

What about Prudhoe Bay? It is only a 250-square-mile outpost on the Arctic Ocean and produces all of Alaska's oil. With millions of square miles of identical wilderness all around, how could this tiny settlement make a difference?

"Good point, but think about the Dalton Highway that was built to service Prudhoe Bay. That opened up those millions of square miles of wilderness to hunters who go in and kill moose and wolves.

My book calculates the fossil-fuel cost of different diets. A guy in Wyoming expends 79,000 K-calories to shoot 150 lb. of elk meat. The equivalent amount of Idaho potatoes costs 150,000 K-cals. Rice and beans from Northern California 477,000 K-cals."

That's great, but I hadn't seen too many elk roaming around my Boston suburb, whereas we are well-supplied with supermarkets. Can a significant number of Americans really live off game?

"There are more white-tail deer now than when Columbus landed because the forest has been opened up and they flourish on the edge of timber land."

> *Reviews of Ted's book spoke volumes about the difference between East and West coasts. The* New York Times *review read much like this synopsis, focusing on his argument and its numerical underpinnings. The* Los Angeles Times *review started and ended with a discussion of the similarities between hunting and sex.*

Janet, Ted's companion from Wyoming, described herself as a "shaman." I asked if she had a day job also.

"Being a shaman *is* my day job. I make a living healing everything from a broken hip to a broken heart."

She looked longer than anyone ever had at the picture of George that I carry in my wallet. She must have stared sympathetically for a full minute before speaking.

"A dog's job is to teach us about love."

Who gave them that job?

"Everybody has a service."

Traveling alone is great when one wants to be schedule-free, but walking around alone at Brooks can be a bit unnerving. Ever the night owl, I was generally the last to leave the Falls viewing platform at night, usually around midnight.

"Don't hike in groups of fewer than four. Don't wear insect repellent. Don't hike after dark because that is when the bears that aren't comfortable with people come out," said the rangers.

My second night there was pretty typical. I was alone, wearing 100% DEET, and at 10:30, darkness was gathering in the thick woods.

As I crested a hill, a 900 lb. boar lifted his head out of the grass and sniffed the air. He was no more than 15 feet from me. I backed away talking quietly, and he didn't get up, pursue me, or even look at me. I bushwhacked around through some tall grass and managed to reach the platform without further incident. By midnight, the light had faded too much even for the video camera I'd brought so I started hiking back to camp. Thick clouds made it much darker than the previous night, and I could barely distinguish trees from bears on the first half mile of narrow trail.

I was glad to get to the road for the last half mile of my walk, but soon had an eerie feeling about a vague shape 50 yards off. Depressingly soon, I confirmed that it was in fact a bear facing me end-on, but I couldn't tell whether he was walking toward me or away from me. He grew larger and larger, lending credence to the "walking toward" hypothesis, then veered off into the woods on the right side of the road. I walked along the left edge of the road and sang Stephen Foster songs. The next night I was charged.

Reenacting *Dido and Aeneas* is tough in our age of fax machines and airplanes, but Ranger Lisa and I thought it was worth a try. When two Jews meet in the wilderness for a date, what do they talk about? How much trouble they have dating Jews.

"I grew up in Colorado and went to Brandeis because I wanted to be with other Jews. However, I quickly discovered that I didn't like East Coast JAP culture. And Jewish men are ridiculously spoiled by their mothers. It took five months in Israel to restore my Jewish identity. Still, I haven't dated a Jewish guy for the 11 years I've lived in Alaska, something my parents weren't too pleased about."

I offered Lisa my standard theory of why American Jews can't get along. Naturally I think of Jewish men as wonderful souls who are willing to dedicate themselves to their wife and kids. If they only dated Jewish women, they'd just select their favorite and that would be it. However, American Jewish men date both Jews and non-Jews. They can't help noticing that their non-Jewish girlfriends are grateful for the good treatment and that the Jewish ones accept it as their due.

"I think Jews of both sexes, but especially men, are spoiled and used to having their way, which makes it hard for them to get along with anyone as stubborn as themselves," Lisa concluded.

We walked out to the viewing platform talking about literature, music, philosophy, and our life histories. It was a real pleasure to talk with someone thoughtful, well-educated, and absolutely direct. Other dates I'd been on seemed like shams by comparison: two people playing roles, each pretending to be what he or she imagines the other person wants. I wondered how could people get to know each other if they were acting. I questioned whether I'd ever been 100% frank with girlfriends or vice versa and, if so, how long it had taken to get to that point.

Lisa didn't miss too much about city life and found that even Anchorage (pop. 200,000) was now too large for her taste. The ever-present possibility of a new start with new people in the city didn't entice her.

"I've adapted to life in small towns or this tiny park. It's a fish bowl, but I can deal with that. I just never do or say anything that I'm ashamed of."

Alone together on the platform in a companionable silence, Lisa and I had time to reflect. Lisa broke the silence.

"The more I look at these bears and their simple lives, the more I am convinced that there is something wrong with the way we live."

My response underscored the gulf between us and the fact that two months on the road isn't sufficient to erase an East Coast Type-A personality.

"I was just thinking that these bears lead completely worthless lives. They sleep half the year, then stand in a stream eating salmon the other half. What's the point?"

Life in Paradise has to end sometime, and that sad morning broke clear and cold. The Twin Otter appeared out of a distant fogbank and splashed into the beach. Wayne, the trim young pilot, helped me haul my 150 lb. of luggage down the beach and we soon arced over the lodge and the falls before climbing into the clouds. I never did get to see the Valley of 10,000 Smokes, where the 1912 eruption blew the top 6000 feet off Mt. Katmai, so I'll have to return. I told Wayne how much I envied him his job, but he feels shackled to it.

"If I didn't have a wife and kids, I'd go back to school and prepare myself for some other kind of work."

The grass *is* always greener.

In King Salmon, I had a nice reunion with two Swiss-German couples, medical doctors whom I'd met in Fairbanks. Meanwhile my mouth had a good reunion with some of their sandwiches—I was getting pretty good at bumming food from the better-prepared. One of the wives, a dark-haired Italianate beauty, graciously switched the conversation from German into her perfect English.

"Europeans are fools, by and large. They leave their carefully selected group of educated friends back home and go into a McDonald's in Kansas. Wow! The workers there aren't as educated as their friends back home. So they go home and declare that Americans are morons.

"What I like best about Americans is that they are delighted to encounter each other abroad and invariably stop to chat. When Swiss meet other Swiss in foreign countries, they take pains to avoid having the strangers recognize them as Swiss."

Touching down in Anchorage, I felt a twinge of lost innocence and community. Oh, I was anxious to get to Photo-Wright's, with its $300,000 dip-and-dunk slide film processor. I thought of the new adventures awaiting me on the Kenai Peninsula. Ethnic restaurants beckoned. I appreciated the classical radio station (KLEF, far better than Boston's) and the well-stocked bookstore/café. Telephones would connect me to my friends.

Would it really have been crazy to abandon my car at the Anchorage airport and stay in Paradise?

11

Kenai Peninsula, Lesbians, Jews, and Strange Bedfellows

July 17 and 18

Anchorage seemed frighteningly anonymous after Brooks Camp. I took to spending most of my time in Cyrano's bookstore/café/arthouse-cinema/alternative-theater. One nice thing about a city of this size is that all the intellectuals congregate in one place. Spending three days at Cyrano's, one would be likely to encounter 90% of Anchorage's literary-minded population.

Anxious to avoid imposing on any of my local friends, and struggling under a load of errands, I decided to stay in the shabby Anchorage youth hostel. A bunch of guys gathered to watch me sort 17 rolls of Katmai pictures, and their praise swelled my already-inflated-beyond-the-manufacturer's-rated-pressure head.

I had to wait until past 2 for my favorite interaction, though. A 24ish Chicagoan was haranguing me from beneath his baseball cap.

"You have to make these pictures available to children. You should put together a book about bears," he insisted.

"Hey, I get enough rejection from women; I don't need any more from editors," I pleaded.

Mercifully ending this exhortation to commercial endeavor, a black guy came in looking very confused and wandered from room to room. My book agent said, "May I help you?" a few too many times to what turned out to be a harmless fellow from Niger studying business at Colorado State University.

"It is a shame that people in Chicago have so many problems with blacks that it creates such prejudice," he opined later when we were alone, then became entranced and glued to the light table by a slide of Emma.

"Did she become your girlfriend?"

He knew I'd only been there a few days, so he must have had a high opinion of my marketability or an unrealistic optimism about American girls.

Anchorage may be a tougher place for nonconformists than the rest of Alaska. I'd met more lesbians in a few weeks in Alaska small towns than in over a decade hanging around Cambridge, home of *Our Bodies, Ourselves.* They either said they were attracted by the tolerant spirit here or complained that they'd been repelled by the men. Yet in Anchorage I quickly encountered a 22-year-old who'd been pushed out of her job here as a legal secretary after three days. Rumors of her lesbian tendencies surfaced, based on her lack of make-up and choice of "severe" navy and white rather than pastel colors.

"I'm physically attracted to both men and women, but time and time again I've put my faith in men and they turned out to be jerks."

Relations between the sexes in Alaska are rather unusual even when boys like girls and vice versa. Alaska should be a paradise for women since the jobs here attract men disproportionately. Sheer numbers aren't always enough to satisfy, though. Women are fond of noting that "The odds are good, but the goods are odd." Men here are allegedly crude, demanding, macho, unreliable, drunk, and irascible.

The "unfair sex" has a slightly different view of matters. I was cautioned several times against striking up anything serious with the more rugged Alaska women.

"If they've been living by themselves in a cabin for 10 years, they aren't going to be able to adapt to you," noted a burly hunting guide.

A woman who had indeed spent a lot of time on her own in remote cabins echoed this sentiment. "I'm used to being alone, and I've become capable of handling everything life dishes out by myself. If I get too close to a man, I am afraid that when he is gone I will have forgotten how to survive on my own."

A Prudhoe Bay worker warned me against "Sloper Girls," whose boyfriend(s) work on the North Slope one week on and one week off.

"They are not exactly whores, but one guy will pay their rent, another their entertainment, and so on. I'm from the Midwest, and one thing that surprised me here was the high level of acceptance of women with multiple boyfriends. Guys will say, 'I know she isn't faithful, but we're here together now and that's all that matters.'"

The drive toward Kenai out of Anchorage has got to be one of the world's loveliest and certainly the nicest I've found within one hour of a city. One drives along one shore of Cook Inlet, which is a little slice of ocean that has worked its way in between two 5000′ mountain ranges. The mountains are covered with stripes of snow and glaciers. For the first half-hour of my drive there was a cloud overhead but sunshine on distant mountains ahead; it was like driving toward Valhalla.

After 45 minutes, I'd reached the sunshine and Portage Glacier. This glacier empties into a beautiful mountain-ringed lake, but thousands of years of global warming have caused it to recede to the point that one can't see it from the road anymore. I arrived just in time to catch the 6:00 PM cruise, and I rushed to get on. The folks operating the boat saw me parking and hollered up to ask if I wanted on. They held the boat and let me on for free, rather than reopen their register to collect $20. We were immediately sailing past intricately sculpted icebergs calved off the miles-long and 700′-thick glacier. Under a blue sky our guide told us how lucky we were with the weather, which is famously rainy in this part of the Kenai. Alaska had been having its sunniest summer in memory, and people everywhere reminded me how lucky I was to be here now.

I spent the cruise on the open top deck chatting with Mike, one of the members. He is 46 years old and looks just like Harrison Ford. He'd spent some years at U.C. Davis studying ecology, but left to play basketball in a minor league in France, leaving his wife behind in Davis to work. Absence did not make her heart grow fonder, and she abandoned him spiritually as he had her geographically. Mike stopped in Anchorage en route to playing more basketball in Australia. He met the woman of his dreams there and stayed to raise two children in Girdwood, population 1600.

"I worked for awhile as a paramedic in Anchorage. Someone with a year's training can earn $100,000/year with a bit of overtime. But I didn't like the pace of the city and the hours so I moved my family back to Girdwood."

Despite his multiple careers, countries, and companions, Mike looked less worn out than most of my friends in their early 30s.

A large black family had been on the boat, and we ran into each other back at the visitors' center. One woman was moving from New Jersey to Hyannis, Cape Cod.

Isn't that where old Republicans go to die? What's it like to be black in a WASP enclave?

"No problem at all. I've been going there since I was 5. People accept us even though we're black and Jehovah's Witnesses. Say, you're Jewish aren't you? Are Jews still waiting for the Messiah?"

I told her the old joke about the unemployed guy who sees the "Messiah Watcher Needed" sign outside a synagogue.

"We need someone who knows all the signs laid out in the Bible for the appearance of the Messiah," says the rabbi. After the rabbi quizzes the applicant for awhile, he says, "You are a real scholar; the job is yours."

"But what about the salary?"

"$11,000/year."

"I can't feed my wife and four kids on that!"

"Well, I admit the salary isn't so good," says the rabbi, "but you can't beat the job security."

Monday, July 19

Tom Bodett fans will recognize Homer, Alaska, as "The End of the Road," and it is a dramatic end at that. The road, which had been heavily populated with motor homes, ends in the world's longest natural gravel spit, extending 4.5 miles out into the Cook Inlet.

I stopped at the airport control tower, and Stan and John told me about their life flying in Alaska. Stan was a cargo pilot out of Bethel, a small Eskimo fishing village, for six years.

"In some ways they are more civilized than we are," noted Stan. "For one thing, they don't look down on prostitution. It's a damp town. You can have alcohol, but you can't sell it. My daughter went to junior high school there, and her Eskimo classmates were happy to trade a night in bed for a six-pack."

Aside from well-priced prostitution, living in the bush involves occasional moose charges.

"They all called off their charge after I fired a shot in the air. I don't hunt. I learned in the Marines that killing isn't a sport."

Stan was happy to be out of the flying business and working for the F. A. A.

"East Coast lawyers and insurance companies have ruined aviation. A lot of manufacturers have stopped making light aircraft because insurance is too expensive. You can't get a lift in a commercial cargo flight anymore because if you aren't paying for a ticket, the insurance won't cover you. Commercial insurance costs a fortune, and you can go to jail now if you only have personal insurance and split the gas with a friend."

Failure to reserve in advance prevented me from cruising over to the mountains on the other side of the inlet, so I bummed around the docks looking at halibut. As far as I could tell, recreational halibut fishing consists of getting up early, shelling out $150, and sitting on a boat doing nothing for the whole day. At the end of each cruise, the 10 biggest fish are hung on a pole, usually ranging from about 200 lb. down to 40 lb. The proud fishermen, a couple of whom will have caught fish that weigh more than themselves, line up behind the fish for photographs. Homer is the halibut fishing capital of the world: a record-breaking 400 lb. halibut was caught near here.

Commercial halibut fishing is permitted only one day a year, and the take is prodigious. I was later to encounter a woman who fed her family for a whole year on "road-kill halibut." Just after the commercial day, she came upon a truck whose doors had sprung open to litter the highway with hundreds of ice-packed halibut.

FANNY

907
FOX

She and her family helped the driver reload his cargo, and he gave them eight fish to take home.

Tuesday, July 20

Groggy but alive, I hopped onto the *Danaina* for the 7:00 AM trip over to Seldovia under a thick overcast. We saw a lot of comical puffins in the water, but the tide was too low to get up close to their nests in the rocks of Gull Island. Our guide pointed out dozens of species of birds, but didn't explain anything about them that would make them interesting to a novice. Huddled inside against the cold, I sat down next to Stephanie, who described herself as the "shikse trophy wife" of a 56-year-old Jewish financial executive. She claimed to have a daughter starting at B.U. in the fall, but it was hard to believe from looking at her wrinkle-free face.

"East Coast women, especially Jewish ones, don't appreciate a man's true qualities. I grew up in Ohio, and you *must* move to the Midwest after you graduate."

Stephanie was traveling with Arlene, her husband's sister and the sardonic wife of a Scarsdale literary agent. We had a cozy breakfast together at 9:30 at the Kachemak Kafe in Seldovia. At the next table, three retired fishermen schmoozed over coffee and pancakes.

Walter had come up here in 1960, and his stiff swollen fingers betrayed several decades working lines. He went away every winter to escape the darkness of Seldovia, population 250. After his first winter here he got married in the spring.

How come he didn't wear a wedding ring?

"Wedding ring?" Walter chuckled. "Everyone here knows who is married and who isn't."

I told Walter that I liked living in a city because it was possible to date a woman, have her conclude that you are a total fool, and date another woman the next week without her being aware of the first woman's low opinion of you.

"True enough, but I don't like starting from Square One with people. If you are a gentle, kind, helpful person, you become known for that in a small town. You don't ever have to 'go in cold' with anyone. I'm not fond of the city. Anchorage isn't even part of Alaska anymore. People there don't know how to survive."

DERBY
TICKETS
SOLD HERE!
ONE

Local girls told me that the ride to Jakalof Bay would be a "nice, basically flat, short ride with views of the Inlet and mountains." I parked my cameras with the harbormaster and set forth on what turned out to be a 24-mile round-trip on a dirt road with 1700′ of climbing. The first few miles offered views only of trees overhanging the occasional rat shack house. Seldovia is allegedly quaint, but what were probably shabby historical buildings were wiped out by the '64 earthquake. Householders have apparently all availed themselves of the local Instant Okie franchise; boats, trucks, cars, and campers in various stages of rusting decay stood in every front yard.

After six miles, the houses thinned out, and I was rewarded with views over the Inlet and harbors. Much of the roadside forest appeared to have been cut 20 years ago, but patches were carpeted by ferns and crowded with old trees. Jakalof Bay consists of a gravel parking lot, a rotting wooden boat hauled up on the beach, and a dock with a few open clam boats tied up. I walked out onto the dock to talk with Sadie Sin, a Great Lakes Indian who moved up here 30 years ago to fish and dig clams.

Sadie claimed to be "an antisocial, ornery, bad-tempered son-of-a-bitch," but he seemed happy to entertain me and two couples from Wasilla (north of Anchorage) who'd come in on their recreational fishing boats. Sadie washed and sorted clams and spoke about his life here as a wild bachelor. He liked to dress up as a woman and sweep the two paved streets of Seldovia free of gravel. Sadie is a musician and is halfway through making a few music videos with his 16 mm movie camera.

Isn't it lonely being the only transvestite music video director in Seldovia?

"I'm alone wherever I go."

My ride back was uneventful except for occasional encounters with Sadie in his ancient Chevrolet Suburban. He pointed out houses that he'd helped build and talked about the folks who owned them. When I got back into town, I stopped for a Coke at the Linwood Bar, whose walls were decorated with numerous photos of Sadie in drag. I took the 4:30 cruise back to Homer on the *Endeavor,* a boat with the best naturalist in town. He was particularly expansive on the "woman's libber bird," which lays eggs and then abandons them to their father for nurturing.

Playful sea otters gathered in groups of 20 or more to watch us pass, including a mother clutching a baby to her breast. Their dark eyes held more meaning for me than all the birds put together, and I recalled a *Wall Street Journal* article about the Audubon Society. They hired a management consultant who reported that the public saw the Society as having a "narrow bird-oriented focus."

Back in Homer, I was waxing rhapsodic over a Skor bar when I ran into Susan, a freckled 26-year-old Washington Stater.

"I do whatever is right for today without worry about tomorrow because tomorrow might never come. If tomorrow it ends, at least I won't have wasted today . . . . Say, you seem interesting. Let's spend more time together."

We meandered about town, then settled down at the Salty Dawg bar. Our picnic table contained Keith Iverson, self-published author of a well-written autobiography, *Alaskan Viking*. He describes his travails in making a life just across the inlet in tiny Sadie Bay. My experience with the Katmai bears was put into perspective by his gripping account of a few minutes in the woods with a black bear.

Keith was treading silently over a moss-carpeted trail when he surprised a napping 300 lb. black bear. The bear tried to run away but in its confusion ran directly into Keith. Physical contact made the bear think that Keith was attacking him and he bit him in the shoulder, then they tumbled down a slope tied to each other.

"I managed to poke the bear in the eye as we got towards the bottom and he ran away."

Any permanent injuries?

"I'd rather face a charging bear than start a conversation with a strange woman."

Keith wasn't carrying a gun and might not have had time to use it if he had been. When he first came here he carried a 44 Magnum pistol at all times until an old-timer advised him to file off the front sight.

"Why?" asked Keith.

"So it won't hurt so much when the bear shoves it up your ass."

Alaskans have lots of pithy bear folk wisdom: "How do you tell the difference between a grizzly and a black bear? . . . When you climb a tree, if the bear follows you, it is a black bear; if the bear knocks the tree over, it is a grizzly."

An alternative answer is, "The grizzly bear jingles when he walks," referring to the tendency of tourists to wear little bells on their backpacks that allegedly warn bears of their approach.

It had been more than a week since I was charged, but I couldn't get two images out of my mind: (1) the bear rising up from nowhere and appearing 30 yards ahead of me on the trail; (2) the grip of his ancient eyes looking down on me from where I left the trail (researchers are now questioning the belief that bears have poor vision, claiming that their visual acuity is about as good as ours).

Susan encountered a stranger, Cid (short for Cindy in an almost California way), a trim 33-year-old elementary schoolteacher about to start teaching in a tiny Eskimo village north of Nome. Cid and Susan joked about the virtues of casual sex: "No, you can't have my phone number." They liked sex but were tired of the mechanics of dating, marriage, divorce, etc.

"The first sexual encounter between two people is always the most exciting," Cid opined. "You never know what to expect. Marriage isn't about sex, it is about boredom."

"I never saw the downside of sex or romance until my dog died," I noted. "I'd had an exaggerated sense of the immutability of my self. I thought that if I were dropped down in a different culture or among different people that I would be essentially the same person. Because I never got depressed or even really unhappy, I thought that I was fundamentally different from all of my friends who were subject to occasional periods of despair. After George died, though, I became just like them; the tribulations of life could cut deep for the first time in many years."

Susan found it a little comical that a man could love a dog so much, but Cid said that every experience was useful. I asked her how the death of a beloved companion could possibly contain anything good. She responded with the wisest and most comforting thing anyone had said to me on the subject for two years.

"George's death enabled you to empathize with your friends in a way that you couldn't before."

I bedded down on the Spit on my sleeping pad, not bothering to pitch the tent because of Homer's reputation for clear skies. It was so dark that one could barely see the nearby mountains, and it finally hit me how far south I'd come from Fairbanks. Cheerful dropouts surrounded me. They'd lived on the Spit for months in tent/tarp palaces, in open defiance of Homer's new $3/night camping fee.

Wednesday, July 21

I limped over to the Latitude 59 espresso café to write my diary, but found it impossible to catch up with the past few days. New people kept sitting down next to me and telling interesting stories.

Glynn had a build reflecting years of physical labor and long white hair reflecting 54 years of thought. He spoke in the gentle tones of his native Mississippi.

"I wanted to reach the truth so I started my own private investigation. It took me a long time, but it finally came to me that everything is in a divine order. Everybody looks for this in God, but they have to look within themselves. They burned Martin Luther after seven years in jail, but the truth of the matter is that for every head there is a different reality.

"I divorced a really beautiful wife in Christmas of '84 after relocating her and our daughter to Prescott, Arizona. I wanted to be totally unattached and not having anything tugging at me. I wanted to be alone and forgotten."

Didn't he feel guilty for leaving his family?

"Don't carry about regret. You can't be free packing all that weight. Chop your toe off and it will hurt like hell, but it will heal. Christianity has ruined our life with lies about how we are born in sin and God will kill you if you don't do right. It is a shame to destroy all those clean fresh minds. Most people never recover from that. All the pain and suffering."

Glynn had traveled all over America and never ran short of feminine company. He spoke well of his Jewish girlfriend from Miami Beach.

"Jewish women treat a Jewish guy awful, but they treat a goy like a prince. Still, I had to leave her. I just recently left a really beautiful woman, a warm body, and a beautiful apartment in Billings, Montana. I'd stayed with her two years, but I had to come here."

How old was she?

"She was 55. I usually date women my own age. I'd go after a 22-year-old if she had the kind of mind I could live with, but for the sake of a body, no way Jose. I'm past that."

Where did Homer fit in his search for the truth.

"Although I had never visited Homer, I had a bizarre dream about four years ago about moving here. I rode my motorcycle down a road downhill. Farther and farther everything was incredibly green, a lot of grass and a lot of water. People lived on stilt houses out on the water, but I could ride my motorcycle out on the dock and had a wonderful reception from people. I flew out of town and everything on earth and sky was either blue or gray. I'd been contemplating coming up here four years ago and made a decision in the driveway: Belize or Alaska. It was around September 1st so I towed a boat through Mexico City and down to Belize and camped out for five months. I took my Honda in my camper also and would ride it out to a point and see the mountains in three countries at once."

Glynn had only been in Homer a few weeks and was settling in repairing boats and doing other kinds of odd jobs.

"I keep noticing strange things about Homer that came to me in that dream long ago. I see birds play games and people laid back and doing their things. People are a little bit mellowed out; maybe it is the long dark winter."

Glynn's friend Dennis, a heavyset guide, sat down with his 6-year-old daughter, Winafred, to whom I was magnetically drawn.

"I can tell that you want to share your life with a child. Take some advice: Find yourself a nice woman with two children. Move in for the winter. Reevaluate your goals in the spring."

Glynn had some final thoughts before getting up to go to work.

"A lot of people in this country emanating love and peace toward Russia changed those people. We can definitely as humans influence what goes on on this planet more than we think. We already do with ignorance."

I talked a little bit more with Dennis, who is such a fundamentalist Christian that he doesn't go to any church.

"Two Christian girls came to stay with our family, and they were horrified to discover some marijuana. I laid out on a table a pen, a knife, a revolver, and a joint. 'Which one is sin?' I asked. They immediately pointed to the joint. 'I can write false witness against my brother with the pen, stab him in the back with the knife, or kill my brother with the gun, but you think the joint is sin.' The girls nodded yes."

I was reminded that the Kenai Peninsula was the only part of Alaska that voted to keep dope legal.

The local museum had an illuminating exhibit on the consequences of the *Exxon Valdez*'s grounding. The slick came within a few miles of Homer. Exxon forked over more than $900 million in penalties plus spent $2 billion on cleanup, yet virtually nothing was accomplished. A lot of the cleanup lasted only a day or two as new oil washed over the same beaches. Ecologists eventually decided that many of the cleanup efforts in fact did more damage than just leaving the contaminated beaches alone. There were a lot of sanctimonious quotations from environmentalists about how evil Exxon was, but it seemed pretty clear that accidents are bound to happen if we don't resolve to make do with the oil we produce domestically. In other words, the enemy is really us, the car drivers, electricity users, and home heaters of America.

Clouds covered the sky just in time for my second cruise to Gull Island. I'd chosen to go at high tide because we would be able to get right up within a few feet of birds by the thousands. The gray day was unfavorable for photography, but puffins and some penguinlike birds grabbed our attention. Seagulls here aren't quite as ugly as ours in Boston, but they aren't much better than flying rats either. Baby animals are always adorable, though, and we cooed over mother seagulls sheltering their tiny young.

Two Alaskan retired schoolteachers compared notes with me about our trips to Israel.

"We just loved everything about Israel!" they enthused.

"That's because you aren't Jewish so for you it was like a zoo," I noted. "If polar bears want to live like polar bears, what do you care since they aren't part of your family? For me Israel is horrifying because it isn't the kind of place American Jews would build but rather has an Arab mentality. Europeans or Americans with a little money cooperate to pave the common street and line it with flowers. Middle Easterners use their first bit of money to build a high wall around their property so

they won't have to look at the ugly street. They line the *inside* of the wall with flowers and hurl their garbage over the wall into the street."

I left Homer late and drove north while the mountains across the inlet were garbed in mist and crowned by a golden-red sunset. I pitched the tent by a quiet lake.

Thursday, July 22

Back in 1984, someone decided Alaska needed yet another park that can be reached only by boat or helicopter and created Kenai Fjords National Park. I finished the three-hour drive to Seward by 10:15 AM and found that both 11:30 boats were fully booked. However, at the last minute, a single place opened up on the best boat in town, which is fast, new, and stabilized.

We took off with terrific speed over the flat water at 11:30, but stopped soon enough to watch a cute otter and then roared out again into the open. Clouds still covered the dock, but warm sunshine bathed us 10 minutes out of port. Seward is home to a fair amount of heavy industry, all of it visible from the water. A Japanese coal freighter took on Healy coal (mined near Denali) from a large conveyor system. A mountain of sawdust proclaimed a sawmill that processes timber from all over Alaska, lately mostly trees killed by a beetle, and sends its output to Japan. As we passed a new concrete structure, our captain said, "That is Alaska's maximum security prison, which holds 400 innocent men."

Homer was full of people spending two months living on the beach trying to see three tiny towns and one inlet; this Seward tourist cruise was full of people spending two weeks living on a bus trying to see all of Alaska. Continuing the "Jews who wouldn't give each other the time of day in Manhattan but who are delighted to find one another in the wilderness" theme of this narrative, Jody, a 30-year-old Atlantan, singled me out and noted that we were probably the only Jews on the boat. She and her husband, Eric, a solid-looking accountant, were here for just nine days escaping their two children. They were enjoying Alaska, but Jody couldn't shake her disappointment at the thrown-together appearance of all the towns.

FJORDLAND

"I thought it would be like Jackson, Wyoming, with rustic Western architecture."

I loaned Jody some New Zealand mittens against the cold breeze, and she invited me to come to Atlanta to meet Eric's 28-year-old sister. This was probably the 15th time since leaving Boston that someone had tried to set me up with a Jewish girl.

After a turkey sandwich lunch of which United Airlines might have been proud, we chased two killer whales that rolled halfway out of the water 100 yards from the boat. They were impressive to see in the wild, but one never got a really good look at their faces or feeling for their size.

We circled into the first fjord and back to the glacier that carved it. The glacier calved with impressive noises from time to time, but the sight wasn't overwhelming from our vantage point one-quarter mile away. Another tour boat got quite a bit closer, but our captain didn't want to put his million-dollar baby at risk.

Sea bird viewing wasn't as good as it had been in Homer, so the main wildlife attraction was a stellar sea lion colony. Their "colony" isn't much of a home, just a few ledges on a steep rock fronted by crashing surf. We stayed 75 yards offshore but still could see 2000 lb. bulls snarling at each other, pups sliding clumsily into the water, and fat happy sea lions sunning themselves. Their population has declined dramatically here to the point that they are on the endangered species list. Nobody knows the exact reason, but commercial fishing is suspected.

Crepuscular light in an infinite variety of colors and intensities spread itself over the mountains as I drove back to Anchorage. Finished photographing the spectacle, I stopped in Girdwood, 35 miles south of Anchorage. Hauling out Samantha to jog her memory for some phone numbers attracted the local Macintosh aficionados. Charles, a good-looking compact ironworker with blond hair and mustache, stopped to give me a few Microsoft *Word* tips and reveal his personal philosophy.

"The most important obligation a person has is to exceed his parents' level of knowledge."

Charles works half the year connecting steel beams and spends the other half in various university programs.

"When I was 18 years old in 1976 I was making $13.56/hour and people said, 'How can you make so much without a college degree; how is that fair?' Well, everything I've built will be here in 200 years. How many people with college degrees can say that society will still be benefiting from their work that far in the future?"

Charles has a B.A. in history and is worried about the state of our economy.

"Look at the ratio of operative to overhead sectors in the economy. In the history of the U.S., the highest ratio was 62% operative during 1942–44 and it is only 11–14% now. This way of looking at things goes back to Alexander Hamilton."

Charles doesn't worry too much about his own job because ironworkers tend to be employed building public works during dark economic times. In any case, his needs are modest, and he only works half the year, spending the other half educating himself.

"There should be a law against working in excess of six months a year. Why do people do it? They're wasting their lives."

Charles led me to an isolated creekside campsite where I pitched my tent around midnight.

Friday, July 23

Being back in a city is a good recipe for frustration. I expect to be able to get things done and am angry with myself when I can't. The U.S. Post Office's "2 days, $2.90" promise turned out to be a joke; I would have to wait two more weeks to see the physical mail that Bruce forwarded from my house. A critical replacement part for my medium-format camera failed to arrive from New York, thus leaving me with a $20,000 50 lb. deadweight. The guy who was going to take me flying had a conflicting business appointment. America OnLine had gotten its act together for awhile and then failed catastrophically. I felt my July 26 ferry reservation (from Skagway, 14 hours of driving away) pressing me. I wanted to scream.

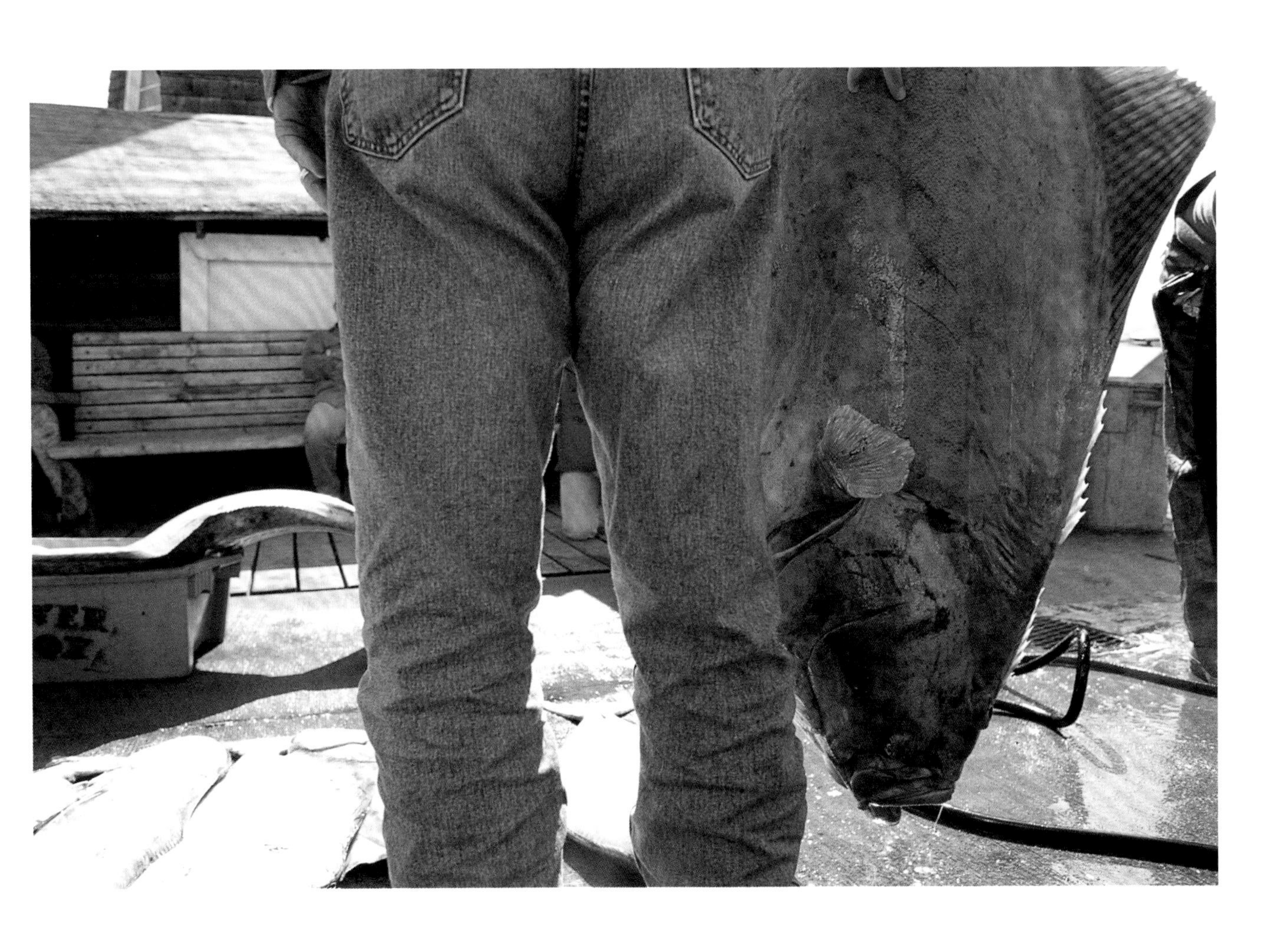

12

Marine Highway to Juneau and South to Vancouver

Saturday, July 24

How big is Alaska? If you are in Anchorage and want to catch a ferry to Juneau or "Outside," you have to drive 900 miles first.

Under mostly blue skies, I said good-bye to Anchorage and drove for several hours through the awesome Matanuska Valley to Glenallen. The highway rides the edge of a mountain range and looks across a glacier-carved riverbed to another range, very much as in Denali National Park. After 200 miles I rested up in a café and then hit the road around 6 o'clock for Tok. With the massive 20,000′ Wrangell mountains on my right and the end of a broad rainbow in front for nearly the whole drive, it was a near-mystical driving experience.

I pressed on past the "Cheapest Gas for 2000 Miles" sign to the Canadian border with the glorious sunset behind me. Thirty miles into Canada, I pitched my tent at the first likely looking spot and collapsed.

Sunday, July 25

Getting breakfast on this stretch of the AlCan provided as good a lesson in rudeness as 10 years in New York City. All the Canadians who want to be in the service industry but whose personality is maladapted to the task seem to have congregated here. "If you don't like the surly service and the shocking prices, you can just drive 250 miles to Whitehorse."

Well, I did just that and, aside from the usual beautiful mountains and Kluane Lake, saw a big white/gray wolf 25 yards from the road. At 5:00 PM, I pulled into Whitehorse to find the town denuded of all of the people I'd met on my last visit. Everyone had gone to the Dawson City Music Festival, six hours north of here. This should give you some insight into what day-to-day life in Whitehorse is like; imagine an entertainment event in Philadelphia drawing most of the inhabitants of Boston.

Klondike Highway 2 to Skagway is one of the most scenic two-hour stretches of road anywhere up here. Half the trip follows a series of enormous lakes through which 19th-century prospectors navigated in whatever scraps of boats they'd managed to bring up from San Francisco. The last bit rides the edge of a gorge to crest at 3290′ White Pass. This is the route of the White Pass and Yukon narrow-gauge railroad, completed in 1899 to service the gold rush.

Skagway provides a warm welcome to the traveler returning to the U.S. and was the first Alaskan town I saw with any character. Anchorage and Fairbanks were built in a series of booms, and most of the seaside towns were destroyed by tidal waves during the 1964 earthquake—a 300′-high wave moving 500 miles/hour can do some damage. Skagway's old wooden buildings were never ravaged by anything other than time, and many have been restored for tourists, who constitute the main industry for the town's 700 residents.

At Moe's Frontier Bar, the "oldest operating bar in Skagway," Samantha attracted the interest of William, a German-American farmer from Ohio in the final stages of drunkenness. His intoxication was perhaps unsurprising for someone who has been here for five months and has spent "$4500 drinking, $500 eating, and had a spectacular time all the way." He is doing maintenance work at a hotel here for the summer, but has to "get back and see what my crops are doing. I don't trust people to do my job." He'd like to stay forever.

"I came up here to fulfill a lifelong dream. I was born 100 years out of my time. I enjoy the outdoors so much that I can't live without it. Once you come to Alaska, it is in your blood. You *will* return."

Sam, a 41-year-old pioneer woman, had just come down here from Anchorage in a motor home with her husband, Ken.

"We came here to see southeast Alaska. The only way to see it is to live here and take the Marine Highway. You have to be part of it."

Ken used to work in Prudhoe four weeks on, four weeks off, and they were very happy together for years. Prudhoe hasn't been paying that well recently, and they laid Ken off in June.

"Now that he's come home it is 'like no, that's a whole 'nother lifestyle.' I appreciate the fact that I have a man who will take care of me for the rest of my life if I so desire, but right now I can't say that I love Ken. Alaska has given me the courage to make it on my own. This is a paradise for a woman who knows how to take advantage of the situation."

I'd pictured Ken as a loutish fellow with dirty fingernails from working the oil rigs and was quite surprised when a lean soft-spoken Texan approached us. He held a beer but was the most sober-sounding person I'd spoken to in the bar. Although he'd just learned from Sam that she wanted out of the marriage (his second), he encouraged me not to be afraid of marriage.

"I've had several wonderful phases in my life, and I know that somehow the next one will be good also."

Ken's attitude reminded me of Socrates's advice: "By all means marry. If you have a good wife, you will be happy. If you have a bad wife, you will become a philosopher."

Ken and Sam invited me to join them in their spacious 33′ motor home for the night, but I pitched my tent a few paces off instead. I didn't want to crowd out their pets: a sweet-tempered Doberman bitch, a playful Husky dog, and an enormously fat gray cat. I had such a good time slapping my hand against the Husky's hollow chest that I didn't get to bed until 3.

Monday, July 26

By 10:30 when I woke, Sam had gone off to her job at the supermarket. Ken invited me in for a tea and a shower. Even after I'd broken the shower head support, Ken left me in possession of the $55,000 motor home while he went to the post office. Ken invited me to Howard and Judy's trailer, where a bountiful picnic lunch awaited. Judy's mother was visiting from Kansas and had made raspberry pie with raspberries picked from local roadsides.

After lunch I poked around downtown Skagway and, not being a souvenir hunter, quickly exhausted most of the diversion available here. I lined up to get on the ferry, but after an hour nothing seemed to be happening. I got out to ask the driver of the van in front of me if I was in the right line. All I could see were delicate feet propped up on the top of the red van's door, then slender legs leading back to a reclining woman with the face of a Spanish aristocrat framed by long dark hair. Lurking in the back were two teenage boys. Judy rolled down her window and told me, in a dulcet Tennessee accent, that the ferry would be late. Judy had a fund of interesting conversation, starting with a story about a friend who had adopted a Czech girl.

"She'd been in a Czech orphanage where conditions were so straitened that a group birthday party was held each month with an inflatable plastic birthday cake. Each child who'd had a birthday that month got a picture of himself."

As we drove onboard, past numerous "stowaways will be prosecuted" signs, one of the crew offered to maneuver Judy's van for her. She refused to give him the satisfaction, so he directed her with the admonition "stop trying to drive and just watch me." Sexism rules here in the wild North. My van is festooned with a bike rack on the rear and the pile of junk inside limits rear visibility. Nonetheless, the same guy just gave me instructions, watched my progress, then complimented me on a job well done.

I started my tour of the ship in the "solarium." As there is typically precious little real sun in this part of Alaska, heat lamps hang over cheap plastic chaise longues. These are highly prized, and a stampede for them had apparently ensued earlier. The winners were mostly two groups from Trek America. Trek America loads 14 people into a van for several weeks and takes them camping through different parts of the U.S. The usual contingent of Germans was supplemented by a lanky Australian girl, a cheerful 26-year-old Dutch printer who'd fallen in love with but been rebuffed by a neurotically thin 23-year-old French-Swiss bleached blonde, and two real live Americans. They were well prepared for the straight four-day trip down to Bellingham, but they weren't the best prepared travelers. At least a dozen people had actually pitched tents on one open deck!

Chilkoot Inlet was so calm that we could hardly feel the boat moving past the stately mountains. We docked in Haines at around 6:00 PM. Haines is famous for its annual gathering of bald eagles. Alaska has more of these birds than the rest of the

NOTICE TO PASSENGERS
PLEASE DO NOT
REMOVE CHAIRS
FROM SOLARIUM
KEEP CLEAR

U.S. combined, and they congregate here in October through January to feed on the last of the salmon running up a river that curiously remains unfrozen. About 4000 birds show up usually, which is less than in olden days but pretty impressive considering that eagles were once hunted mercilessly by people anxious to increase the supply of fish. Biologists concluded that the birds mostly ate "spawned-out" salmon that were about to die anyway and were of no commercial value (salmon actually start to decay as they swim upstream and are rather moldy by the time they spawn). Fans of Big Government might wish to know that the Feds used to pay a $2 bounty for every pair of talons hacked off of our national symbol; now they give you a free trip to The Big House if you so much as insult a member of this endangered species.

Most guidebooks rate Haines a fairly ugly little fishing village, but I'd heard people describe it as their favorite spot in southeast Alaska. I just had to see for myself, so I took advantage of our two hours in port to hop a taxi with Judy and the kids to beautiful downtown Haines. Had they not been shrouded in thick clouds, the surrounding peaks running down to the water would have made for a dramatic setting, albeit not very different from the rest of southeast Alaska. However, the town's buildings are solidly in the boomtown mold. Even the fabled harbor isn't much to look at. Virtually all boats in Alaska are newish fiberglass or steel affairs. That quaint wooden fishing boat you might find in New England? The murderous elements here sent it to the bottom a long time ago.

After dinner we cabbed back to the boat, and Judy found that she'd left her tickets in her van. A crewman didn't want to let her board, but she remained impassive and unperturbed. Judy was the first member of her northern Italian/English family to attend college, and she got there through sheer tenacity.

"I was the parent after age 7."

Sure of her correctness and possessed of iron determination, Judy was used to having her way. She'd married at 19 and divorced at 27. The divorce was her idea—no man had ever left her—but it was still incredibly painful.

"It isn't that one mourns the loss of the partner; one is sad for the death of dreams of doing things together," Judy noted.

With two boys to care for, Judy has stuck to practical education and careers. She got a degree in psychiatric social work but now has a hospital administration job. Jason, her 14-year-old, is a professional actor in Memphis theater, while Justin, the 12-year-old, is more devoted to video games. The three of them were so close both physically and emotionally; I wondered what it would be like to marry a woman with kids and know that a big part of her heart would always be reserved for her children.

Sitting with Judy and her family, I plowed through *Touching the Void,* a shocking tale of two English guys who climbed a 21,000′ mountain in the Peruvian Andes. On the way down, Joe fell and broke his heel and leg in a way that twisted his knee into a pretzel. Simon lowered him down 300′ at a time and then lowered himself down with frostbitten hands. Halfway through each descent, Joe had to unweight the rope so that Simon could move a knot through a piece of climbing equipment. On about the seventh descent, Joe was just hanging in midair. Thus did matters stand for about half an hour. Then Simon's snowseat began to collapse, and both climbers were about to fall to their death. Simon cut the rope and Joe fell into a crevasse. When Simon reached the opening of the crevasse, he could hear no response from Joe and left him for dead.

Simon made it back to base camp laboriously and spent a few days recuperating there. Meanwhile, Joe crawled out of the crevasse, down a glacier, and into camp. He did this with excruciating pain in his leg and no food or water for three days. Simon was about to break camp when he heard Joe's screams for help. Joe eventually got back to civilization and, 10 weeks after the last of six operations, was climbing again in the Himalayas.

Clouds mostly obscured the moon, and darkness blotted out what is supposed to be wonderful scenery. By 10:30 PM people started to sprawl out on the loungers and lost all sense of shame. Jason and Justin couldn't stop laughing at a German fellow whose blanket had slipped off, revealing hairy legs and comical underwear. We drove off the ferry at 1:00 AM, more than two hours late, and drove straight to Mendenhall Lake campground. Judy and Justin slept in their van; Jason and I each pitched a tent in the woods.

You may have had your rope cut in the Peruvian Andes. You may have taken over Bugs Bunny's job testing artillery shells for duds (by striking them on the tip with a hammer; the ones that didn't explode he set aside as duds). You may even have gotten married. But you don't know the meaning of fear until you've slept next to a

14-year-old with a loaded double-barrel shotgun. Judy abhors guns, but her brother insisted that she take a shotgun to Alaska for protection from the bears.

Tuesday, July 27

After a little bit of hiking around a grayish lake fronting the massive Mendenhall Glacier, I visited the Alaska State Museum in downtown Juneau. I especially enjoyed the exhibit on the Russian period in Alaska, which was from the 1740s until 1867. Russia was worried that the discovery of gold in Alaska would bring in a flood of people and that they'd not be able to hold the colony. They were worried about British encroachment and saw American ownership as the best practical outcome. It was actually the Russians who pushed us to buy the place for $7 million.

Why does every city with a hill call itself "little San Francisco"? I have two arms and two legs, but I don't call myself "dark-haired Robert Redford." Some of Juneau's streets are steep, but not because there are hills; rather, the city is cut into a mountain side like Honolulu. With under 30,000 population, Juneau survives on two industries: state government and milking cruise ship passengers. Alaskans have been talking for 20 years about moving the capital to a small town near Anchorage but are never quite ready to spend the money to do it. Alaska's Inside Passage is one of the world's most popular cruise routes, and Juneau is the only city the passengers see after Seattle or Vancouver. Three enormous ships were in port today, and their passengers thronged five blocks of souvenir shops hawking everything from fudge to Eskimo Ulu knives.

I started my bike tour of Juneau by the cruise ship dock and from there rode up 250′ to the top of one of the city's highest hills. Some of the views are impressive, but industrial blight and the lack of a Golden Gate Bridge makes comparison with San Francisco a bit absurd. Once over a bridge to Douglas Island, a residential suburb, I looked back at Juneau fronted by the Gastineau Channel. The channel was a beehive of activity, with float planes roaring past dozens of big ships. Sunshine broke through a few clouds, continuing the streak of extraordinarily good weather.

After 13 miles my feet were hurting from my too-tight bike shoes, so I decided to drop into a bike shop. I had a brand-new pair of Shimano bike shoes that fit nicely, but couldn't get them to engage securely in my SPD pedals. Rey and Hans at Mountain Gears figured out the problem: Shimano's shoes recess Shimano's cleats too much to ever fit in Shimano's pedals. With this kind of engineering a Japanese company manages to control 98% of the mountain bike component market. It is kind of heartening that they aren't invincible on the one hand; on the other, if they leave so many loose ends, why can't American companies compete in this area?

After a light dinner, I drove to Salmon Creek power substation to meet eight guys for what was described as an "easy ride with just a little hill at the beginning and a couple of slightly technical parts at the end." The English have nothing to teach Alaskans in the department of understatement. Quite a few tourists here noticed that "just go four blocks down and take a right" might involve 20 miles of driving. Well, the "little hill" turned out to rise 500′ in about 300 yards. A few people walked most of it, but I was determined not to be seen as an "East Coast wimp" and managed to make it up in the saddle.

After grunting nearly straight up the mountainside, we cruised on a flat gravel road for awhile before turning off onto a singletrack trail. The singletrack began with big trees horizontally across the trail three feet off the ground.

"Slightly technical." Uhh . . . yeah.

Each time we came to a creekbed the trail would dip down about 5′ and then rise up again steeply with boulders, roots, and railroad ties in the way. Many of the guys managed to bunny hop over nearly all of the obstacles, executing maneuvers I'd only ever seen in competition.

It was the stairs that got to me.

The first set of three stairs dropped down four feet; Hans and Rey went down without blinking. The next stairs rose up about 4′ to a wooden bridge. Each biker would pull a big wheelie and hit the stairs with both wheels at once, then pedal like crazy to scramble up to the top. Just to the side of the stairs was a rocky 10′ slide down to the stream. It wasn't long before Darren fell off the stairs and dumped himself and his $2500 Klein bike down the slope. Several parts of both the bike and Darren's body needed trailside repair.

Nearly everyone was riding $3000 titanium bikes with shock absorbers, but no one laughed at my pathetic clunker. There was a lot of good camaraderie and no macho posturing over who could ride which sections and who couldn't. The forest scenery was well worth all of the effort. Huge ferns and extensive mosses gave the place an enchanted flavor, and it looked like old growth whether it was or not. Mosquitoes weren't a problem, but some kind of biting black fly was pretty irritating when we stopped.

Going down was truly terrifying. We dropped 750′ at high speed over rocks and roots that felt much larger now. The thick forest and gathering darkness made it tough to see as well. I'd wondered why all these experienced bikers were riding brand-new machines, but the final toll provided an answer: one derailleur smashed into pieces by a rock, another thrown out of adjustment, sheared-off brake and shift levers, numerous scratches to bike frames and human legs. You're lucky if a bike lasts one season here.

We sailed from Juneau at 2:30 AM. I took a delicious, copious, free shower on board and went upstairs to the solarium deck to sleep. All the "food warmer" bunks under the overhang were taken, but I preferred to sleep in the open anyway. I spread a Thermarest on a chaise longue, stripped, and crawled into a down sleeping bag. The mountains of Juneau receded into the distance, black under a crown of bright sky. The fresh breeze, glass-smooth water, scattered overhead clouds, and stars made for a magical 15 minutes of contemplation before my tired body collapsed into sleep.

Wednesday, July 28

A cloudless blue sky spread over forested hillsides in the morning. We hugged the coasts of numerous little islands and passed through so many channels that none of the passengers could say with confidence where we were. The beaches were dotted with the occasional deer or Indian fishing settlement.

I lunched with Gil and Shavit, an Israeli couple fresh out of the army. They were seeing the world for a year before going to university. Gil had fallen in love with what he thinks is the U.S.

"You have it so easy here. You can work just a few months a year and yet live better than 99% of Israelis. The scenery and wildlife here are incredible; there is nothing on this scale anywhere in Europe," Gil said.

I reminded him that coming to Alaska, the least densely populated state in the U.S., from Israel, the most densely populated country in the Mediterranean, wasn't the best way to get perspective on ordinary American life. Had he been to New York City?

"We spent a few weeks there with relatives. It was wonderful. There is so much freedom and open space. It would be a dream to settle here."

At 3:45 PM we sailed past Mt. Edgecumbe, an extinct volcanic cone, and docked in Sitka. This island was once the capital of Russian America and currently is home to about 8500 people. Taking advantage of the rare sunny weather, I hauled my bike out of the minivan and pounded out the seven miles to town. The road hugged the shore and afforded beautiful views out over the water, but the population seemed curiously housed. Half the people live in houses that are quite stylish by Alaskan standards, and the other half live in rusting trailers squatting on the ground. Newish Japanese cars are often parked in front of the trailers, so it isn't poverty *per se* that has reduced people to this, just indifference to their temporary home between fishing trips. I earlier echoed Thoreau in arguing that people put too much time, money, and effort into their shelter, but a cluster of rusting old trailers is pretty ugly. Hey, consistency is the hobgoblin of little minds.

From smack in the middle of downtown one can see snow-capped granite peaks, dark green forests, the Gulf of Alaska, a rebuilt Russian Orthodox cathedral, and hundreds of fishing boats. I wheeled into Sitka National Historical Park and learned some of the island's history.

Russians started their settlement of Alaska in the Aleutians and were primarily interested in otter pelts. Otters, the only marine mammal without insulating blubber, have incredibly fine fur. After they'd decimated the Aleutian otter population, the Russians decided to exterminate the fur-bearing critters of southeast Alaska and built a fort here in 1799. Local Tlingit Indians, armed with modern weapons, captured the fort and killed most of the Russians.

Forgiveness in warfare is not a traditional Russian value; they came back in 1804 with a gunboat and beat the Tlingits this time. After their victory, the Russians moved in whole hog, tarting up the town so much that it called itself the "Paris of the Pacific." To this day, Sitka claims to be the cultural center of the southeast, despite the loss of population that ensued when the capital was moved to Juneau in 1900. I missed the June chamber music festival and the July 4th ax-throwing contest, and hence was unable to verify this claim.

Totem poles once used by Indians to decorate houses have been beautifully restored, then incongruously strewn along a wide one-mile trail through the tangled fairy-tale 10,000-year-old cedar forest that was the 1804 battleground. In addition to the massive root systems of overturned trees, one can see the harbor and the Indian River from the peaceful trail.

Downtown Sitka sports two blocks of touristy shops for the cruise ships. I picked up a few chocolates and raced back to the ferry just a few minutes before our 6 o'clock departure. I never did find much evidence of Sitka's Russian flavor, unless you count the filth-spewing ancient pickup trucks that rushed by me on the island's one road.

Thursday, July 29

Sleeping outside again was lovely for awhile, but at 5:00 AM a steady cool rain began to fall. I retreated under the deck and was roused at 6:00 AM by a retired couple. Not only do those over 65 get to ride the ferry for free, they get to spend a full hour rustling around in plastic bags and talking loudly while others are trying to sleep. Where were Karin and Walter now to sing the praises of America's traveling senior citizens?

At 8:00 AM, I drove off the ferry into Petersburg, a fishing village of 3500. As in every other town in southeast Alaska, my car radio found only two FM stations: a gospel station and Alaska Public Radio. If you listened to the public radio station carrying NPR news you might think that southeast Alaskans were just like folks anywhere else in the U.S. But then *Morning Edition* is interrupted by local news, 99% of which concerns where to find animals to hunt.

Samantha and I ensconced ourselves at La Café Agapé.

"*Agapé* is a Greek word from the New Testament meaning unconditional love, the God kind of love," explained Lavonne, the proprietrix.

You can probably guess which radio station she'd selected.

Lavonne was preparing the annual Christian retreat for her three children and other members of her Faith Christian Fellowship. They'd had good weather in three previous years because "children's prayers are always answered."

How did she square that with the recent flooding of the Midwest?

"Maybe they just weren't praying."

At Petersburg Fisheries, I was greeted cordially by Bruce, manager of PFI's relations with the fishing fleet. Although PFI owns four massive factory boats, it buys most of its fish from thousands of small operators. PFI does whatever it takes to support small-timers in the ocean. They send a tender to visit fishing grounds and haul the catch back 80,000 lb. at a time in a refrigerated hold. They send their float plane out with spare parts to boats. "Petersburg fishermen have a reputation as some of the best all over Alaska," Bruce noted. "You'll find Petersburg boats crabbing the Aleutians and spread out all over the southeast."

Patrick, a handsome 35ish bachelor with dark hair and mustache, manages the 600 seasonal workers in the cannery itself. His competence and confidence were palpable as I observed him talking to workers and customers (two of whom are Canadians supplying Ontario fish and chips shops with 5 million pounds of frozen halibut each year). Patrick walked me around the plant, beginning on the dock. A salmon starts its journey into the cannery from the seawater-filled refrigeration hold of a boat. An enormous pump on the dock pumps water and fish up to the dock while a worker stands hip-deep in foaming dead-fish-filled water in the hold. His job is to move the pump intake hose around to gather up all the fish. Four pleasant college kids on the dock sort the fish into bins. Some are discards, some are useful only for roe.

Patrick didn't want me photographing the fish disassembly areas, so we headed straight to where glistening orange roe is separated from fish guts and packed up to be sent to Japan. After my tour of the working cannery, I have one piece of advice: Don't take any nice clothes to your job here; even stuff that I left in the car smelled like fish afterwards.

I went to neighboring Chatham Strait Seafoods to get an idea of what Patrick hadn't shown me, but my request to take photographs was politely brushed off due to "insurance problems." Rick, a machinist who keeps their 90-year-old custom-made equipment up and running, walked out of the office with me and noted that "they think no one will eat canned salmon if they see people up to their waists in fish guts. It is all clean, the FDA lives here, but it isn't necessarily pretty." Rick gave me a tour of a nonoperating line. Fish come in on a conveyor and are manually aligned with their gills under a clamp. They roll down another conveyor with their gills clamped and a knife chops off their head. A really frightening machine slits open their bellies and a rotating brush eviscerates the fish before a final section chops off the tail. Until

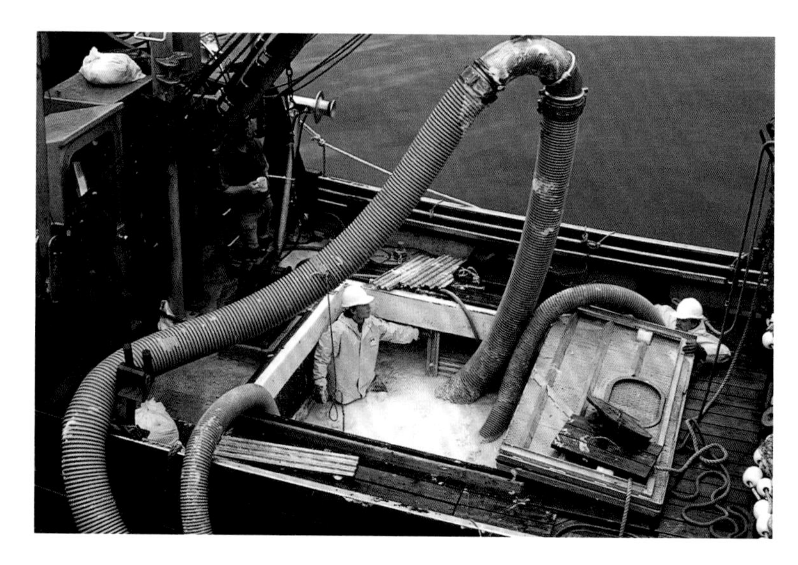

the early 1900s, this job was done by Chinese laborers, and the mechanical replacements are called "Iron Chinks." In fact, I saw one with that appellation cast into its faceplate.

From conversations with cannery workers, I pieced together a portrait of their lives. They get paid only about $6/hour, but they work 18–22 hours a day and rack up the overtime.

"Four hours of sleep feels normal to me," noted Pam, "and I just sleep in my office in my clothes. All I have to do is hand out equipment. When someone needs something, they just knock and wake me up."

Her friend Pat doesn't worry about falling asleep and injuring herself.

"My job is just inspecting fish. Anyway, the cannery is pretty safety-conscious. Guys who stuff fish near rotating knives have their hands secured with steel cables so that they can't get within six inches of the knife."

Petersburg's gloomy weather made me face the fact that I wasn't ever going to succeed with America OnLine. I decided to switch to CompuServe, an allegedly more reliable competitor of America OnLine's. Hooking up to CompuServe's 20-year-old mainframes involved hours of trial and error and voice calls to their 800 number. Thoroughly frustrated with America's commercial computer networks, I decided to seek solace in religion. I accepted Lavonne's invitation to the "Are You a Slave?" lecture at the Faith Christian Fellowship. A reformed alcoholic was supposed to explain how Jesus saved him from bondage to alcohol.

An older woman welcomed me warmly and pressed my hand in both of hers, asking, "Are you alone?" She seated me in the middle of a square chapel with a suspended ceiling and fluorescent lights over pews comfortably padded and covered with red polyester. The white walls were bare save for a map of the world with Alaska enlarged and three banners ("Christ Lives," "Jesus is Lord," "Because He Lives We Too Shall Live").

I arrived in the middle of singing by three women in front with the congregation joining in, mostly waving their hands in the air and sweating profusely. Having spent much more time at MIT than in synagogues or churches, I assumed that each sermon would build upon the previous sermons much as successive calculus lectures might. I was therefore surprised that Lloyd, the local pastor, said a lot of things that should have been basic to most of his parishioners. Obvious or not, everyone seemed happy to hear it all said again, and Lloyd was rewarded by the congregation. Every 15 seconds they said, "Amen" or "Praise God."

After the collection plate was handed 'round, the main event began with an introduction from Cindy Rhorer, the ex-alcoholic's wife.

"We feel so blessed to be here in Alaska. The only time we've been here is flying back from Moscow through Anchorage. We felt blessed to be in America and kissed the ground. It isn't that our country is so great, but that other countries are so bad."

Don't be quick to accuse Cindy of obstructing international understanding. She has visited many poor countries filled with "new Christians who don't know a lot about the Devil." In many of these blighted spots, she has healed the sick. Her prayer cured a man of his color blindness and gave a hip to a woman who was born without one.

Richard Rhorer walked on in a black shirt, flowered silk tie, and gray suit. This 50-year-old makes up for his weak chin with a California, longish, blond hair style and trim body. His home church is in Irvine, California, and he reminded me of nothing so much as an L.A. rental property agent. Rhorer was a captivating dynamic speaker who made good use of wild gestures and bulging eyes.

My previous experience with religious ceremonies was limited to established churches. Two points that struck me here were references to the possibility of backsliding and leaving the faith and constant reminders that this church serves only a select group of enlightened folks. Established churches want everyone to come and listen, in the hopes that maybe someday they'll learn. Rhorer told people time and time again that "if you want to hear about <Jezebel, rituals, etc.>, you're in the wrong place."

Self-improvement via confrontation with the Devil was the main theme of the sermon. Rhorer contrasted the obvious efficacy of Jesus versus secular systems such as EST. Stepping down from the podium to pace back and forth in front of the first pew, he reached out to the crowd with his hands.

"How many of you have had a dream, a vision, a heart, something that you know is a vision from God? [Thirty percent raise their hands.] Don't quit; that is the seed the Devil wants. The Devil is only afraid of the anointed. He fights whenever you start to get good at something worldly, e.g., singing. That is why it is tough to get good at things. God wants you to be successful financially. He has a plan for you laid out in Deuteronomy. But the Devil puts obstacles in your path. If you look the Devil in the face, he won't have anything to say to you. You can be successful."

Rhorer had me fairly well convinced that the Devil was in fact an omnipotent being behind most evil, but his last comment about a sickly little human being able to stare down the Devil let the air out of the Devil for me. Is the Devil stronger than we are or isn't he?

Rhorer ended the evening by exhorting everyone to return for the next four evenings and also buy some of his previous lectures on tape. I chatted with the congregation and Lloyd, the pastor, while people were milling about. Nearly everyone in the room had been cured of some kind of substance-abuse problem by Jesus.

After the revival meeting, I went to Tent City, where enormous tarp palaces cover wooden platforms over the boggy forest. Cannery workers pitch ordinary tents under the tarps and live there for the summer, with hundreds of people sharing two small bathrooms and a coin-op shower with a tiny hot water tank ("a good time to take a shower is 2:00 AM"). America, where everyone lives well . . . .

There was space at a couple "guest platforms" hard by the noisy shelter/kitchen and parking lot. I pitched my tent in a light rain and went into the shelter to find Gil and Shavit with a couple other Israelis from the ferry strumming the guitar and singing American songs. They told me about their evening at the city dump. Twenty black bears came down from the woods to feed and cavort among the garbage.

"You didn't have to fly all the way to Katmai to see bears," they enthused.

Friday, July 30

As the *Malaspina* pulled out of Petersburg, I was shocked to see a crewman picking up paper cups, cigarette butts, and other assorted trash, then throwing it all overboard. Thus did we slip away into the gray passage.

Although the weather wasn't the best, I had pleasant reunions with people I'd met everywhere from Skagway to Petersburg. My most interesting new friends on this leg were Tom and Lisa. Tom is a classical reserved German-Minnesotan who might have stepped out of one of Garrison Keillor's Lutheran hamlets. His spare tall physique is in perfect keeping with his modulated speech and quiet competence. Lisa grew up as a nonobservant Jew in Los Angeles and leans more toward sensitivity.

"Do you like yourself?" Lisa asked over pizza.

Tom rolled his eyes and said, "Another one of your unanswerable introspective questions."

"I'm stuck with myself so it doesn't make any difference, and therefore I don't ask the question," I said.

Tom nodded his approval of this response.

RV living proved so seductive that Tom and Lisa eventually bought Rancheros de Santa Fe Camping Park in New Mexico. "The good news is we'll be closed for four and a half months during the winter."

Tom studied mechanical engineering as a Navy ROTC student at U. of Minnesota but never fell in love with working as an engineer in industry. "It really isn't much of a career." Lisa quit her job selling radio advertising time, despite her boss's cautioning, "You're committing financial suicide." They left Ventura, California to spend 16 months on the road in their 22′ motor home. Although they arranged for their mail to be forwarded, people who called themselves friends very quickly proved themselves unwilling to go to the effort of writing a letter. It really upset Lisa at first.

"I wonder if they ever really were our friends."

They've gradually become more tolerant of people who've been sucked into the yuppie lifestyle and jokingly ask old friends to "add a 'write Tom and Lisa' reminder to your Day-Timer."

Tom and Lisa have fallen completely in love with the road.

"We could spend our lives out here and never see it all. We've had to learn to relax and enjoy where we are and not worry about what we're missing."

Saturday, July 31 and Sunday, August 1

Ketchikan is the first Alaskan port of call for most cruise ships. I'd seen a lot of cruise ads showing young attractive people dancing the night away, but the average age of the passengers getting off the three ships in port was somewhere between 65 and

dead. In fact, a cruise ship radioed ahead for an ambulance on one of my days in the Southeast and then 15 minutes later radioed to ask for a coroner instead. There had been an "unattended death" of an 80-year-old passenger.

Ketchikan's waterfront is nicely restored and has the full array of services that you'd expect from Alaska's fourth-largest city (a population of just 13,000 is enough to secure that title). Tourist attractions, however, are heavily concentrated in the totem pole department. Totem poles are fabulous, but you can see them just as well in the museum in Vancouver as here and with about as much authentic context.

I chatted with the usual colorful cast of Alaskans. Esther, a Tlingit Indian, makes traditional button blankets. Esther was born here 78 years ago, and although a few of her nine children have ventured "down South," she wouldn't consider living anywhere else. Esther doesn't cherish romantic notions about Ketchikan, either. "There's crime here just the same as anywhere else."

As I breakfasted in style at the counter of the Roller Bay Café, Susan, who looked like a young slip of a girl, sat down next to me. I was shocked to learn that this 24-year-old is the mother of two children, six and seven. Susan has been going to community college in Santa Rosa, California, but hopes to transfer to Berkeley, thinking that her status as a single mother will earn her preference. She has no regrets about her divorce.

"We were too young to get married. He's a nice guy, but we weren't meant to be together. I can't imagine getting married again. Why would I want to have to sacrifice myself every day just to get along with another person? I already sacrifice enough for my children."

The highlight of my Ketchikan visit began when I was pushed into a Taquan Air Otter by Doug, the burly pilot. This is just a "single Otter," with one humongous engine in front. For 90 minutes Doug's narration came through my noise-blocking headset. After lifting the floats off the harbor surface, Doug overflew the monstrous local pulp mill and headed inland over Revillagigedo Island. Indian-owned land with massive clear-cuts swept underneath the left side of the plane while national forest land, which is being more gently raped, lay to the right. Doug, a paunchy 45-year-old, explained that the Feds prohibit logs cut in national forests from being exported whole; such logs must be turned into some kind of intermediate or final product. However, in true Third World style, logs from Indian land are merely loaded onto a ship and sent to saw mills in Japan.

One of the first sights Doug noted was a helicopter parked high up a mountainside. Although there is a fairly extensive network of logging roads on this island, many logs are lifted out by helicopter to the nearest road. Once we got into Misty Fjords National Monument, which encompasses part of Revillagigedo Island and the mainland across a channel, signs of despoilment evaporated. The landscape here resembles Yosemite in many ways: bare granite walls of astonishing sheerness, green forest trying to clothe the naked granite, still lakes reflecting surrounding peaks. Traditional Yosemite Valley features, e.g., squalid tent cities, buildings, and traffic jams, are all fortunately missing from this landscape.

It is possible to see portions of Misty Fjords by taking an 11-hour cruise, but I think our low-flying plane gave me a much better idea of the terrain. How Doug kept the wings off looming granite walls and spotted mountain goats at the same time was a mystery to me, but we got good looks at clusters of the gentle animals up at 3000′.

After poking our way into a hidden valley, we circled and dropped down onto a long lake completely cut off from the rest of the world by ridges 1000′ above. Doug shut down the engine and let us walk out onto the float. The airplane is a great way to see Alaska, but the noise that continues to resonate in one's head for an hour or two afterwards keeps one from getting a complete feel for a place. It would have been nice to stay here with a good friend for a day or two.

Sunday night through Tuesday morning, August 3

I thought that there would be nothing like a 40-hour ferry ride for writing letters, polishing up *Travels with Samantha,* and reading a few thick books. However, this is everyone's last leg on the Marine Highway, and the atmosphere is a bit like a New Year's party. For many, it is nearly the end of their vacation, and for everyone it is a bittersweet farewell to The Last Frontier. Although I managed to finish Barry Lopez's *Arctic Dreams*, I spent most of my time with old and new friends.

Like my previous rides, this trip was blessed with good weather, unruffled seas, and a smattering of wildlife: 15 killer whales, the occasional beach bum deer, and miscellaneous birds. It all went by so fast, and I realized that experiencing the wilderness of southeast Alaska would have required a few weeks in a sea kayak.

One conversation served to underscore how Alaska had changed me. Ever since I'd been skipped from third to fifth grade and lost most of my friends, I'd wanted people to like me. I was telling a story on the boat to a handful of friends and strangers, and a Jerry Garcia wanna-be from Seattle interrupted me.

"Aren't you afraid that if you use language like that, people will think you are a sexist?" he demanded.

I responded without thinking, "To tell you the truth, if people don't want to take the time to get to know me, I don't care what they think."

13

Vancouver, Victoria, and Olympic Peninsula

Tuesday, August 3

With a small harem surrounding me, I drove off the Alaska Marine Highway at 10:00 AM. Although Alison, Elke, and Jo-Anne each managed to make do with one backpack, the minivan was now stacked to the gills and riding so low that we couldn't drive over a crush-proof cigarette pack without a sickening dragging sound. As we headed up the Interstate toward the Canadian border, I noticed how much easier it was to travel with three companions rather than one. I didn't have to make conversation, just drive and listen.

"The girl with the German passport will have to have it stamped at Immigration," said the smiling fellow in the little booth. In fact, we all had to show various IDs to an unfriendly woman. Although we weren't detained for more than a few minutes, we felt unwelcome.

Our first taste of British Columbia was uninspiring. We drove through the flat fields of the Fraser Valley and then built-up areas until the highway simply ended in a residential neighborhood. Elke was determined to pay no more than C$6 per night for a bed so she and Alison asked to be dropped at a backpacker's hostel near the railroad station, which turned out to be Vancouver's highest crime neighborhood.

I dropped Jo-Anne at her friend's house in the chic Kitsilano district and proceeded to my friend Jim's office at the University of British Columbia. Jim and I took in the university's Museum of Anthropology, the pinnacle of high-culture tourism in

Vancouver and notable for its collection of totem poles. I was stunned by the quality of the work, especially by the warlike Haida Indians. The Canadian government never managed to sign a treaty with the Haida, who are therefore suing to reclaim all of British Columbia's coast and fishing rights. I thought I was tired of totem poles, but Jim was able to bring most of the figures to life for me.

East Ocean Hong Kong Restaurant lies outside Chinatown, like all of the really good Chinese restaurants here. Lest your surroundings in a modern office building cause you to suspect the restaurant's authenticity, East Ocean brings your dinner to the table flopping around in plastic buckets. Jim and I regretted that we lacked the Hong Kong matron's ability to inspect the gills and eyes of the rock cod, and we simply asked our waiter to "please kill these animals, cook them, and bring them back." Jim says that it is the influx of Hong Kong Chinese that is responsible for this presentation; 10 years ago, everything brought to your table was well-killed.

Jo-Anne had promised to meet us later in the evening, but when I phoned her friend's house, I was told that "she met some friends and went away with them for a week-long bike trip." When I returned to the table, Jim said I looked stunned.

"I was just rejected, but it was by a woman I only met yesterday. This is much better than being rejected by women in Boston. In Jo-Anne's case, I can say to myself, 'She wouldn't have rejected me if she knew me better.' What I hate is when women who know me perfectly well reject me."

Not one to let humiliation spoil an evening, I let Jim take me toward the beautiful sunset by Stanley Park. The First Law of Photography is that whenever you see something really beautiful, you won't have your camera. My seven cameras were in my van; I was in Jim's car. I helplessly watched the sunset drip liquid gradations of red behind the mountains around the city.

Jim treated me to gelato in a chic West End café, right next to a high-rise apartment block known as "K-Y Towers" (this is the area of town popular with homosexuals). As we walked back to the car along the dark seawall path, it was nice to see how many young women were still out. This isn't Central Park in terms of either crime or fear of crime. Drug dealers and gangs kill each other, mostly with knives, but the average Vancouverite is able to enjoy the city at all hours and in almost all neighborhoods.

"Strip joints in Boston are really grimy, and you feel sleazy going into one. You have to see how different they are here," Jim pointed out. I had no experience for comparison, but I was surprised to see how clean, well-lit, and sober "The Cecil" was. Customers were neatly dressed and hardly anyone smoked. There were only a handful of women customers, all sitting at tables with counterculturish men. Entertainment at The Cecil consists of multiple TVs showing sports and a big stage in the center. The stage is equipped with a hot tub and a small fountain. Men who really want to get involved with the show sit "lip-side" on the edge of the stage, while friends who want to converse sit at tables farther back.

Jim and I walked in during the middle of the Amateur Night stripping contest. We saw four women, one of whom looked no more than 15, display themselves for five minutes each while prancing around the stage to pop music. The music was played at a moderate enough volume that we diehard nerds were able to carry on a mathematics and computer science discussion. The girl who looked 15 won the contest. After the contest was over, we watched two professional strippers. Jim revealed for me the mysterious formalized structure of the strip. During the first song, the woman dances around the stage fully clothed. The second song leaves her topless and the third bottomless. She spends her fourth song writhing on the floor, disporting in the fountain, or lolling about in the hot tub.

Patrons left to themselves will simply sip their drinks and watch quietly. An announcer periodically reminds the audience to "show her how much you appreciate her," at which point a desultory howling rises up only to die a few seconds later. Strippers appear to enjoy their work and are treated with some deference, as are the cocktail waitresses, who are conservatively clad. Jim used to have a tenant who called herself an "entertainer." In fact, she stripped for a living, and Jim learned something about their culture: "Don't touch any of them; they all have boyfriends who are bikers."

Considering it was my first time, I think I acquitted myself well. We spent about 20 minutes sipping our drinks and then left at 11:30. Jim told me I'd done much better than his last out-of-town guest, an MIT faculty member friend of ours.

"He got so excited that he spilled a glass of beer all over me."

Jim's neighborhood is full of friendly young families. Everyone has young children, and six women were due in one month recently.

"This is British Columbia. Once any animal gets here, it thinks it is time to spawn," Jim noted.

I was overjoyed to find messages on the answering machine from both Elke and Jo-Anne. Jo-Anne hadn't left town, and they both wanted to go to Vancouver Island with me.

Wednesday, August 4

A week cruising down the Nile River builds strong friendships. I hadn't seen Michael for 18 months, I didn't call him until noon on my last day in Vancouver, and he'd just spent 12 hours driving back from the dragon boat races in Calgary. Yet he treated me like royalty. Michael rolled up to Jim's house in his new Mazda and introduced me to his parents. His mother was born in South Africa and his father in Hong Kong, but the family has become thoroughly Canadian. Michael speaks pretty good Cantonese, but he wouldn't be too happy to live in Hong Kong, which he has visited several times.

"It is the only city I know where if the walk sign comes on and you don't move off the curb immediately, someone will push you off."

We drove to a medium-size Chinese restaurant nearby that was packed with big round tables. A party of two would feel out of place here amidst the enormous (all Chinese) families chowing down. It was a bit hard to talk over the din, but we managed to catch up on old times.

Michael took a six-month leave of absence from his engineering job here and worked as a wildlife photographer in Africa. I met him toward the end of that assignment, which he looks back upon wistfully. He'd like to escape the routine again, but his boss cringes at the thought of losing him.

Michael is in his mid-30s and still living at home. I asked his mother why she hadn't introduced him to any nice Chinese girls.

"That's his department," she said abruptly.

"When I'm traveling, it is no problem to meet women. But here at home, they get irritated when I talk to them," Michael mourned.

After dinner, Michael showed 400 slides from his six months in Africa (less than 2% of the 600 rolls he exposed). Just one photo of mating cranes would have been worth the entire trip.

"All of these animals will be gone in a decade or two. These countries are facing choices about whether to feed animals or people; they are going to choose people," Michael noted.

His observations about animal behavior betrayed substantial learning, but also his western nose. He introduced quite a few animals with "these smell really bad."

Thursday, August 5

I'd pictured Vancouver Island as a rugged parkland with occasional small towns inhabited by sea kayakers. Traversing the east coast via a heavily used divided four-lane highway reveals an island that is heavily populated, packed with fast food chains, and quite industrial. Elke, Jo-Anne, and I took a 90-minute ferry ride to Nanaimo and then started the 60-mile drive toward Victoria.

Jo-Anne illustrates what a wonderful person can be produced when Australian openness and directness is mixed with education, intelligence, and a certain amount of ambition. She moved to Toronto six years ago with her Australian husband and has been working as an actuary. Just recently, Jo-Anne shed her husband and the grueling Toronto pace in favor of the outdoorsy life centered around Vancouver.

Elke came to Michigan as a Fulbright Scholar a year ago. She calls herself "East German," in direct defiance of the politically correct lingo over there. Elke has the kind of passionate response to literature, art, and life that so many people have lost. She can appreciate a Shakespeare play, a beautiful city, or a photograph with the

wide-eyed wonder of a child mixed with the sophistication of a well-educated 25-year-old.

I had been a little apprehensive about traveling with two people who'd only met three days before, but Elke and Jo-Anne sorted themselves out into complementary roles. Jo-Anne sat in the front seat and expertly navigated; Elke lounged across the back seat and supplied us with country-western tapes from her collection.

We spent the afternoon among an eye-popping explosion of artistically placed flowers in Butchart Gardens, Vancouver Island's #1 tourist attraction, then drove to McDonald Park, the closest provincial campground to the metropolis of Victoria. All 30 campsites were taken, but three happy-go-lucky Dead Heads from Ontario agreed immediately to let us share their site.

Paul was raised in England but lived in Canada a bit as well. His seven years of following the Dead on tour was recently cut short by some vaguely described brushes with the law in California.

"Did they dump you at the border?" I asked.

"No, I just ran."

I noted that most of my friends who toured with the Dead gave up after a few months because they couldn't shake their middle-class values.

"I'm trying to get mine back," Paul responded.

Friday, August 6

Nobody can organize like a German girl. I'd been meaning to clean out the disgusting cooler for over a month; Elke hadn't been in the car 24 hours before the cooler and all the Tupperware containers were washed. After washing the cooler and showering, we drove to downtown Victoria under gorgeous blue skies. I immediately got on my bike to tour the city alone. I hadn't gone more than two miles before I ran into Alison. She insisted that I come with her to Castle Craigdarroch, built on the top of the hill by John Dunsmuir. Dunsmuir was a Scottish coal miner who came here in the 1850s and became western Canada's richest man. He built a stone castle and fitted it with wood carvings and stained glass just in time to die.

After the castle tour, every aspect of which delighted Alison, we drove to Chinatown for dim sum, which Alison had never had. Despite her sober lobbying job in Washington, D.C., Alison told me how irresponsible she feels at age 31. She skips and jumps along the street and dates a 22-year-old bike messenger.

"Can you believe it? I've never dated a man who wore a suit to work."

Alison hadn't fallen in love with Alaska.

"A place needs history to be interesting. Europeans destroyed the native cultures in Alaska, but haven't been there long enough to build interesting cities of their own."

After I dropped Alison at the fast ferry to Seattle, I got back on the bike to tour scrubbed-up beflowered Victoria some more. Like all capitals, this city prospers on the "tax the many to enrich the few" principle, and public places are extraordinarily nice for a town with a small population (250,000 including an endless suburban sprawl). Most of the downtown shops cater to tourists, however, and it is difficult to get a sense of the real city life, especially on a fine summer's day.

Elke's sensitive nose sniffed out the finest "clash of cultures" photograph in the city: teepees and a totem pole on the front lawn of the enormous stone parliament building. Measured by weight at least, European culture seems to have triumphed by a factor of a million to one.

We drove down the west coast of Vancouver Island to Sooke and camped in the city campground, right next to the Sooke River. I tossed the car keys to Jo-Anne and Elke and biked down the 50 km Galloping Goose Trail, a former railroad. Hard work was rewarded with good views over the Sooke Inlet, a lagoon, and a large freshwater lake. I rode back on little country lanes past peaceful sheep farms, little marinas, and lots of forest. It changed my opinion about Vancouver Island.

Saturday, August 7

Elke and I bid farewell to passportless Jo-Anne at the ferry terminal and hopped a ferry across the narrow channel to Port Angeles, Washington. As the ship rolled in a slight swell, I fixed my eyes on the horizon and recalled Jackie Mason's "there's nothing sadder than a Jew with a boat" routine. Port Angeles was ugly and slightly shrouded in clouds; I felt strangely little joy at entering the U.S. for the final time this trip.

After a swim in the local 25-yard pool, where Elke revealed why East Germany used to win all those Olympic medals, we considered how best to enjoy Olympic National Park.

The main portion of the park is a 40-mile square surrounding the Olympic Mountains, a ring of 6000+′ peaks including 8000′ Mt. Olympus. These mountains

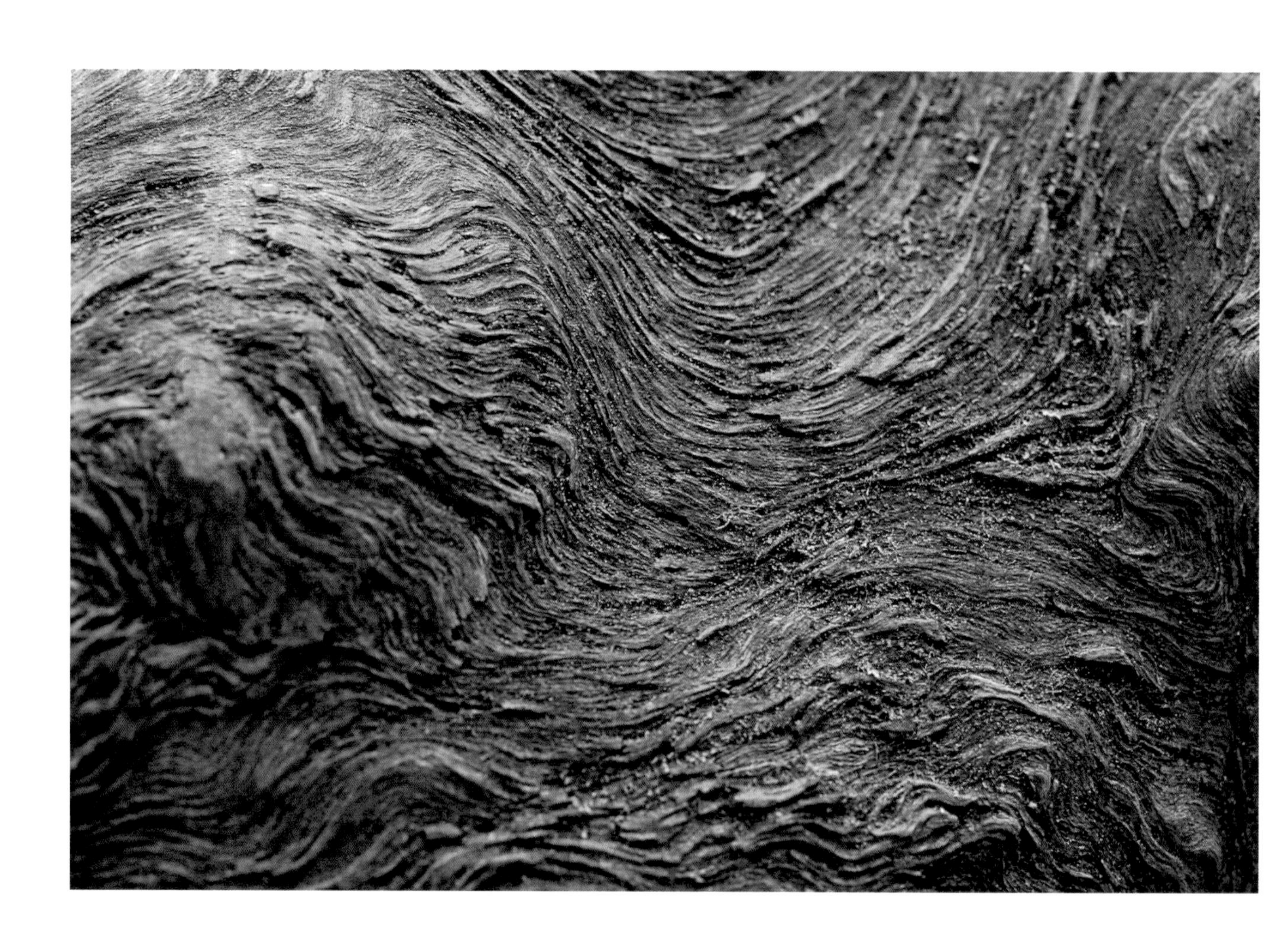

were cut off from the rest of the continent by glaciers until about 12,000 years ago. A unique ecosystem evolved here, and many species of plants and animals common in the nearby Cascades are missing from the Olympics, grizzly bears for example. After hanging out with Jo-Anne and Elke, I developed a particular fondness for the Olympic marmot; he lives in a colony with two adult females and their children.

Twelve feet of rain falls each year on the ocean side of the mountains, creating rain forests and glaciers. The continental side is drier but still plagued by weather that can only be called miserable. As an afterthought in 1953, a big section of coastline was tossed into the park. It looks a lot like the Oregon coast. Lush cliffs meet violent sea.

Sunday, August 8

Elke and I started our tour in the Hoh Rain Forest, named for the Hoh Indians who inhabit this area. We slowly hiked around the eerie Hall of the Mosses trail. Huge trees hung down their twisted moss-covered branches. I forgot to bring my 20mm lens and mosquito repellent; stupid, stupid, stupid. We were beset by mosquitoes just enough to leave Elke's beautiful face a mess but not quite enough to justify a run back to the car. I gave Elke a two-hour photography lesson.

"What separates snapshot from art is a tripod and Fuji Velvia film," I noted. "You have to learn how to use manual exposure on your Nikon and remember that the camera assumes a world that is 18% gray. If you point it at something white, it thinks the world has suddenly gotten brighter; if you point it at something black, it thinks the light has dimmed."

"I always wanted to meet a man who could teach me about photography and computers."

With fantastic manual dexterity and inherent style, Elke prepared a scrumptious lunch. I'd been eating in restaurants and going hungry or snacking when far from civilization. Elke wanted to live out of the cooler. Rather than get on a soapbox and preach about how much more noble it would be to live her way, she simply shopped, organized, and cooked.

After a shower at the Rain Forest Hostel, we drove down Highway 101 to Ruby Beach, part of the coastline portion of Olympic National Park. Enormous piles of driftwood littered the bottom of the cliffs. A blanket of clouds covered the land and the first few miles of sea. The sun eventually sank low enough to illuminate the undersides of the clouds, the cliffs, and the enormous rock formations in the surf. It was pure sorcery but didn't last.

After dark, we camped at South Beach. Elke was desperate for some couscous and soup, so I promised to boil up water with my brand-new stove and pot. Problem 1: fill stove with fuel. Solution: find motor home and beg. A retiree lent me his genuine Coleman funnel and fuel filter. Then he got some pliers so we could open the fiendishly child-proof fuel can. Problem 2: find recently purchased pot. Solution: tear apart car in the dark for 30 minutes; find motor home and beg. Problem 3: pressurize stove with pump for the first time in the dark without reading all the instructions. Solution: spend 30 minutes fruitlessly pumping without realizing that one is supposed to hold one's thumb over a little air hole; cry like a child.

Joel's girlfriend Denise (Chapter XIV) demonstrated a contrasting female attitude in a subsequent phone call. Without even knowing about the contretemps with the stove, she called me a wuss for eating in restaurants rather than cooking for myself.

Elke made sandwiches. I felt like a total failure as a man, but Elke never criticized or betrayed the slightest trace of contempt or disappointment.

Monday, August 9

We stayed in the tent until quite late listening to the rain fall on the fly and soak through sleeping bags and various other interior items. Anxious for a tourist attraction, we followed signs to the Hoh Tribal Center. As the state highway entered the Indian reservation, we could feel the federal dollars stroking the car's undercarriage. The road took on a creamy smoothness that was nothing short of delicious. The 200 Indians on this reservation live in rather attractive houses whose yards are festooned with satellite dishes.

The Tribal Center turned out to be a dumping ground for Indian schoolkids with nothing to do on their summer vacation. Elke called Mauricio, a Colombian she'd met in Juneau.

"He's going to fly to San Francisco to meet me, rent a car, and then drive me down the coast to Los Angeles. He doesn't have any hopes of getting involved; he's just trying to be nice to me for showing him around Juneau. Colombians are Catholic; they're very conservative about such things."

Right.

We spent the rest of the day eating, driving through one downpour after another, and eating some more. Elke shattered some of my misconceptions about East Germany. I'd thought of Communist East Germany as a drab, gray, joyless place full of people dying to get out and move to the West. Elke had been perfectly happy growing up under the old regime and isn't particularly fond of the new system.

"One thing I have trouble adjusting to is the concept of property. We didn't go walking through people's front yards, but everything else in East Germany was public. You never had to worry about whether you were trespassing because everything belonged to you in some sense."

Clothing at least wasn't gray. Elke's high-fashion wardrobe predated Unification. If she and her friends couldn't afford something, they sewed it themselves. Sometimes less is more anyway.

"I hardly owned a bathing suit until I came here; I can't believe how prudish Americans are."

I reminded her that we couldn't all be young, 5′ 6″, and 120 lb.

Politics has never been Elke's main interest, but she told me about East Germany's five political parties, including the dominant socialist unity party (SED). Elke only voted once, but she was satisfied enough with the system to vote voluntarily for SED.

"East Germany was very safe, very community-oriented, there was good day care for kids and a lot of good opportunity for women to work. I am very sorry when I see how materialistic many of my old friends are becoming. I really don't like the values of West/Unified Germany. Even things that are supposed to be better are in fact worse. Bureaucracy, for example, is much worse in Unified Germany."

Elke is so well-educated and speaks such good English that her deficits jarred me. She'd never heard of Jack Nicholson, Cary Grant, Stanley Kubrick, or any other Hollywood icons. "I've only had three years of American movies, you have to remember." She'd never heard of Gummi bears, staples of West German childhood. A lot of attitudes that I'd thought of as German aren't very prevalent among East Germans according to Elke.

"In my experience the difference between East and West Germany is greater than the difference between West Germany and the U.S."

Speaking of the U.S., how had she found it?

"I really enjoyed my first six months here, but then began to see people as living on islands separated by phone answering machines, connected only by wires to the outer world. There was too much space. I tried to immerse myself in American culture, but then stepped back. I began to reject American things, to try to hold onto my German culture. I was so happy whenever I heard someone speaking German. Now I think I am better at appreciating both cultures."

A couple overheard part of this conversation in a restaurant, and the wife came up to our table. She peppered me with questions: Where did you go to college? Where are you from? What are you doing now?

Elke smiled and said, "That's what I love about America; that would never happen in Germany."

Tuesday, August 10

Hurricane Ridge is supposed to afford views to Victoria in one direction and Mt. Olympus in the other. Elke and I hiked for two hours but never saw much more than a few hillsides in front of solid white cloud. We drove back down to Port Angeles to find sunshine and a nice ride through the Olympic Peninsula toward Seattle. A golden sunset kissed the treetops as we rolled onto the Bainbridge Island ferry and drew across the waters of Puget Sound toward the tall buildings of downtown.

The trip had been going far too well. Hospitable people everywhere, sunny weather in Alaska, the lingering spell of Katmai, relatively crash-free driving. What I really needed was the pain of staying under the same roof as my beloved ex-girlfriend

Rebecca and her new boyfriend Dave. I dropped Elke at a friend's and arrived at Rebecca and Dave's house at 10:30 PM to find them together in the kitchen. Rebecca had dyed her hair red and was wearing knee-length jeans and a punk top; she looked more like a rock groupie than a physics Ph.D. Dave, a soft-spoken guy of medium height, looked more like his social work day job than his drumming night job. He was a good listener and rather reflective.

Rebecca tried to start about five arguments that we should have had five years before, but Dave and I got along surprisingly well. Rebecca had told him I was a "nerd," and he was pleasantly surprised to find my belt free of calculators or other paraphernalia.

I had a joyous reunion with my letters and stayed up until 2 reading them and writing replies. Although I'd not felt lonely for some weeks, I was suffused with warmth every time I opened a friend's missive.

BREMERTON

14

Sleepless in Seattle, Sightless in St. Helens, Pummeled in Portland

Wednesday, August 11

I picked up Joel at SeaTac Airport. Joel and I go back to 1979, when I was an unusually immature sophomore at MIT and he was an unusually mature senior. Joel's a physics professor at Berkeley now and has probably changed less than anyone else I knew at school.

Joel still stands 5′ 10″ high on his stocky legs, hides his face behind a black beard, and wears the "physics wardrobe" (flannel shirt with one tail untucked hanging over faded jeans). At 35, he holds the same vaguely liberal political views; he wasn't even radicalized when his Ph.D. project, a terrifying room-size free-electron laser, became a cornerstone of Reagan's Star Wars project. Joel hasn't changed his taste in reading, still turning to English literature and the *New Yorker.* Although encumbered by home ownership, he's never bought a TV, decent stereo, or much else.

Joel was staying with Adi and Viola, two West German academics. We'd planned on going out for dinner, but Elke and her hostess Julie surprised us with a salmon feast.

Adi started off the conversation by waxing rhapsodic on how wonderful the Brave New World of computer software was. Joel, such a computer algebra wizard that his first date with a Harvard girl was helping her with Macsyma, looked amused.

"Where is the innovation? Macsyma was written by MIT graduate students 25 years ago and is still better than any of the new commercial computer algebra systems."

"Electrical engineers have been so innovative that a business can be run with $1000 of hardware, but commercial software is such a mess that they'll spend tens of thousands on adaptations, hand-holding, and baby-sitting," I piped up.

"Look at how wonderful *Windows* is," Adi gushed.

"The last real innovation in software was the spreadsheet," I noted. "Visicalc is more than 10 years old. A vintage 1980 Apple II could do word processing and spreadsheets, which is about all the average PC user can do today. Other supposedly new applications existed on big computers and are available to the masses today because hardware is cheaper, not because new kinds of software have been written."

Adi moved the discussion over to politics. He and his liberal friends are delighted with Bill Clinton's first eight months. I pressed to find out what Clinton had done to make them so happy.

"Er . . . Well . . . Hmmm . . . Uh . . . He changed an administrative rule on abortion counseling; a woman can now be told about the availability of abortion by doctors at government-funded clinics."

After I stated my hope that the most powerful man in the world should be able to do something more substantial, Adi said, "You are really cynical about everything."

It stunned me for a minute. After a month in Alaska, I wasn't used to people making such quick character judgments. "Perhaps commercial software and politicians aren't the things about which I am most optimistic," I conceded.

Thursday, August 12

Rebecca and I had reversed roles. I used to have a real job and would take her out; she was in graduate school and would use my washing machine. Now I'm in graduate school and using her washing machine; she has a real job and took me out to breakfast.

The great tragedy of science and engineering right now is that there are 10 times as many Ph.D.s as academic jobs. I tried to convince Rebecca, currently doing research, to use her Ph.D. to get a teaching position.

"It doesn't matter where or what. The very act of standing in front of students a few hours a week and teaching them will give you the confidence to do good research and writing. That is why academics go so quickly from craven graduate students to awe-inspiring professors. Science and engineering research are inherently depressing. You spend all your time working on a problem confused. If you cease being confused, it means that you've solved the problem and move on to the next one. Thus, 99% of your time is spent in a state of confusion."

We parted warmly, even if our reunion underscored a friend's philosophy: "We need to see ex-girlfriends occasionally so that we remember why we aren't with them anymore."

Joel and I pushed our way out of Seattle through a maze of espresso shops, upscale, downscale, sit-down, stand-up, walk-in, drive-through . . . even McDonald's serves the stuff. They were all full of ex-Angelenos enthusiastic about their new life here in the Northwest: "Yeah, man, I lived in L.A. for 40 years and was really aggressive; I've been here six months and have totally mellowed out."

L.A. is getting to be like Ireland: a place that can't sustain its population and is filling up the rest of the world with its emigrants. Come to think of it, an Irish-Angeleno would feel perfectly at home here: it rains all the time and the freeways are jammed.

One of the nice things about Boston is that the population hasn't grown since the highways were built. You'd think that, with a 10-lane highway punched right through the center of town, Seattle would have good transportation; you'd be thinking wrong. Seattle has the fourth worst traffic in the U.S. Traffic crawled for 20 miles out of town.

We rolled north through various ugly waterside industrial areas before finally turning off the highway to follow a lovely river valley into the heart of the Cascades. Like Going to the Sun Road in Glacier National Park, various highways into Yellowstone, and I-280 in San Francisco, Washington Route 20 claims to be "America's Most Scenic Highway." It pales a bit next to some of the other claimants, but it is a beautiful drive by any standard. One starts with farms and distant mountains and finishes with sharp granite peaks.

SMOKED
BLACK COD
WHITE TOTEMS
MasterCard
VISA
LIVE
OYSTERS

After camping in a half-empty national park campground and eating dinner, Joel and I lay on the ground and watched the meteor showers that had peaked the night before. The sky was absolutely dark. An impressive meteor cut through the sky every two minutes or so and often left a trail visible for seconds afterwards.

Friday, August 13

If you want to know how the Swedes manage to keep themselves in pickled fish and boring cars, stop by the brand-new North Cascades National Park visitors' center. Six $3000 Hasselblad medium-format projectors dissolve onto the center screen while New Age philosophy is drummed into one's head through the sound system. It is amazing how blandly acceptable New Age philosophy is to environmentalists worldwide, rather as Christianity would have been in Hester Prynne's New England.

Tibetan monk chants melted into a soothing voice-over.

"We are all star-born. The sun is our father; the earth is our mother. We are all one people striving toward harmony. Change is Nature's constant."

To complement the vagueness of the philosophy, no image was allowed to remain sharp on-screen for more than a fraction of a second. Almost all of the time two or three images were dissolving together, fuzzing up all of them. "Welcome back to Berkeley," I told Joel, who was looking visibly nauseated.

Following a ranger's suggestion, we biked from Colonial Creek campground to Ruby Creek, a distance of 8 miles. The first 1.5 miles was pretty tough, straight up an 800′ hill to Diablo Lake Overlook. I started to kick myself in the parking lot—this would have been the right place to start. Hydroelectric power uglifies the landscape to some extent, but a series of dams makes 159,000 kilowatts of electricity and impounds two beautiful green lakes. My first thought was one of sorrow for wilderness subdued and lost. My second was that if civil engineers hadn't cut this highway into the mountainside, it would have been pretty tough to see the scenery from a bike.

The two most destructive forces in the universe are man's desire to be with woman and the automobile; disaster is certain when the two are combined. I plucked my bike from the safety of the minivan to admit Alison, Elke, and Jo-Anne. There is in fact no good way to carry bikes outside a minivan. Roof racks whistle, put the bikes out of reach, and invariably result in a collision with an overhanging branch, bridge, or building. My brilliant solution was a $290 folding trailer hitch rack. My bike hadn't been on it more than a week before some unfelt impact had bent its big chainring. I couldn't use half my gears so I turned back to get the car; Joel went on another 30 miles to conquer 5500′ Washington Pass.

Experienced bike tourists know that prevailing winds dictate the right way to travel in North America: west to east and north to south. Going east to west in the Cascades meant fighting a 30 mph headwind today. Most of it was downhill, but oftentimes the wind reduced my speed to a crawl. Dropping down that last 800′ hill gave me some speed that the wind couldn't kill; I hit 47 mph despite touching the brakes a bit.

As Joel sweated his way up the pass, I walked to Rainy Lake under cloudless skies. The easy trail winds its way through primeval forest to yet another eerily glowing glacier-fed lake. This one is especially pretty because a 500′ waterfall plunges into the far side and the whole lake sits in a bowl surrounded by steep faces.

At the Washington Pass Overlook, I spent a fair amount of time taking pictures of wind-gnarled trees with the Cascades receding into the background and a plunging valley below. I picked up a chilled and tired Joel at the Lone Fir campground, and we drove on to Winthrop. This town was founded in the 1890s by a Harvard man, named for a Yale graduate, and is a tourist trap to be proud of today. It has more of an Old West feel than any place I visited in Alaska. We talked our way into the last campsite in Pearrygin Lake State Park, which was packed with boaters and families. Joel borrowed a pot from the happy extended family next door and came back confused.

"They don't seem well educated, yet they have four motor homes and a $6000 Jet-Ski."

The only people Joel sees either have Ph.D.s or are homeless. His vision of America is the standard left-wing one: the economy is profoundly unfair, the middle class is nonexistent, less than half the population has health insurance, and only a few people have enough money to secure material comfort anymore.

87% of the American population in 1993 was covered by some kind of insurance, including Medicaid and Medicare.

"Joel, this is America. We are rich. These people have been working since they were 18 or 22. A house costs $80,000 where they live; they don't spend money on exotic restaurants; they don't fly to Europe every year. You aren't part of the financial elite, Joel. In fact, virtually every California public schoolteacher your age makes more than you do."

Saturday, August 14

Eastern Washington is amazingly dry. We drove for three hours down a river valley flanked by barren hills, which would be described as "brown" by most Easterners and "golden" by Californians. We saw enough irrigated apple orchards to understand Washington State's claim to being the apple capital of the U.S. The most interesting thing about these orchards is how frost is averted. Huge wind machines dot the orchards, each one powered by a big electric or propane motor. When frost threatens, these are fired up and somehow the breeze prevents frost from forming.

We reached Wenatchee (pop. 40,000) around noon. It was the first real town we'd seen since the Interstate, where "real" in America is defined by having a McDonald's and 24-hour supermarket. While we shopped, someone stole the water bottles off my bike. I was sorry to see my bike further crippled and sorrier to have been a crime victim, but it struck me that this pilferage wasn't bad considering that I'd been traveling for months with $1000 of possessions in a canvas roof pouch.

Joel and I toured Wenatchee bike shops in search of a Shimano SG 46-tooth chainring. Jamie, a pleasant 17-year-old lifelong Wenatcheean, had the right part and proposed to replace it while Joel and I lunched.

"Just damned good food," the local diner's sign promised, but our counterman gave us a bonus lesson on how the town was being ruined by Mexicans.

"We give these people free education, health care, and college education. But we won't do anything for a homeless American. 'Get a job, you bum,' is all we have for them."

That day's Wenatchee newspaper carried the same sentiment from California Governor Pete Wilson: "Illegal aliens are stealing $2.3 billion a year in services from the people of this state."

In addition to the message of international understanding, we learned that Wenatchee has more police per capita than just about any other town in the U.S. There are federal, state, city, and county police from various overlapping jurisdictions. "This is in between Spokane and Seattle so a lot of drugs come through here," explained the counterman.

Back at Jamie's repair shop, I got the bad news that it wasn't my $20 chainring, it was my $90 crankset. A comedy of errors ensued that consumed a couple more hours, but Jamie never charged me a cent for labor.

After a night in the Ottawa City Jail, the next logical step on the ladder was . . . Leavenworth. Heavy overcast prevented the Cascade foothills approaching Leavenworth from being really scenic. However, the town itself was something one doesn't often see: a faithful replica of a Bavarian tourist trap town. Beautiful flowers hung in pots from every half-timbered building. Murals of German alpine scenes festooned the walls. Yes, there was even an Edelweiss Restaurant. Leavenworth lacked only Japanese tourists to be truly convincing.

The federal penitentiary is actually in Leavenworth, Kansas.

Highway 97 from Leavenworth to Ellensburg crests magnificent Swauk Pass (4100′) and then rolls downhill for miles. One of us should have done it on a bike, but we didn't see it coming. My AAA membership paid for itself a little later. Instead of taking I-82 down to Yakima, I noticed little scenic dots on the parallel Washington 821. This turned out to be a magnificent road through Yakima canyon. Golden hills rose up from each side of a swift river. The flat road, gently rolling downhill, tailwind (we're going north to south here), and sparse traffic made this irresistible to Joel. He got on his bike and pounded out 16 miles while I went ahead in the car, stopping to write or photograph occasionally. Even the weather cooperated, with the clouds parting just enough to let the sun splash some of the hills.

If the preceding paragraph doesn't sell you on the scenic route, consider the fact that the Interstate goes right through Yakima Training Range where your vehicle may contribute to our nation's security by serving as a weapons testing target. The Interstate also gets you closer to the Department of Energy's Hanford Reservation. Once proud manufacturers of H-bombs, the Hanford folks are now rather ashamed of contaminating eastern Washington and its residents with radiation.

As the sun was just setting, we passed up the urban scene in Yakima to press west to Naches. The glorious death of the day outside contrasted rather sharply with the interior scene. Joel removed his biking tights and parked his sweat-soaked underwear-clad butt directly on the upholstery. Then he cranked the ventilation system in hopes of blow-drying his nether regions. I wanted to puke.

Sunday, August 15

AAA's little black dots barely did justice to the glory of Washington 410. This is a miniature version of Glacier's Going to the Sun Highway despite making no claims of any kind for scenic beauty. I deposited Joel just before Chinook Pass and quickly became envious that it wasn't me riding. The descent from the pass is probably one of the best bike rides anywhere in the world. One wouldn't have to pedal for 10 miles or so while being entertained by fabulous Cascades scenery. Mt. Rainier's glacier-covered flanks loom in the distance when the clouds clear; this baby is 14,410′ high, the fifth highest peak in the Lower 48. Without any high neighbors, it is much more distinctive than California's 14,495′ Mt. Whitney, our highest.

After driving up 4000′ or so to the Mt. Rainier National Park visitors' center, I walked to Glacier Overlook. While Joel was thinking how I'd martyred myself and let him enjoy the bike ride, I enjoyed one of the nicest hikes of my life. Wildflowers in all the meadows exploded in a riot of blue, purple, red, and yellow. Mt. Rainier cooperated fully with my hike, brushing away its veil of clouds just as I left the visitors' center.

Full sunshine made walking a bit hot, and I was glad to stop 1.3 miles from the parking lot at Glacier Overlook. I shared a fabulous view down the river valley and over to Mt. Rainier with Marty, a schoolteacher from Seattle; Adrianne, his Jewish lawyer girlfriend; Robert, a rugged friend of theirs; and his charming twin daughters. I commented to them that in my peregrinations through North America, among the happiest people I'd met were schoolteachers. They are the only large group in the U.S. with both the free time and money to indulge in real travel. Marty agreed that "most people have one or the other." He teaches his middle school children that they should expect to change careers five times in their lives, extrapolating from the current average of three.

Naomi and Marie asked about my life in Boston, and at the end, one of them stated simply, "You're really interesting to talk to." I repaid the guileless kindness of these 12-year-old twins by eating their Fritos and drinking their water.

A cloud rolled in and covered the trail for my return voyage, but two deer quietly sitting by the trail more than made up for the lack of sun. By the time I got back to the parking lot, the fog was so thick that I couldn't see the snack bar

50′ away. Joel was already there, looking pretty good for a man who'd conquered the hill.

Joel is a much more patient person than I am, not that he should be proud of that distinction, which is rather like being a dwarf among midgets. Nonetheless, as we wound our way through fog-shrouded overlooks and depressed little towns, it struck me how comparatively poor were his skills in appreciating the backwaters of America. He had a hard time avoiding greasy food and shaking his condescension toward unambitious small-towners. Even if one can hide it in one's voice, it isn't possible to get to know people for whom one hasn't a genuine respect.

Going to public school for 10 years was like swimming in molasses. My mind couldn't breathe or move. I regret my stunted brain, but looking at Joel I appreciated that the worst legacy of public school was my conviction that I was a genius.

Factory schools necessarily give all students identical straightforward assignments. It is inevitable that some students will take a bit longer to complete these assignments and become discouraged. Students who are slightly quicker than average are in some ways just as unfortunate. Like Don Quixote triumphing over the herd of sheep, they come to believe that they are great intellectuals as they polish off the trivial assignments of the factory school. Unfortunately, the school writes checks that the world won't cash. Real-world problems don't present themselves in neat packages and not everyone can learn to think in new ways at age 18 or 22. Even worse, someone who is convinced he is superior to the rest of the human race is likely to be robbed of contact with his fellow man.

Freshman physics at MIT gave me my comeuppance. Every week I stared at a whole sheet of problems that I was sure I could never solve even if I lived to be 100. I'd never learned how to work on a problem for more than 10 seconds, so I was stuck with a knotted stomach and a panicked brain. Fourteen years of struggle with these kinds of problems in and around MIT taught me, by imperceptible steps, that I wasn't actually better than the average person. If a slight increase in the difficulty of the problems rendered me just as helpless as those poor souls in junior high, then who was I to hold myself above anyone? Without consciously trying to do anything differently, I found myself able to have real conversations with people from all walks of life.

I decided to look at my students next semester at MIT and try to figure out if they were learning this valuable lesson. I also decided to try to figure out if the lesson was worth $27,000/year.

MONDAY, AUGUST 16

We felt our way up toward Windy Ridge through thick fog and a palpable devastation. Mt. St. Helens erupted in 1980—*13 years ago*. Purple wildflowers grew over the graves of thousands of trees blown down by the blast. Joel-the-hypernerd wondered why they hadn't all broken off at the base as one might expect for a uniformly strong trunk pressed sideways by a uniformly applied force. I conjectured that neighboring trees shielded each individual tree to some extent, especially around the bottom. Joel's spirit of inquiry must keep him from ever getting really bored, even if it is death in a singles' bar.

"No shoulder. Vertical edge," read the sign but it should have added that this wasn't one of the 12 sunny days they've had here this summer. Steady drizzle and fog made the 80 winding civilization-free miles to Cougar extremely wearing. Washington State is remarkably desolate. We had driven 52 miles on a heavily traveled national forest road without encountering a gas station; one can't do that on the Alaska Highway. Washington is more backward than Alaska in other ways as well. Some folks here have never been out of their hometown. Virtually everyone living in the backcountry of Alaska has at least a dim memory of somewhere else.

We reached the Interstate and Burgerville, a McDonald's clone that operates only in the Northwest ("Inconveniently located for most of America"). Their menu board lists the number of "Northwest Newcomers." So far this year 86,868 people have immigrated into Oregon and Washington, supposedly because they can't live without Burgerville.

True love is driving 14 hours from Berkeley to Portland to pick up your boyfriend. We met Denise, Joel's girlfriend, at her sister's house at 3:00 PM. I was in a state of shock from six hours of driving either through fog on mountain roads or on an overloaded I-5. Denise's sister had just walked in after two months away to find her life in disarray; my signature bull-in-a-china-shop style of arrival didn't soothe her. Denise was in an ugly mood because she'd just driven 14 hours with a carful of

stuff that Joel and I requested but didn't need. A dark cloud seemed to hang over the house.

After reorganizing my van to accommodate Denise, we set sail for the Oregon coast through Portland's rush hour. Kazuyo had sat primly in a space she'd made for herself between cooler and cameras; male hitchhikers had generally sprawled out over the miscellaneous stuff; Elke had molded herself into the backseat like a cat. Denise tossed the cooler into her sister's backyard, hurled the rest of my stuff into the back, then presided over the newly created throne like a queen.

"Did you ever drive a school bus?" Denise asked. "Because the way this thing is wallowing over the road, I assume you must have."

We were going 65 through beautiful farm country down to Tillamook, but hostility continued to emanate from the back seat.

"Can't you get this bus moving any faster? . . . When was the last time you guys took a shower? It is much nicer to be backpacking because then you aren't crammed into a small car with a bunch of smelly people."

Denise defies categorization, but I'd start with this: a charter member of the "men: can't live with 'em, can't shoot 'em" Berkeley school of feminism. Joel and Denise comprise a virtually complete set of the world's knowledge. Joel knows physics; Denise knows everything else. She knows biology, nutrition, philosophy, literature, politics, history, and the price of tea in China. Although she isn't a lawyer, economist, or engineer, she regularly makes fools of all three in her court appearances on behalf of California's public utilities commission, which regulates utilities. She's studied at Berkeley and Harvard, but knows so much more than the run-of-the-mill credential-grubbers that it would be insulting to list her degrees next to her name.

Denise's tall athletic physique, comprehensive learning, and the lordly manner of one raised in the Bay Area make her probably the most formidable woman I know. The only thing that keeps Joel from being utterly crushed is his broad general knowledge and unshakable inner conviction that a woman does not have the right to criticize him.

I'd loved Denise the last time I'd visited Joel in Berkeley: "Joel, this girl is sexy, smart, lively, and caring. She's just what you need. Marry her." One should never underestimate the force of circumstance, however, and traveling puts as much of a strain on human relations as anything.

After two and a half months on the road, I'd learned how to be satisfied with much of what life threw my way. Joel had jetted out of his carefully controlled life at home into chaos. Thus with Joel, I'd ensured harmony simply by giving in to all of his requests. It cost me little and made him substantially happier. However, with Denise it wasn't enough to give in; one had to give in with the proper attitude.

Amid an atmosphere of tension and recrimination, we reached Cape Lookout State Park with its nice stretch of coastline and 250 superdeveloped campsites. We're talking free hot showers and today's Portland paper in a vending rack. Joel and Denise set up camp and cooked a salmon dinner while I walked up and down the beach photographing the sunset on the cliffs, waterfalls, and twisted trees.

Tuesday, August 17

We woke up to a rare-for-this-area beautiful blue sky. A bit of mist hung between the huge trees of the coastal forest. Denise was in an easy-going, yet perspicacious mood.

"This is the kind of weather that makes some Okie weekend tourist say, 'Ma, we found paradise. Sell the farm and let's move up here.' They don't realize that it rains the other 51 weekends a year."

This is one of only two places on the Oregon coast where one can be on the coastal road and not be on packed-with-motor-homes Highway 101. That makes for much more pleasant cycling. We surmounted some good-sized cliffs and were treated to grand views over the water. Pounding surf has carved gaping tunnels in enormous rocks standing in open water. Today's waves crashed and boomed through these holes carved by their forebears. Scenery, sun, headwinds, 1600′ of climbing, and 31 miles made us happy to relax on the beach until sunset.

Wednesday, August 18

We escaped coastal fog by driving inland to the Columbia River Gorge, drenched in sunlight. Multnomah Falls is a thundering 600′ cascade visible from I-84. Joel noted that "this must be a maxima of beauty multiplied by accessibility."

Although moving inland was a good idea, three hours of driving with Denise reduced me to a pathetic state. Denise moved to the front seat, took over my life, and made it hell. She assumed it was her right to control the car temperature, stereo

volume and music, and overall noise level by opening her window at 60 mph. It might have been a pleasure to be a gracious host and yield to her, but I wasn't given the chance. She just took everything as her natural due. After asking Denise, "Are you absolutely sure you don't have any Jewish ancestry?" I regretted my earlier expressed stereotype of Jewish girls.

I dropped Denise and Joel at Denise's sister's and wished them a good trip back to California. I was anxious to show my genuine affection for Denise and smooth things over after a sometimes-difficult couple of days.

"It would be less trouble to have married and divorced every woman I've ever met than to spend one afternoon with you in the passenger seat."

Even a week later it was hard for me to imagine having thought and said this; Denise is a treasure.

Despite being given only a few hours of warning, old friends Dwight and Karla welcomed me warmly into their cliffside home in the Portland suburb of Lake Oswego. I had hardly stepped over the threshold when Karla said, "You must have laundry to do; let's start it now." By the time I'd begun to consume the delicious salmon barbecue they'd prepared, all the tension of the previous two days melted away. I'd remembered 8-year-old Emily as the world's sweetest child, always ready with a kind word or deed even for her frighteningly violent younger brother. Thirteen-year-old Emily was just as charming but she shocked me by challenging her father. She showed signs of becoming almost as scornful of parental wisdom as I had been. Little Brother was off at camp, so I couldn't see whether or not his testosterone-poisoning had abated. Emily's saintly tolerance hadn't persisted, though.

"There are many days when I don't speak a word to Harlan."

Thursday, August 19

Suburban America can lead to distressing contentment, self-satisfaction, and complacency. However, if you really want to relax for a day, there is no better place to spend it than inside a lovingly organized suburban homestead. Emily and I had the house to ourselves: stocked kitchen, three comfortable living rooms with interesting art on the walls, ample office and recreation supplies, pool, hot tub, view out to the coastal

mountain range. We spent most of the day going through 50 rolls of slides for a Yellowstone-through-Seattle slide show. After eight hours, bears, mountains, people, and cities all looked exactly the same.

Friday, August 20

Two days with Dwight, Emily, and Karla left me feeling warm and completely refreshed. It felt as though I'd been comfortably at home and today was the first day of a new trip.

If my friends weren't enough, going to the Lake Oswego post office was actually a life-affirming experience. Not only was the last machine-gun massacre a distant memory, but customers and clerks were so happy to see each other that it was almost a party. The local Schwinn dealer was scarcely less friendly, replacing a few rattled-off pieces of my bike for free.

My heart went thump as I got onto Interstate 84 East. This was the beginning of my return to Boston. Just as I had become perfectly adapted to life on the road, I was headed home. Three weeks remained to me. It seemed cruelly short and made me wonder.

What can a person possibly see in just three weeks?

15

Portland to the Promised Land

AAA puts their magic dots next to I-84 as it follows the Mighty Columbia from Portland up to the high plains. The river has been substantially tamed by a series of dams and no longer carves its gorge with such ferocity. Nonetheless, the dry sculpted hills on both sides of the river are spectacular, as are the whitecaps on the mile-wide river stirred up by the relentless 30 mph wind. Despite unwelcoming weather, the river was teeming with hundreds of expert windsurfers. This is supposedly one of the best places in the world for the sport, but I wouldn't try to learn here, what with other guys roaring past at 25 mph and waves big enough to break an ankle.

"Warning, last Burgerville for 26,000 miles," read a billboard reminding me that I was leaving the Pacific Northwest. A couple hours out of Portland and one realizes why so many braved the hardships of the Oregon Trail back in 1843 ("the cowards never started, and the weak died along the way"). With a little irrigation, this is some of the richest farmland in the world. Eastern Oregon's plains burst with fields of wheat and corn surrounded by grassy hills for grazing cattle.

Every hour of driving brought clearer weather, and I was enjoying the late afternoon light shining on the alternately green and golden hills. The eastern half of Oregon is so dry, vast, and open that it is difficult to remember that it is part of the same state as the wet, densely forested western half.

After six high-speed hours, I encountered a massive storm system centered above Baker City. My first view was of a dark patch in the sky with three wide rainbows coming down. These were the widest, richest, most saturated rainbows ever. As

I drew closer lightning appeared on the hilltops. Not your average everyday lightning thrown down by Zeus on unworthy earth-treading mortals. Lightning thrown sideways across hilltops, stretching horizontally for at least half a mile. Zeus fighting with other gods. As I entered the storm, heavy clouds shrouded the lightning, which was now only perceivable as an ominous general illumination.

MIT freshman physics was 14 years ago, but I remembered that an electric field can't be established inside a Faraday cage.

"I am surrounded by the car. The car is made of steel. Steel conducts. Charge will flow through the body instantly to counter the externally applied field that leads to lightning. Lightning will therefore go around the car."

Repeating this mantra didn't entirely banish my primal fear. Something about storms prevents rational thought.

> *This is easily verified by picking people at random to ask why it is safe to be in a car during a lightning storm. "Because of insulation from the rubber tires" is the common answer. "Is air an insulator?" you may ask. "Yes," they'll respond. "Then a lightning bolt that has punched through a mile of air is going to be stopped by an inch of rubber?" "I think so."*

SATURDAY, AUGUST 21

Boise boasts many attractive stone or brick buildings, including the classical State Capitol, and retains some historic charm despite a few 15-story monstrosities. Lunching at a yuppie French/vegetarian/Tex-Mex café, I perused the *Boise Weekly* alternative newspaper. The Idaho Shakespeare Festival was concentrating on the lighter side of romance this summer (*Midsummer Night's Dream*), but the destructive lust and state coercion of *Measure for Measure* has spilled out right onto the cover page. It turns out that fornication, cohabitation, and adultery are still criminal offenses in Idaho. My favorite is the sodomy law:

> Every person who is guilty of the infamous crime against nature, committed with mankind or with any animal, is punishable by imprisonment in the state prison not less than five years.

It would be a shame if a modern-day Angelo appeared to enforce these laws because every other woman in Boise was a tall, beautiful blonde.

Driving from Boise to Salt Lake helped me appreciate how much space we Americans have. Half of the four lanes were closed, and traffic was squeezed into one lane for each direction. This was August, the peak travel month, and there is only one Interstate linking the two biggest cities in the region. Yet traffic merely slowed from 65 to 55 mph.

Just before the Utah border, I passed a casket manufacturer's truck emblazoned, "Drive Safely, Heaven Can Wait" and "Giving Dignity to Life (TM)." The highway surface improved as I left Idaho, but the few traces of civilization disappeared. There wasn't a McDonald's for 200 miles, just ranches and farms and "No Services" signs tacked to the infrequent exits.

Here in Zion, one of the evils of life that has been banished is getting lost. Virtually all towns in Utah, from the smallest right up to Salt Lake, are organized on a Cartesian coordinate system. If you need a map to find an address, then part of your brain is on hold. If you can't find Temple Square, which is smack in the center of the grid and well-signed, then you have no brain at all.

Temple Square, "Dedicated to the Sacred Principle of Religious Freedom," is a compact confection of gleaming white buildings, freshly scrubbed twenty-something women giving tours in 15 languages, and mostly well-dressed respectful tourists. Slumping in lumpy contrast to this prosperity are, well, bums. Down-and-outers of various descriptions line the public sidewalks near the entrances to the square holding signs: "Stranded; need money to get bus back to L.A." or "Drug-free mother with three kids needs help."

Temple Square has two visitors' centers explaining the faith of the Church of Jesus Christ of Latter-Day Saints. Series of paintings illustrate the Old Testament, the New Testament, and the Book of Mormon. I stopped first at the genealogy database public access terminals. The Mormons have the world's largest collection of birth and death records. They do this because they have an answer to an Enlightenment criticism of Christianity: If Faith in Jesus is the only way to get to Heaven, then a lot of virtuous Indians and Chinese are out of luck. Would a benevolent God have really set up the world so that people who were unlucky to be born in a place without Jewish/Christian bibles would all go to Hell?

Mormons answer this with a resounding "No!" They are going to convert all the dead souls they can find to the LDS church. Individual Mormons like to convert their own ancestors but also take upon themselves the selfless task of converting (dead) strangers. Souls are eternal, by the way, and the dead soul retains its freedom to reject Mormonism and salvation.

Dead Greenspuns will apparently all rot in Hell for awhile; there weren't any in the database.

Legacy draws full houses every hour in the plush Joseph Smith center, a refurbished 1911 grand hotel. A big screen and 70 mm projectors grace the 500-seat theater. *Legacy* is as engrossing as any Hollywood picture and beautifully photographed. The story starts with a young woman's 1830 conversion in New York. She watches her brother die with 16 other Mormons in the 1838 Haun's Mill (Missouri) massacre. State governors were shown ordering troops to tar and feather or expel Mormons.

This isn't as bad an infringement of constitutional guarantees as it appears. The Bill of Rights originally restricted actions only by the federal government. In 1833, the Supreme Court specifically wrote that the Bill of Rights did not restrict actions by state governments (Barron v. Baltimore). It wasn't until the Fourteenth Amendment's ratification in 1868 that the U.S. Constitution guaranteed civil liberties for individuals against the states.

A period of comparative peace follows, with proselytizing in England and painstaking temple building in the thriving settlement of Nauvoo, Illinois (pop. 15,000). The murder of Prophet Joseph Smith by a mob in 1843 darkens the mood again. The final exodus to Utah, lead by Brigham Young, doesn't look like much fun: hard miles through Iowa, up the Platte River through Nebraska into Laramie, Wyoming, then across the Green River and down into Salt Lake City.

David, a retired Salt Laker, and his son Doug, an engineer from California, sat next to me. They were quite anxious for me to join the 8.5 million Mormons, as was Doug's wife Sue, a convert 23 years ago (and now mother of six).

"We like Jews, especially Israeli Jews, and pray for the Jews to return to Israel because that brings Jesus closer."

"You can pray all you like, but until Israel gets proper heating and air conditioning, they'll pry my American passport out of my cold, dead hand," I responded. "Hey, and speaking of Israel, I know the Lord moves in mysterious ways, but my visit there really jarred my common sense: *this* is the promised land?!?"

Mark Twain had the same sentiments back in 1869: "Monotonous and uninviting as much of the Holy Land will appear to persons accustomed to the almost constant verdure of flowers, ample streams, and varied surface of our own country, we must remember that its aspect to the Israelites after the weary march of 40 years through the desert must have been very different."

"Israel was just a way station," Doug explained. "Around 200 B.C., God moved a couple of tribes of Jews out of the Persian Gulf in boats, and they sailed for the real Promised Land: America. Descendants of these tribes became the American Indians."

So Mormons reject the theory that American Indians came over from Siberia?

"Absolutely."

How could the Jews, a people for whom literacy is the *sine qua non* of adulthood, evolve into illiterate Indians?

"That's all explained in the scripture. Basically it came down to internecine conflict."

It is not too hard to argue that North America is the best piece of real estate on the planet, but isn't Utah a little inhospitable to be Zion?

"'Zion' means different things in different contexts. Salt Lake isn't Zion. Joseph Smith identified the Garden of Eden in Missouri, and that is where the church is going to build Zion and the New Jerusalem eventually, as soon as enough land has been bought up."

Is it going to be like John Calvin's theocratic Geneva, where civil authority was used to coerce people into obeying religious law (a woman was fined for "making a rude noise in church")?

"Absolutely not. We think the U.S. Constitution was divinely inspired. Mormons don't want any more power than that of excommunication."

How can they have such faith in a document and system that had failed them in their time of need?

"It is true that the Mormons petitioned President Van Buren to do something about Missouri's illegal extermination order, but he made a political decision not to," Doug noted. "However, we have faith in the American system."

Sunday, August 22

After hearing the Mormon Youth Symphony and Chorus perform in the Tabernacle, I walked out into the blinding light of Temple Square. Keith dropped out of high school in Illinois and moved here nine years ago.

"I was on my way to Vegas and never made it."

Dressed in denim work clothes, he holds a cardboard sign reading, "Out of Work and Homeless; Please Help."

Won't the Mormons help him?

"They are better at helping their own. Oh, I could go to their work center and stay for three days, but they don't pay you, just give you credits against food and clothing. A friend of mine came here from Boston. He'd been baptized in the church but never practiced. He went to see a bishop, was looked up in the computer, and the bishop put him up in a hotel room for two weeks. He got a job within two days. They take care of their own.

"I'm living in an abandoned apartment right now. It's pretty good; nobody bothers me. But I shouldn't have quit my last job. My girlfriend wants to get a place together. I didn't like working in that restaurant, but I only made $9 yesterday from tourists. And every time I light a cigarette, a Mormon will come over and say, 'I wish I had enough money to smoke.' They say it is a sin, but they do it. A friend of mine is an archaeologist and he says, 'You should see the stacks of whiskey bottles I've found at old Mormon sites.'"

Does he personally know any polygamists?

"I've seen quite a few walking around Salt Lake. The most flagrant was a guy from southern Utah. He had 16 wives, but they couldn't touch him. Legally, he'd only married the first. She signed something giving her consent to the other 15 living with them."

Trying to learn about polygamy in Temple Square is a bit like trying to learn about the Nazis in Germany; it is the part of local history that outsiders find most interesting, but nobody wants to talk about it. Young Mormons around the temple go by "Brother Joe" or "Sister Judy" or whatever, but there is a class of folks who go by "Elder Smith" or "Elder Jones." Elder Pomeroy, a graying information resource, gave me a good education on the subject of polygamy.

"Joseph Smith had a divine inspiration in the early 1840s that led to the institution of polygamy. There wasn't a shortage of men or anything, and in fact Prophet Joseph was very unenthusiastic and unhappy about the idea."

> *Mark Twain looked at the Mormon women in 1872: "I warmed toward these poor, ungainly, and pathetically homely creatures. . . . 'No—the man that marries one of them has done an act of Christian charity which entitles him to the kindly applause of mankind, not their harsh censure—and the man that marries sixty of them has done a deed of open-handed generosity so sublime that the nations should stand uncovered in his presence, and worship in silence.'"*

Smith and Twain's sentiments notwithstanding, the U.S. government was downright hostile to polygamy from Day One.

"My great-grandfather was a polygamist, and he was fined and chased by U.S. marshals in Arizona Territory. The Church fought for religious freedom all the way up to the Supreme Court in the late 1880s, but ultimately lost. Congress passed a law that would confiscate all church buildings, funds, and assets if polygamy continued. Although this practice had been ordained by God, Mormon theologists tried to reconcile it with passages in the scripture requiring obedience to civil authority. Polygamy was abandoned in 1890 and that paved the way for Utah's statehood."

I subsequently asked a "man-in-the-street" Mormon if he knew any polygamists.

"Only two. One lives in Colorado City, Arizona, where there is a community of about 2000 polygamists. Economically, they manage to live fairly diversified lives, winning construction contracts all over the West. My friend there has three wives in one big house. The other is my aunt. Her husband read the scriptures carefully and took a 19-year-old girl as another wife. My Aunt, who was 40 at the time, was very angry, and my father (her brother) wanted to kill the polygamist. But my uncle eventually convinced everyone that this was the right way to live, and they've worked it out."

Do they sleep in the same bed?

"No, it isn't the kind of wild sex party that people imagine. In fact, the old polygamists used to maintain each wife and set of children in her own house. They wrote in their diaries about how difficult it was. They really didn't want to do it."

> *Oddly enough, the last time I was in Phoenix, local TV news was abuzz over some litigation in Colorado City. A dispute there over property spilled out into the federal courts and all the lurid details of life there became public. One litigant complained that another had stolen two of his wives and added them to his harem of seven.*

My last stop in Temple Square was the new Mormon Museum, which recounts the history of the migration of the Mormons and the rigors of the Mormon Trail. An exhibit upstairs documents the design and decoration of the Temple, finished in the 1890s and off-limits to non-Mormons. The structure is a bit heavy and graceless, but one can't fault the church for skimping. They sent a group of their best artists to Paris for a proper education. When they came back to Salt Lake they did some nice Impressionistic paintings for the interior. A golden statue of the Mormon angel, somewhat unfortunately named "Moroni," adorns the top.

I walked out of the museum mostly astonished by how they underplayed the vicious persecution of Mormons by their fellow Americans. I was upset that I'd learned so little of the failure of the Constitutional guarantees in grade school. The unfairness of the taking of Indian lands was covered in great detail, but the Mormon experience, which offers a much more disturbing caution to our present age, was hardly mentioned. Nobody seriously expects a repeat of the European/Indian conflict if only because we already took all the Indian land that we wanted. However, conflict between religious cults and the state is ongoing. Just ask David Koresh, the Rajneeshi, or even the Christian Scientists. Given the erosion of civil liberties over the last decade in the name of the Drug War, all Americans might do well to ponder the Mormon experience.

Gorgeous two-lane roads through coal and uranium mining country took me to Moab, Utah. I listened to Ishiguro's *The Remains of the Day.* When I read this a few years ago, it didn't resonate with me. On second encounter, Ishiguro's English butler reminded me of many of my friends. He's sacrificed everything in order to do his job well and at a late age begins to question whether it was worth it.

Monday, August 23

There are two ways to become Christian in Utah. One is to fall in love with a Mormon missionary. The other is to ride the Slickrock Trail.

> O man, citizenship of this great world-city has been yours. Whether for five years or fivescore, what is that to you? Whatever the law of that city decrees is fair to one and all alike. Wherein, then, is your grievance? You are not ejected from the city by any unjust judge or tyrant, but by the selfsame Nature which brought you into it; just as when an actor is dismissed by the manager who engaged him. "But I have played no more than three of the five acts." Just so; in your drama of life, three acts are all the play. Its point of completeness is determined by him who formerly sanctioned your creation, and today sanctions your dissolution. Neither of those decisions lay within yourself. Pass on your way, then, with a smiling face, under the smile of him who bids you go.
>
> — Marcus Aurelius before Slickrock (12:36)

> Dear God, thank you for making me emperor. I shall forever hallow Thy name for keeping my gonads off the top tube. Would it test Thy greatness to keep me from sneezing so I don't get a face-first tour of Negro Bill Canyon?
>
> — Marcus Aurelius on the Slickrock

FOOT

Even setting aside the politically incorrect canyon, the names of Slickrock features are not comforting. "Hell's Revenge" and "Abyss" jump out of the map. The trail was created in 1969 by a motorcyclist. He painted white stripes on the rounded sandstone features for 14 miles and about 200 dirt bikers each year were crazy enough to attempt it. Several years ago the trail was discovered by America's mountain bikers, and they've inundated the town to test their mettle.

This used to be known as "Nigger Bill Canyon," after a 19th-century sheep farmer who lived in the area. A proposed name change to "African-American William Canyon" was defeated in favor of the current compromise.

There is a 2.5-mile "practice loop" alternative to the main trail. It isn't any easier than the main ride, just shorter. This is no small consideration when one considers the 100–110 degree heat and unavailability of water on what is normally a very strenuous four-hour ride. Slickrock winds through a landscape of fantastic beauty: red sandstone sculpted into towers, canyons, squatting lumps, and the Colorado River flowing through it all. Scrubby trees soften one's immediate environment, and the 12,000′ La Sal Mountains covered with trees and/or snow provide a pleasant backdrop.

Here is a typical sequence of the Slickrock. Step One: Survey the landscape from the top of a 40′-high lump. Step Two: Bike straight down the 30-degree side into a pit about the width of your bike tire. You've two choices here: don't brake or brake. If you don't brake, you'll crash into the pit at 35 mph. If you brake, little bumps on the way down will hurl you over the handlebars at 15 mph. Whatever you choose, remember to get off the brakes and adjust your weight so that your bike doesn't get stuck in the pit and send you flying over the handlebars and into the next rock. Step Three: Start up the next 40′ lump. The 30-degree slope will have you standing on your pedals in the lowest of your 21 gears. Remember to keep your weight forward or you will lift the front wheel and fall off the back of the bike. Step Four: Get to the top exhausted from the heat, climb, and thinnish air at 4500′. Step Five: Drink from your dwindling water supply; go to Step One.

Here is a less typical, but even more invigorating section. Ride along a horizontal contour of a 25-degree slope, amazed all the time that your bike tire grips the sandstone. Stare in disbelief as the trail makes a tight 180-degree turn. Contemplate getting off the bike but realize that stopping will start you tumbling sideways down a 100′ slope to a dry canyon bed. Make the turn realizing that a 5-degree error in steering will plunge you straight down the same slope. Repeat three times then go to preceding sequence.

A combination of aerobic fatigue, 97-degree weather, and stark terror left my energy reserves and water bottles dry at the end of the 2.5-mile loop. After a refreshing dip in Ken's Lake, a lovely reservoir, I drove back to downtown and hung out at Mondo Espresso in front of Kaibab Bike. Terry and Rebecca dipped into a $3000 Italian machine and served me a fine ice and fruit slush supplemented with an education on the local mind-set.

"We called contractors just after we moved here, and they came over and gave us estimates. After three weeks we wondered why they hadn't showed up. Friends clued us into 'Moab Fever,' which might otherwise be described as laziness. People come here and throw away their calendars and watches. Every business is open 7 days a week, the supermarket is 24 hours a day. Knowing the day or date is almost worthless information. One time I had to dig out a supermarket receipt to figure out what day it was."

The bike rack in front of Kaibab is a lot like the valet parking lot of the Beverly Hills Hotel: Lycra-clad drivers drop off the world's most expensive custom-made machines plus a bunch of absurdly expensive mass-produced ones. At Kaibab, however, all the machines are American and most are badly dented and scratched. Clark, the shop's assistant manager and some visitors were chatting about how lonely life here can be for a single guy in this town of 6000. Apparently it is not the place to meet that Lycra-clad beauty in the Raleigh ad.

"I've ridden here every day for four years and can count on the fingers of one hand the number of single women I've seen on the trail."

In nearby Arches National Park, I hiked 1.5 miles to the perfectly formed Delicate Arch. Germany's goodwill ambassadors were out in force. Christina is in her last

year of gymnasium and came here with 20 other Germans in a tour bus. She's hardly spoken any English since she came here and not gotten to know any Americans.

"People look at me funny when I smoke in shops here. We all smoke in Germany, what is wrong with people here?"

I explained to her a bit about American smoking etiquette. Would she smoke around a fellow German with a respiratory problem?

"People like that should stay home."

I wasn't surprised to learn that Christina's tour was organized by Marlboro cigarettes. I wondered what our Joe Camel protesters would think about a cigarette company sponsoring youth travel.

A large group of folks sat on a rock overlooking the arch while a smaller number walked around having their pictures taken right up against it. One family sat themselves down smack underneath the arch. They were looking out over a canyon with their backs to us. A thirtysomething German kneeled 40 yards away with his camera.

"Do we all have to take your picture? There are other places to sit, you know," he hollered at them in heavily accented English.

It dawned on me that this might well be the best way to motivate a German, i.e., to convince him that he could be a better citizen. Most Americans, however, instinctively know that the best way to motivate a fellow American is to convince him that he could do you a favor, e.g., "*I* would really appreciate it if you would . . . ."

Delicate Arch at sunset inspired the burning of a whole roll of film. I clambered up to a car-sized arch-shaped hole in one wall and mounted an ultrawide 20 mm lens on the Nikon. The rim of the hole was in shadow, making a black frame for the picture. Delicate Arch sits in the middle of the frame, with the La Sal Mountains behind, all glowing warmly in the setting sun.

Moving closer to the 46′-high arch, I used a tripod and small aperture to turn the setting sun into a starburst over the red rocks of the foreground. Almost everyone else left, but I stayed to capture the moon over the arch and the La Sal Mountains with 15- and 30-second exposures. I finished up where I'd started, capturing the same scene of hole-framed arch in the fading twilight before hiking down the dark trail.

Tuesday, August 24

Utah's Route 128 is devoid of its Massachusetts namesake's biotech and computer firms, but its path at the bottom of the Colorado River's canyon more than makes up for it. Dams at numerous points on the river keep river levels constant so that a good highway can snuggle right up to the riverside, making for an almost entirely flat bike ride. Enormous sandstone cliffs tower above the road while lush vegetation flanks the silty river. It would have been a perfect ride had the temperature not been about 100.

Cruising smoothly through a beautiful canyon at 13 mph with a cool breeze in my face, I had to admit that pavement has its advantages. The silence was broken only every five minutes or so by the passage of a car on its way to Colorado.

Her Isuzu Trooper loaded with bike and camping gear, Lisa sat on a streamside rock reading *Zen and the Art of Motorcycle Maintenance*. Only about 15% of her elfin tawny body was covered with shorts and halter top.

Lisa has been out of college for three years and wants to do something with her degree but can't get the travel bug out of her system.

"I can save $5000 in one winter waitressing in Vail. Then I'm off. My first trip was a $600 five-month tour of France, England, and Ireland. I hitchhiked with ex-cons, stowed away on ferries, and ate spaghetti and porridge until it made me sick to look at either again."

Was she alone?

"Just as I was leaving the U.S., my friend Brett said, 'I've always wanted to do that.' He quit his law firm and came with me. We were barely speaking to each other after a few months. He was always flaunting his Yale degree but never really impressed me or anyone else with his learning or intelligence.

"'Why did you take this trip, Brett?' I asked him.

"'I wanted to have some stories to tell,' he responded.

"'So you are working on your travel résumé.'"

I figured this would be the ideal time to tell my one lawyer/biker joke: "If you are driving along and see a lawyer on a bicycle, why don't you swerve to hit him? . . . Because it might be *your* bicycle."

Brett fell in love with Lisa, but only managed to join her substantial stack of broken hearts.

"Men fall in love with me because of my independent spirit and then want to hold me; I don't understand it."

After a photo safari to Dead Horse Point, overlooking Canyonlands National Park, I stopped back at the Lazy Lizard, where Michael, a German university student, asked me how I'd liked Berlin. I told him how interesting I thought it was, especially the tension between Russian and German monuments, the Nazi history, and the Turkish neighborhoods.

"Don't you think attitudes in Germany have completely changed?" he asked.

"Frankly, no," I answered. "I'd say the attitude toward Turks today is more or less the same as it was toward Jews in the Old Days: 'Here are a bunch of outsiders living off of us Germans who've worked hard for centuries to build this society.' Furthermore, I'd heard quite a few well-educated good-hearted Germans say many of the same things about Jews that the Nazis did."

This set off a firestorm of criticism from all sides.

An English guy said that what the Nazis did to the "inferior races of Europe" was no worse than what the U.S. did to the Indians. In fact, he went on, "I've been here for four months, and Americans today are just as racist as Germans ever were."

Had he heard any American advocate any kind of action against someone because of his race?

"No, but I saw a bumper sticker on a car here that said, 'Zap Iraq.' . . . Anything the Germans might have done is ancient history. Young people today are completely different and much more educated about the world. The main threat to the world today is the U.S."

Colin, a New Zealander, said it was unfair to criticize the Germans because the Israelis were as bad as the Nazis ever were.

"I got through the border in a few minutes, but they spent an hour questioning an Arab going through. Palestinians can't vote or work."

Colin was unaware of the distinction between Arabs in the Occupied Territories and those in Israel proper. I asked him if New Zealand would be happy to give the vote and full political rights to a group of people who had evinced no desire to be part of New Zealand and in fact had fought several unsuccessful wars to take over the country. Colin changed the topic.

"Well, I think it is really obnoxious that Jews consider themselves the chosen people and that Israel gives special treatment to Jews. Isn't it time to move beyond religious labels?"

Colin had traveled all over the world and had found only one constant: Israelis are obnoxious and unwelcome everywhere.

"There are lots of hotels and restaurants where they won't even let Israelis in because they are so rude. Why aren't they better ambassadors for their country?"

The only one willing to distinguish the Nazis from other world malefactors was Michael, the German student.

"No one else was as organized as the Germans."

He understood why Jews were a natural target for the Nazis, though.

"They controlled all the banks and media and were dominant in medicine and law. There were 2–3 million Jews in Germany then."

I tried to defuse the argument by reminding folks that I hadn't passed judgment on anyone but only said that I didn't think German attitudes had changed much.

"The main lesson I would expect Germans to draw from World War II is that attacking the U.S. and Russia simultaneously is a bad idea. Why would attitudes about racism have changed? Attitudes that are deep-seated in a culture aren't going to change easily. One doesn't learn about people by killing them; one learns by living with them. Americans who have day-to-day contact with different cultures tend to reevaluate their stereotypes. Unfortunately, since there are essentially no Jews left in Germany, that option isn't available to Germans."

Michael violently disagreed with this.

"There aren't any young people who are anti-Semitic in Germany anymore. Germany today is full of Jews. In my life, I've actually met five."

A famous Nazi saying was "500,000 unemployed; 500,000 Jews. Solution is very simple." Although this slogan might be faulted for its inclusion of women, children, and elderly, the 500,000 number is well-grounded in a German census of 1920. By 1937, only about 365,000 Jews remained in Germany, less than 1% of the German population. These constituted less than 5% of Europe's Jews. Germany's Jewish population rose by 180,000 when it merged with Austria, but fell dramatically during the Holocaust. At the end of the war, 5,000 German Jews had survived clandestinely and 12,000 as spouses of Aryans. Between 1948 and 1964, 9000 of these 17,000 survivors emigrated to Israel (sources: Atlas of Jewish History *and* The Jews in Germany*).*

Wednesday, August 25

Humidity, clouds, and rain greeted me in the morning, reminding me how tame our desert really is. In the Sinai, it rains once every three years or so, and there isn't a shred of vegetation anywhere. Everything here is covered in grass, brush, or trees because it actually rains fairly regularly.

It was a beautiful drive south along the edge of Canyonlands National Park. Violent crosswinds and occasionally heavy rain made for dramatic driving; this is not the place to bring the Volkswagen. In a convenience store in Monticello, I met Larry and his wife, a Navajo who'd been placed with a Mormon family near Salt Lake.

"Our mothers wanted the best possible educations for us. The local Bureau of Indian Affairs school wasn't any good so it was a choice of boarding school or taking advantage of the Mormon program to place Indian children with families."

Were their parents horrified that they'd converted to the LDS church?

"No. They saw it as part of adapting to modern culture."

In their designer clothes and jewelry, I had to admit that they appeared to be some of the better-adapted Navajo I'd met. What had drawn them to Monticello?

"I haven't gotten a job here yet, but my wife has a good job with the local uranium tailings cleanup operation."

John, an insurance agent, added that "they just finished spending $200 million cleaning up mill tailings here. It was really fine sand, and it blew out over a bunch of fields. A lot of people actually used it as building material so now their houses are slightly radioactive. Brilliant, eh?"

Uranium cleanup is a big industry in Utah right now. A classical form of contamination was caused by the "big heap" system. High-grade ore was dug out of the ground and processed. Low-grade rock was just piled up and left out in the open for 30 years. It wasn't radioactive enough to be used in bombs or reactors, but it was still hotter than normal. Three decades of wind blew radioactive dust from these piles all over portions of Utah. Now government contractors roam around thousands of square miles in special sniffer tractors finding radioactive topsoil so that it can be scraped up and buried somewhere.

John was the last Mormon I talked to in Utah and the first who had any sympathy for David Koresh. In light of their own persecution by the government, weren't they firm believers in the words of Frederick Douglas: "No man can put a chain about the ankle of his fellow man without at last finding the other end fastened about his own neck"?

"Koresh was molesting children" was a typical reaction.

How did they know that?

"We read it in the newspapers."

How would an 1840 newspaper have described their own religion?

"Hmmm."

John thought the government should have left Koresh alone and said that quite a few Mormons in southern Utah shared his thinking. "Folks here support the Indians' right to use peyote as a matter of religious freedom. A lot of people were also cheered by the jury verdict in Idaho acquitting Randy Weaver."

John told me about Monticello's history.

"This is one of the few cities in Utah that was not settled by Mormons. We have a Catholic church here and a large Hispanic community, which was here decades before the Mormons."

As we parted, I got a good illustration of the cultural difference between Boston and Monticello: I set the yuppie alarm on my $18,000 van before running into the convenience store; John left the motor running on his $30,000 Acura Legend.

According to a report in a friend's gun magazine, Idaho resident and small-time gun dealer Randy Weaver was approached in October 1989 by a federal undercover agent interested in purchasing sawed-off shotguns. The two shotguns Weaver sold the agent had barrels just under the legal limit of

18". Eight months later, Weaver refused an offer to become a government informer and was indicted for the sale of the guns.

In January 1991, Weaver and his wife Vicki stopped to help motorists in a camper stranded at the side of the road; federal agents emerged from the camper, put a gun to Weaver's neck, and pushed his wife to the ground. After a federal arraignment, Weaver returned to his cabin in the woods, vowing never to cooperate with courts or government; he was later indicted for failure to appear.

In August of 1992, U.S. marshals—heavily armed and camouflaged—surrounded Weaver's cabin. Weaver's 14-year-old son Sammy, his Golden Retriever Striker, and neighbor Kevin Harris were out hunting when an agent fired into the dog without warning. Sammy shot back with his bolt-action hunting rifle and was shot first in the arm and then in the back as he was running toward the cabin. Harris shot and killed a U.S. marshal and made it back to Weaver's cabin.

Following the death of the marshal, the cabin was surrounded by FBI and BATF (Bureau of Alcohol, Tobacco, and Firearms) agents, U.S. marshals, and Idaho state police and national guard. The media also showed up in force, characterizing Weaver's cabin as a "mountain fortress" and later as a "bunker."

When Weaver came out of the cabin, moving toward his son's body, he was shot in the arm by an FBI agent. The same agent shot Weaver's wife in the head as she stood in the doorway holding her infant daughter. Press reports maintained that Vicki had been "killed in an exchange of fire" or in a "gun battle" although these were the only two shots fired.

Weaver and Harris surrendered. After a 36-day trial for murder and other felony charges, Harris was acquitted of the murder charge by reason of self-defense. Weaver was acquitted of the gun charge first brought in 1990. Agents said they had never considered just knocking on the door to arrest Weaver.

The report in the gun magazine I saw probably overlooks a few unsavory facts about Weaver, but the Wall Street Journal *has run very similar accounts.*

INDEPENDENCE PASS
Elevation 12,095 feet
CONTINENTAL DIVIDE

16

Colorado

"I was diagnosed HIV-positive in 1984. I've been very lucky to be one of the few without symptoms. I decided to spend some time giving back and now I'm going to enjoy. I was experimenting at just the wrong time, in the late 1970s. I tell young people today, 'Sex is wonderful, sex is exciting, have fun with casual sex, but use a condom.' I get really scared when I hear that the fastest growing incidence of AIDS is among college students. These people are throwing away their exuberance."

Arthur was Colorado's first gay rights lobbyist. He has spent seven years without pay, living under the shadow of HIV, trying to insure anonymous HIV testing for Coloradans. The passage of Amendment 2 to the Colorado Constitution is a fresh wound.

> Shall there be an amendment to article II of the Colorado Constitution to prohibit the State of Colorado and any of its political subdivisions from adopting or enforcing any law or policy which provides that homosexual, lesbian, or bisexual orientation, conduct, or relationships constitutes or entitles a person to claim any minority or protected status, quota preferences, or discrimination?

"Colorado is on the cutting edge of civil rights circumscription. Christian organizations such as Focus on the Family are staging a hegemonistic coup d'état here. Colorado Springs never stopped growing, even during the recession when Denver was contracting. Christians were moving into Colorado Springs from out of state."

Arthur told me that there are 55 Christian organizations based in Colorado Springs who apparently take seriously the state motto: *Nil sine Numine* (Nothing without Providence). They've put all kinds of unusual laws before the voters, such as

"All literature available in stores that would be potentially damaging to minors would be prohibited from sale."

I'd never met anyone with AIDS before and only knew a few old people with lingering terminal illnesses. George had the good grace to drop dead a few days after he began exhibiting symptoms; he would have died within 24 hours if he'd not been in intensive care. Here was a witty, charming, handsome, athletic, upbeat, optimistic person whose days were numbered. Arthur lives more and with more enthusiasm than most people I know; it was inspiring. That doesn't mean Arthur is a Pollyanna.

"I don't make friends easily. I had a few close friends, and they have all died of AIDS. Recently I've been making the mistake of trying to turn acquaintances into friends. It doesn't work for me."

I spent an hour or so every day talking with Arthur at the Lazy Lizard hostel in Moab, Utah. He was just starting on a two-month tour of the West. We joked about our complementary physical limitations. I can bike all day but suffer from standing or walking. Arthur hikes four to eight hours a day but can't risk biking because a small cut might cause him to bleed to death. The more I saw Arthur, the more seriously I took Marcus Aurelius: "Live not as though there were a thousand years ahead of you. Fate is at your elbow; make yourself good while life and power are still yours."

At age 20, my heart of hearts knew that I would live forever. George's death planted the idea in my mind that not everyone lives to realize his dreams. About one year later, a doctor told me that the pain in my joints might be caused by a terminal rheumatic disease. I decided to take the New Zealand trip I'd always dreamed of, but didn't immediately change my philosophy. Arthur's example of purposeful living and service to others reaffirmed my commitment to subtle changes I'd made in my life since returning from New Zealand.

I'd been introduced to the ugly side of insincerity by a girlfriend in Boston six months before my trip to New Zealand, where two months' total respite from insincerity made returning to Boston positively revolting. It nauseated me to see a man call another his friend and then beg off dinner invitations week after week. In the eight months since I'd returned from New Zealand, I had faithfully kept my vow to make time for a person within a few days of him contacting me or not call him "friend."

Meeting Arthur cemented in my mind the value of accepting gifts from others with real respect, especially the gift of time. I'd planned to drive more or less straight to Aspen on the Interstate. Arthur spent half an hour out of the time that remains to him drawing out a backroads tour of Colorado. When I thought that Arthur might very well be dead before I returned to this part of the country, I decided to take his advice doubly seriously.

Anyone from Colorado for Family Values might have predicted that a gay rights activist's tour of Colorado would start on Highway 666. This rolls through pinto bean fields into Colorado. I'd expected to see a "Homosexuals: we love you but we hate your sin" sign, but all I found was one bumper sticker reading, "Jimmy Carter is no longer the worst president we've had." Farms gave way to ranches and national forest as I turned north towards Telluride.

Coloradans' mental maps don't contain route numbers but rather pass names. I paused halfway up the Lizard Head Pass (elevation 10,222′) to chat with a national forest volunteer. Dave, a retired Oklahoman, educated me about the forest.

"A raw fir log is only worth $75 at the mill and $250 at retail. Aspen is worth even less since it is just ground up for particle board. They have to strip a whole mountainside to make a few thousand dollars profit, but it is what they know how to do so they keep doing it. Most of this forest is off-limits to logging now and is just used for recreation. The trees we are replanting now will be ready for harvest in 75 years, but nobody expects logging to continue then. All the trees cut then will be privately grown."

Heavy overcast dulled the scenery a bit, and most of the wildflowers had already died. It should have been a spectacular drive all the same, but Alaska had spoiled me and I was beginning to feel like Ronald Reagan: "A tree is a tree—how many more do you need to look at?" I wanted wildflowers lining the road, glaciers worming down from the peaks, and iridescent water at the bottom.

Telluride was a mining town until 1979, when the mines closed up. Grubby mines were replaced by grubbier realtors and attorneys as the town became yet another rich folks' retreat. Aspen isn't too bad, but mention Vail with its reasonably priced condos and people here shudder. Samantha and I took a table at the Between the Covers bookstore/café.

Telluride's rich kids didn't lust after Samantha. In fact, they scorned her charms.

"I'm waiting for a really advanced computer," noted Judd, 19-year-old lifelong Telluridan, "one that uses fiber optics inside."

Why would this be better?

"Because everything would work much faster then. It would have better graphics and be easier to use."

Despite my reassurance that the signals inside a modern computer propagate at 90% of the speed of light, Kevin looked up from tending bar and agreed with Judd wholeheartedly.

Alan spends his summers here painting houses and winters as a perpetual master's student in Boulder. His interests are fine arts and Buddhism.

"Boulder is one of the best places in the country to learn Buddhism, although I've spent a lot of time in Tibet and Nepal also."

Fresh from Oregon, I asked him if the Bhagwan Shree Rajneesh's philosophy had been orthodox or not. In particular, I was curious to know about the doctrine that people are prevented from thinking clearly because of pent-up sexual frustration and that the solution is to get rid of it with free love.

"Orthodox Buddhists would have found very little to criticize in the Rajneesh's teachings. That doesn't mean they would have approved of all aspects of his community, though."

Alan told me Boston was one of the best centers of Buddhist education, but I said that I didn't think I could ever escape the effects of 29 years of immersion in East Coast cultural values.

No Western experience would be complete without meeting a blue-eyed Jewish girl named Lisa. After 13 years as a successful decorative artist in Manhattan, catering to the filthy rich desire for *trompe l'oeil*, Lisa moved out here a few months ago. "I meet a lot more people here than I ever did in New York. One doesn't just stop and talk to people in Manhattan. Here it is like summer camp." Her main problem is that the local contractors are all bums, and the city government won't approve her septic design for love or money. The "New York Minute" (the interval of time between when the light turns green and when the guy behind you honks his horn) is a poorly understood concept here. Lisa admires men because they won't take "no" for an answer from a woman.

"You shouldn't let rejection get to you. Don't give anyone that kind of control over your emotions. When they reject you, they are saying more about themselves than about you."

A large group of hippies came in from their commune in New Mexico. They were here to attend the mushroom festival, several days of lectures and other events about all kinds of mushrooms (i.e., not just psilocybin). They livened up the café considerably, beating their Middle Eastern drums with occasional interruptions to go outside and smoke.

"How does your Mom feel about your not going to college and living this way?" I asked a nose-ringed cotton-dressed Earth Daughter.

"She just wants me to be happy."

At midnight, I rolled into the town campground, which was completely full. I begged hospitality from Pisa and Hans, who were eating dinner at their picnic table by the interior lights of their ancient VW camper van. I could barely make out a large dog curled up in front. Both guys were unshaven and wearing bandannas, which lent them a piratical appearance.

"What kind of dog is he?" I asked.

"A Shepherd/wolf cross."

Friendly?

"Only to good people."

THURSDAY, AUGUST 26

Telluride is the end of the road; I drove back west to Placerville and then up north through the Dallas Divide to Ridgway. "This is another tiny Colorado mining and ranching town that lives off tourism now," said the clerk at the local bookstore/café.

"I've lived up on the mesa for years, without any services of any kind. I was alone for a long time, but recently I found a man who wants to live this way also so we're together."

It was scary to contemplate ending up with a woman this independent, someone who would be perfectly happy to be alone for the rest of her life: "Thanks for the five years of marriage, honey, but I think I'm going up on the mesa for the next decade or so."

After a soak at Ridgway's "clothing optional" Orvis Hot Springs, I hit the road for Black Canyon of the Gunnison National Monument. A river goes to all the trouble of slicing its way straight down through 2700′ of rock, and it doesn't even rate national park status. That's what comes from being right next to Utah. The walls of the Gunnison's canyon are much steeper than those of any of the sandstone canyons of the Southwest, mostly because the water drops so fast. The perfectly smooth rim road made for fabulous biking, especially because I could bike out to overlooks that motorists had to walk to. Sunset on the nearly vertical gray walls of the canyon wasn't much to write home about, but the light was beautiful on fields, ranches, and distant mountains as I drove down to Montrose.

I drove through darkness to Delta, where I pitched my tent at the local KOA.

"There are only four people here tonight; camping season ended a few days ago," noted the proprietress. After dinner at the local Mexican joint, I went to the bar in back and chatted with the mostly Hispanic crowd. Did they think Colorado was being taken over by Fundamentalists? What did they think of Amendment 2?

"All it says is that homosexuals can't be considered a minority like blacks or Hispanics or whatever. It is perfectly fair to give special treatment to people who were kept down based on their skin color. But why should homosexuality be given equal status with something that can't be changed?"

Friday, August 27

The drive to Carbondale is listed as scenic, but it passes a lot of ranches and coal mines. This is the Colorado of Ayn Rand. Real men subdue Nature and brag about their achievements in a Homeric manner.

> This—she thought, looking at the mine—was the story of human wealth written across the mountains: a few pine trees hung over the cut, contorted by the storms that had raged through the wilderness for centuries, six men worked on the shelves, and an inordinate amount of complex machinery traced delicate lines against the sky; the machinery did most of the work.
>
> — *Atlas Shrugged*

> There are enough miles of tunnel in this mountain to reach San Francisco and back.
>
> — roadside sign near coal mine

Over a smoked chicken enchilada at Carbondale's finest restaurant, I read the email harvested from CompuServe. It had taken three months, but I'd finally gotten a commercial network to work for me, albeit at a price. CompuServe charged me as much to receive an Internet message as the Post Office charges to carry a physical letter 3000 miles. I wondered why people think computers are efficient and always complain about the Post Office. Also, I noticed that I didn't really want most of my mail anymore.

When I started the trip, I was so lonely that every contact from friends made me feel warm inside. By now, however, I'd learned to make connections with people quickly, and a dashed-off note from a work-obsessed friend didn't add much to my felicity. Even if America OnLine hadn't severed my electronic link with the world early on, my whole idea of taking this trip with my friends in cyberspace may have been flawed. Most people stuck with the same problems, faces, and tasks every day don't want to hear about the panoply of experience that is available to the traveler.

After driving uphill to Aspen and finding that the gondola wouldn't take bikes ("we consider the mountain too steep"), I rode the Rio Grande Trail, an old railroad bed that starts right in downtown Aspen. It is a beautiful riverside ride, beginning with little waterfalls, interesting trees, small-scale canyons, and generalized woods, and ending with views of the sewage treatment plant and airport just before one is dumped into a housing development. The airport speaks volumes about the kind of people who come to Aspen; it is packed with small personal and business jets. The really big and really small airplanes favored by the Common Man are nowhere to be seen.

Having completed 15 miles up and down the trail, I biked around the town's central residential and business districts. The rich live well here, with their $2.5 million townhouses, Toyota Landcruisers, and neo-Victorian architecture. It isn't that striking until one remembers that this is probably a third or fourth home for many of the people nominally here. A "no growth" policy adopted some years ago means that even a dumpy two-bedroom condo goes for $300,000.

Aspen was an amazingly rich mining town until the U.S. went off silver and onto the gold standard. Stately 100-year-old brick buildings attest to the mining wealth. The town's revival began in 1944 when big-shot executive Walter Pepke came out here. In a perverse reversal of *Atlas Shrugged*, he did not come to escape the IRS and build a more perfectly selfish union. Pepke decided New York executive life wasn't fulfilling enough and started the Aspen Institute for Humanistic Studies. I didn't stay in town long enough to figure out its real purpose, but it sounds a bit like the Bohemian Grove with more babes, less nudity, and fewer drunk Republicans. Prominent statesmen, business leaders, and intellectuals gather here to receive and exchange wisdom. Albert Schweitzer came to the U.S. only once, and it was to hang out here.

Businessmen may occasionally start things, but it takes the U.S. Army to finish the job. The 10th Mountain Division built the world's longest single chairlift here. After the war, hedonist Eurotrash ski bums crashed Pepke's exclusive party, and Aspen as we know it was born.

The nexus of Aspen hedonism is the Paragon, a huge nightclub, restaurant, creperie, and sidewalk café by a pleasant pedestrian mall.

"This used to be the best restaurant in town back in 1972. I was just a kid then when I bought it, ripped everything out, and turned it into a disco. Nobody here even knew what 'disco' meant," related Teddy, the trim handsome owner. "I brought in the best acts from all over the U.S., and there was a line halfway down the block every night. The *Wall Street Journal* even did an article on us."

Some big nightclub operators from New York and L. A. bought the place but sold it back to Teddy when they couldn't sustain $10 million/year in revenue. Teddy lives mostly in Paris now with his French girlfriend.

"I only came back to get her son started in the business. I'm training him now, and I'm going to hire a manager for the winter to train him then. After graduating from school in Arizona, I came here to work at the Institute in the food and beverage department. I felt important just looking at the guest list every day. In some ways, the nightclub business is fabulous; one is getting paid to socialize."

As my crepe came (nothing like a second lunch to maintain that typical American physique), we were joined by Renee, a local businesswoman. I asked her about the five recent suicides in Aspen, a subject of some concern considering the population is only 6000.

"I knew two of the five, one a 56-year-old pediatrician, the other a 43-year-old woman. I hate to say this, but I think it was because they'd never been married. I've been divorced for 16 years, but I know that I'll always have my three wonderful children and eventually grandchildren. If I were this age and never-married, I'd be really depressed."

Renee must have noticed the incipient slash marks on my wrist, for she quickly pulled out a photo of her beautiful (yes, and Jewish) 24-year-old daughter in Boulder and suggested that I look her up. Renee, Teddy, and I talked while I porked down both a dinner and a dessert crepe. They encouraged me to stay and explore, and Teddy comped my bill, but I could feel my September 8th meeting staring me in the face.

Before running away from town, I dropped into Eddie Bauer, presided over by Charles, every girl's dream ski instructor. He had toured Western Europe for a few months on his mountain bike.

"I feel like an idiot. Based on what I'd read for years in the American media, I thought of Eastern Europe as shabby and gray so I skipped it. Now I'm going around the world with my bike for 18 months, and I'm going to see everything I missed. I figure I can do it for 10 to 15 thousand dollars."

How does Charles fund his trips?

"I work three jobs here and can save about $600–1000/month. I don't have a car, one of the jobs pays for a ski pass, and I share a room in a house for $400."

What about the Aspen image of cozy couples?

"In my house there are two guys in one room, two girls in the other. Just about everyone here has to live this way, so people are used to it. If a couple wants privacy, they sneak off to the living room when everyone else is asleep. It isn't the way I want to live, but there's not much choice."

Teddy had told me that Pepke chose Aspen because he was particularly fed up with "one man putting himself on top of another man," something he found rampant in New York City. Yet some Aspenites now work three jobs and have to share a room while others never work and can drop $40,000 on a toy car to sit in front of their third home.

Everyone told me not to drive over Independence Pass (elevation 12,095′) because the weather wasn't so good. They didn't tell me the road was winding, guardrail-free, and only one lane wide in many places (yes, there is two-way traffic; don't ask me how it works). When I got to the top, though, a magnificent sunset was spread over the tops of the mountains. A roadside lake with a boulder in the middle made the spot a lazy photographer's dream.

It was just past 9 when I rolled into Leadville. Next time someone from Denver brags about it being mile high, just remind them that Leadville is fully two miles up. Leadville was all about mining until a few years ago. The population declined from 100,000 in the late 1800s to 12,000 in 1980 and now consists of 4000 shell-shocked souls. I dined and diarized at The Grill, a Mexican place 10 blocks off the main highway and hence safe from tourists. The owner's son told me that the biggest excitement here at the Grill was when Art Garfunkel, Nicholson, and Jimmy Buffett got drunk here in 1977. It must have been more exciting when Oscar Wilde visited in

1882: "I read [the miners] passages from the *Autobiography of Benvenuto Cellini*, and they seemed most delighted. I was reproved by my hearers for not having brought him with me. I explained that he had been dead for some little time, which elicited the enquiry 'Who shot him?' They afterwards took me to a dancing saloon where I saw the only rational method of art criticism I have ever come across. Over the piano was printed a notice, 'Please do not Shoot the Pianist; He is doing His Best.'"

The locals decided it was too cold for me to tent, so I slept in a beautiful guest room. One good thing about shrinking towns is that everyone lives in a nice house. As I fell asleep between soft sheets, it occurred to me that I would be very happy to spend another six months on the road. I'd rolled into Aspen, a poor man in a rich man's town, and made three friends in five hours. Nature had provided me with a magnificent show at sunset. Strangers had given me food and shelter.

Saturday, August 28

Vail was built by more 10th Mountain Division alumni, and it stretches for a few miles along I-70. One can go from Interstate to gondola in 10 minutes. Vail is just 30 years old and as democratic as Aspen is exclusive. They want everyone to come here, ski, and buy a condo (at one-third the price of Aspen). "Wanna-be Bavarian/Swiss-German" has taken root with a vengeance here. Pedestrian malls in the town centers, Bavarian architecture, and hanging flower baskets make the European experience complete. One can ride all the mountain bike trails for free if one is willing to grind up from 8300′ to 10,350′; I opted for the $16 lift pass.

Warm sunshine and high altitude's late spring burst of wildflowers greeted me at the top of the California-made gondola. Vail sits in a national forest, and views south of the "back bowl" stretch out civilization-free as far as one can see. I was in no mood to dispute Vail's claim to being the world's largest ski resort after seeing dozens of little lifts scattered throughout the back bowls.

After meandering among the high meadows, I coasted down six miles to Vail Village on a bumpy dirt road at 25 mph. After I got off the bike, I continued to shake—just like Wile E. Coyote after a mishap with some Acme spring products. The next mountain bike is *definitely* going to have a suspension.

I-70 out of Vail is a remarkable road punched through Loveland Pass. It is a tremendous climb up to a final tunnel at the top. My air-conditioner cut out but I didn't complain; the roadside was littered with overheated underengineered European cars. I'm not sure the scenery from I-70 is any less spectacular than what one sees from the little roads of Colorado, but there isn't much time to appreciate it at 50 mph (uphill) or 80 mph (downhill). There was time to be awestruck by the engineering achievement. I won't gripe about paying federal gas tax anymore.

Route 6 ducks off the Interstate into a mysterious 200′-deep winding narrow canyon. After I turned north on 93, the landscape turned into open flatland. Just before Boulder, I donned my lead BVDs for the breeze past the Department of Energy's Rocky Flats facility. Local legend has it that you will grow a second head out of the side of your neck after 10 passes.

I'd passed nearly all of Boulder's 80,000 inhabitants before realizing I'd arrived in town and starting to hunt for old friend Liz's house. Liz and I have circled around each other for nearly 15 years. We were MIT undergraduates together. We both worked in industry long enough to appreciate academia and sate our materialism. We were graduate students together in the same computer science research group at MIT, our offices just a few steps from each other. The main divergence in our lives is that Liz trained for the U.S. Olympic rowing team (her boat finished fifth in the 1988 Olympics) and I, . . . well, . . . spent a lot of time with my dog.

There are two styles of hospitality that I've come to appreciate. One is the intense European style. You can't pay for a meal, wash a dish, rent a car, or see a sight. Your host is with you every minute of every day showing you around and taking care of you. This style gave rise to the expression, "Fish and houseguests begin to smell after three days." One can't stay very long under the European system, for one would feel badly about being a burden.

America by contrast is so vast that visits can stretch to weeks, and our style of hospitality has evolved accordingly. Liz is a consummate American-style host: "Here are the house keys, the round one is the key to the guest bike lock. Use the Jacuzzi anytime. Help yourself to whatever is in the fridge. Here is the map drawer, laundry room, computer terminal, Macintosh printer, ... Stay for a couple of weeks if you like." The "my house is your house" philosophy leaves one free to run errands, explore the city, and see one's host in a natural setting.

Sunday-Wednesday, August 29-September 1

Seeing friends, attempting to accomplish things, and a rushed feeling poisoned my ability to be a perspicacious traveler. Boulderites could sense that I was just going through the motions and wasn't really interested in their lives. I asked a politically correct cotton-dressed shopgirl in the downtown pedestrian mall why she moved here.

"I don't feel like being interviewed," she huffed.

Boulder is supremely comfortable in some ways. There are great cafés, sushi bars, bookstores, parks, and libraries. Shops allude to Amendment 2 with "hate-free zone" signs. There is an overarching sense of superiority that one can acquire merely by moving here. "We know how to live, unlike those chumps in flatland (most of the rest of the country), trafficland (California), or environmental rapeland (the rest of Colorado)." Unlike Ayn Rand's self-sufficient Colorado community of elitists, however, this one is forced to depend upon the people for whom it has contempt.

Boulder's economy survives on federal money spent at Rocky Flats to make or clean up after nuclear weapons, at a National Institute of Standards and Technology laboratory, and at the National Center for Atmospheric Research. The University of Colorado sucks in tuition from rich parents sending their kids to the ultimate four-year party. It is a leech city like Washington, D.C.. Rush Limbaugh would have a field day here.

What is it about the act of selling a man an automobile that turns a human being into a monster? A dozen bike shops continent-wide had performed minor repairs, given me advice, and showed me around without ever expecting a dime. None of them were dealers for L. L. Bean mountain bikes, and none thought I'd ever return. As recently as Carbondale, Colorado, I'd been thanked for stopping by when all I did was ask for a restaurant recommendation.

Car companies love to whine and beg at the doors of Congress.

"Consumers are being mean to us, suing us for killing them or for breach of warranty. We need protection."

I had to go to two dealerships and a Firestone shop before I could be confident that the brakes and transmission on my five-month old minivan would make it back to Boston. All the time I thought of the study where 20% of Americans said they'd rather have a tooth pulled than take a car in to be fixed.

Did I leave Boulder without charming Jennifer, Renee's beautiful daughter? *Au contraire.*

"I can't believe my mother gave you my phone number. You could have been an axe murderer," Jennifer greeted me.

I sent Jennifer a draft of this chapter, and her reaction was much funnier than anything I wrote about her: "You make me sound like a world-class caustic nympho bitch."

An axe murderer! I was affronted by this attack on my masculinity—the axe having been a woman's murder weapon from Clytemnestra right down to Lizzie Borden—but I swallowed my indignation and took another tack. Didn't she think that her mother's extra decades of experience might enable her to judge men's characters more wisely than she?

"No way! Mom likes the ex-convict type."

17

Don't Cry for Things That Can't Cry for You

Wednesday, September 1

Cousin Tony took me out to lunch at his golf club, with his wife Carol and daughter Debra. They lived in Ecuador for many years before Carol's insistence that they move back to her hometown of Boulder paid off. Debra is working at a company that trains executives for overseas assignments.

"The really hard part is not getting Americans to adapt to life abroad, but easing the transition for families coming here from the Third World. They can't believe that it is possible to do anything productive, creative, or fun if one has to cope with children, laundry, and household chores."

Carol gave me directions to Denver and I-70, but Tony contradicted her. His approach would have taken me 15 miles out of my way on a two-lane road. When I mentioned this, he gave me the same directions that Carol had, without acknowledging that she'd been right in the first place. I want to get married so that I can be right all the time.

Under a big sky, Denver flashed by without revealing more than a glimpse of skyscraper clusters and petroleum farms. Fields of wheat and corn sweep up to the edge of the Rockies here. After three hours of driving through flatland, I was still shy of the border. The little hamlet of Burlington beckoned with the 1905 Kit Carson County Carousel.

"It was built by the Philadelphia Toboggan Company in 1905. It is the only one in the U.S. that has all of its original paint, which was protected by varnish over the years. That's why it is a National Historic Landmark," said Cheri, a cheerful high school senior.

To show me the lengths to which tourism officials in her part of Colorado will go, Cheri trotted out her *Colorado's Outback* brochure. It describes "the other Colorado," which supposedly bears some resemblance to Australia's Outback. Australian or not, it is either "as wild as your imagination" (per the brochure) or "as flat as Kansas and almost as Goddamn wide" (if you ask me). The brochure didn't explain the county's name, though, so I asked Cheri.

"I don't know why we named our county after Kit Carson. He killed 1000 Navajo Indians and did a bunch of other bad stuff. I think he only passed through here anyway."

While Buck Mulligan shaved his way through a BBC dramatization of *Ulysses,* I passed the "leaving colorful Colorado" sign and rolled into the Kansas Welcome Center around sunset. A large AIDS education poster is featured in front of endless wheat fields. I learned that this part of I-70 is named for Dwight Eisenhower, born and raised here in Abilene. He got part of his inspiration for the Interstate system, funded in 1956, on a 1919 Army convoy trip; it took 62 days from Washington, D.C., to San Francisco.

With my nose pointed directly east, the bulging rising full moon hung directly in front of me for 20 minutes. I pondered the hidden meaning of signs proclaiming, "Every Kansas farmer feeds 92 people . . . and YOU."

Thursday, September 2

Determined to get to Kansas City before the art museum closed, I kept the cruise control on for six hours and missed Historic Kansas. Kansas was the site of sometimes-violent conflict between pro- and anti-slavery contingents just before the Civil War. Each faction established its own communities, and it would have been nice at least to see where John Brown got his bloody start.

I also missed Tourist Kansas. I missed Walter P. Chrysler's boyhood home in Ellis, "a city with a rich past and a promising future." I came within a mile of the Sternberg Museum, "the best kept secret in Kansas" and holder of the "world-famous fish-within-a-fish fossil." I blew by the Dwight D. Eisenhower home and library. I did not detour up to Leavenworth, the first town settled in Kansas, where federal offenders kick back in the Big House. Most bitterly disappointing, I missed Hays's Barbed Wire Museum, which "contains hundreds of different types of barbed wire and tools used in making and stringing barbed wire."

Kansas is so determined to remain thoroughly boring that someone tossed all the interesting parts of Kansas City over to the Missouri side of the river. As I crossed the border, I settled upon a simple system for making Kansas just as interesting per hour as the average U.S. state. All you need is a car that goes 300 miles per hour.

None of my 13,500 miles had taken me through any black neighborhoods, and it was a novelty to drive block after block without seeing any white faces. Segregation persisted until I arrived at the Nelson Atkins art museum, where some fraction of every penny you've spent on Hallmark greeting cards has been put to work for culture.

Thomas Hart Benton, who painted in Kansas City around 1940, said, "I'd rather my art were exhibited in saloons where normal people can see it than in museums." A typical vaulted-ceiling marble-floored museum gallery is devoted to his work. My favorite is a crowded portrait of Hollywood as a sham machine running on cheesecake. Figures, equipment, and sets crowd every portion of the canvas. *LIFE* magazine commissioned it but wouldn't print it because of the half-naked woman in the center; they changed their tune a year later after the painting won a big award. Benton's major series depicting the settlement of the U.S. are displayed as well. One shows pilgrims in New England and another cowboys in the Wild West, but the theme is the same: white guys turn Arcadia into a living Hell for red guys.

The Hudson River School is well-represented here, with a Moran Grand Canyon and a Bierstadt Yosemite. Kansas City residents are treated to a good selection of modern art, ranging from a classic Nevelson to a wild chainsawed and painted laminated plywood Arnoldi. If I'd been willing to brave sheets of rain, I might have seen the world's biggest collection of Henry Moore sculpture.

Back on the black side of town, I stuffed my face at Arthur Bryant's famous barbecue joint. Kelly, a 28-year-old practical nurse, sat next to me with her 3-year-old daughter Shanell.

"I was only 12 when my son Donell was born, and it was a bit of a struggle to get through high school. But I managed and now I'm getting some more advanced nursing degrees."

Does the segregation here bother her?

"Oh, I've got white friends; even if neighborhoods aren't all that integrated, I never feel out of place. Some folks say there isn't anything to do here, but life is what you make of it."

Driving east through a heavy rain, I reflected upon my conversation with Kelly. Whenever hard-working yuppies complained about all the single mothers living on Aid to Families with Dependent Children (AFDC) unfairly soaking up their tax dollars, I used to nod my head in agreement. Assuming Kelly had been on AFDC at one time, she was about the 15th AFDC mother I'd talked to at some length. It struck me that I liked all of them much better than the typical yuppie grubbing his way up the ladder of consumerism. I began to think that if yupsters were willing to work 80 hours/week in pursuit of that bigger BMW or sailboat, then they shouldn't complain about having to support a few women content with a 1950s standard of living.

Horrified by these thoughts, I stopped in Foristell, Missouri, just short of St. Louis, and looked around for a Republican deprogramming center.

FRIDAY, SEPTEMBER 3

We will dance the Hoochee Koochee,
  I will be your tootsie wootsie;

> If you will meet me in St. Louis, Louis,
> meet me at the fair.

After tanking up for 89 cents/gallon (!) I drove into St. Louis and visited the Gateway Arch. Eero Saarinen was born in Finland in 1910 and came to Michigan with his family in 1922. He studied architecture at Yale and won a design competition in 1947 for a westward expansion monument (presaging the choice of an immigrant Yalie's design for the Vietnam Memorial). The wheels of government turn slowly; construction was started in 1962 and finished in 1965. Saarinen died of a brain tumor in 1961.

I watched an inspiring movie on the arch's construction. Huge steel plates came in by train from Pittsburgh and were assembled into triangles on site. Each triangle comprises an outer skin of stainless steel and an inner one of carbon steel with space enough in between for steel tendons. Once welded, a triangle would be hoisted into place on top of one arm and its tendons attached to those sticking out of the preceding triangle. Five hundred tons of force were applied hydraulically to stretch the tendons, and then concrete was poured in between the inner and outer steel plates. (The arch weighs more than an aircraft carrier.)

Because of its 600′ height, the arch presented unique construction problems. Each arm had to support its own weight until 450′ had been reached, when a temporary support strut was inserted between the arms. Until then, the arms couldn't lean on each other or on outside scaffolding. Ground-based cranes couldn't reach high enough to lift new sections onto the arms, so tracks were laid on the outside wall of each arm for an arch-based crane. Every scene in the movie shows guys perched a few hundred feet off the ground with no safety ropes, yet remarkably none of the forecast 13 deaths transpired. Finally, joining the two sides required jacking the two arms apart a bit and hosing one down with water so it wouldn't expand in the heat of the sun. Thousands of people thronged underneath to watch, and I was saddened to think that Saarinen didn't live to see his triumph.

A tram system worthy of Rube Goldberg takes one to the top of the arch in a claustrophobia-inducing five-person capsule. The capsule twists with a lurch a few times

to keep the occupants upright during the four-minute ride up. How's the ventilation? Make sure your fellow riders are wearing deodorant. Once on top, you can lean on an inner portion of the triangle and stick your face against a small glass window to look nearly straight down. It is nauseating. Curiously, the thriving metropolis of St. Louis stretches as far as the eye can see in the supposedly open West whereas the farms of Illinois present a much more open picture back East. I didn't contemplate this paradox for long; feeling simultaneously claustrophobic and acrophobic, I was delighted to ride the tram back down and walk over to the riverbank to check for signs of the Flood of '93. Everything looked normal until I realized that city workers weren't changing street light bulbs; they were removing river mud. Then I noticed that the Riverboat McDonald's was floating in what used to be its parking lot.

After a quick look around LeClede's Landing, the yuppie/jazz riverside nexus of St. Louis, I drove through downtown and stopped at the old train station, which has been redeveloped into a fancy hotel and shopping mall. Sandra tended bar and told me about her flood experiences.

"I don't personally know anyone who lost a home, but I do think that most of those people were pretty stupid to build on a floodplain. What struck me most about the flood was driving along the highway and seeing a restaurant roof sticking out of the water; I used to go there every week. For that matter, the highway itself was under water for weeks; an Interstate highway! Then there were all those private airplanes at our local airport. When the levee broke, there wasn't time for most people to fly their planes to safety."

"Works of art by world-renowned dog artists such as Sir Edwin Landseer, Arthur Wardle, Percival Rosseau, and Jean Baptiste Oudry are to be found in the collection of The Dog Museum," read the brochure that lured me to this wealthy suburban neighborhood, where signs of the flood were nil. The museum outgrew its New York City beginnings and came to the middle of Queeny Park here in 1987. I expressed my disappointment at the lack of Samoyed pictures to the woman running the show.

"We take whatever is donated to us."

Computer fans will be pleased to note that advanced technology is at work here matching people with the right breeds. I answered a bunch of personal questions using a touchscreen to see if either of my favorite breeds, Samoyed or Golden Retriever, would come up. My perfect mate is apparently the West Highland Terrier, a yapping 10 lb. old lady's dog. I don't care how lonely I get; I'm not going to try computer dating.

> The state is exceptionally well and evenly drained.
>
> —*AAA TourBook for Missouri*

> Water Over Road.
>
> —warning sign on Highway 94

Half a mile after the sign, my trip from St. Charles, Missouri, to Alton, Illinois, was abbreviated by 10 miles of this main road going underwater; this was *September,* three months after the Flood of '93. Cars rested by the road, recently uncovered by the receding waters, their interiors encrusted with river mud. Farmhouses stood isolated in flooded fields. Ruins and bare foundations dotted the landscape, along with debris and sandbags, but the area wasn't as devastated as I'd expected. First, the places I visited had never been densely populated, and second, the fields and trees appeared to be coming through unscathed.

Listening to the tunes of St. Louis Radio KYKY, I crossed the Mississippi into Illinois an hour before sunset. KYKY faded somewhere on the Interstate, and I had to choose a "W" station for the first time since June 4th, when I'd left St. Paul. I was back East.

SATURDAY, SEPTEMBER 4

Inspired by Kerouac's pre-Interstate adventures in a book-on-tape edition of *On the Road,* I meandered on "scenic" backroads through Indiana and up the Ohio River Valley into Cincinnati. Gritty industries line the riverfront road, then a gleaming downtown whizzed past from my superhighway vantage point. Before I knew it, I was dumped into the extensive park that surrounds the city's art museum. Dog owners, families, and lovers played around fountains.

Two seconds of watching Lily walk through the parking lot reintroduced me to a part of myself I hadn't seen for 14 years. Lily and I were sophomores together at MIT back in 1979. My memory of our first conversation has faded a bit with the years, but I remember one thing clearly: after one hour, I knew that I wanted to spend the rest of my life with her. Circumstance conspired against us, though. We were young (15 and 18). The subtlest miscue from one would slash the other to the bone. During my three years at MIT, I never thought about physics or math except for during brief lulls that separated tempestuous thoughts of Lily. Depending on where we were in our on-again, off-again romance, the thoughts might be bliss, hope, anger, pain, regret, or curiosity.

We went our separate ways in 1982, she to design bleach factories in Cincinnati and I to write software in Silicon Valley. I rested secure in the knowledge that we'd certainly marry one day; we just needed a little time apart to grow up. Lily punctured my self-inflated balloon in 1984 by marrying someone else. How could she be happy without me? How could a Chinese-American girl, raised in New York City, who was a cynosure at MIT, be happy in a white-bread suburb of Cincinnati?

Years passed but we never grew distant. Lily's voice on the phone would sound as familiar as those of friends I saw every day in Boston. Her infrequent letters kept me apprised of important developments. This was my first trip to Cincinnati to see her, though, and I didn't know what to expect.

Lily bounced across the art museum parking lot with her gymnast's posture and sunlit smile and changed my world. Everything I'd ever felt for her came back in a rush; I never wanted to be parted from this woman. We strolled a bit obliviously through the collection and out into the park. All the years and miles of separation melted away; we might have been continuously together until the day before.

Although Lily was always a superstar at whatever she did, she doesn't work anymore.

"Mike makes enough for me and the kids. I'm just not materialistic enough. I got pushed into MIT and chemical engineering by a bunch of well-meaning people who thought they knew what was best for me. I was too young to make an intelligent choice."

Next time something you buy falls apart, consider this: among our friends from the MIT Class of '82, only a handful are actually designing products. The

rewards of an engineering career in America are apparently insufficient to retain the talents of the best-trained engineers. Lawyers keep litigating, doctors keep medicating, MBAs keep managing, but our engineer friends have mostly thrown up their hands and said, "Why bother?"

The more I listened to Lily, the more clearly I remembered how I'd loved her and the more jaded seemed my current approach to love. I might love a woman deeply, but if questioned rationally could come up with a list of pragmatic reasons why we'd not be optimal mates. "I love her with all my heart, but perhaps it would be easier to marry someone <more vivacious | American | who wants kids | who can carry more camera equipment>." I hadn't become bitter and pessimistic after getting hurt, but these kinds of thoughts poisoned love just as surely. The only person I could remember loving absolutely without reservation recently was George, and he was, well, a dog.

Alaska had made me a better listener, and I finally got Lily to explain why she wouldn't marry me. *My Fair Lady*'s Henry Higgins was never my conscious idol, yet Lily remembered my imitation of him as my least attractive quality.

"I didn't want to live your life. I wanted you and I wanted me. I wanted to have a life together and a life for myself and watch you enjoy a life of your own. Maybe things would have been different if we talked about it, but we were too busy hurting each other. I was hurt for months, but I was mad for years. And that was all before I left MIT."

Lily took me back to her new Tudor house in the distant suburbs (big houses, small trees). Mike and their two adorable daughters joined us for dinner, then Lily and I sat up talking past midnight.

SUNDAY, SEPTEMBER 5

Just like old times: Lily got five hours of sleep and had more energy than I after nine. As I pulled out of the driveway, I thought about how pointless it was to have spent all that time and effort chasing other women if none of them made me sparkle inside like

Lily. I didn't let myself get depressed with these thoughts, however. Even if 95% of her heart was committed to husband and children, the leftover 5% was still worth a lot. Our joy in each other's company had survived 14 years and one marriage; I felt fortunate just to have known her.

Tourist attractions are thin on the ground in the 13 hours between Cincinnati and Philadelphia. I got really excited about a Scenic Overlook off I-71 out of Cincinnati; it turned out to overlook "Ohio's longest Interstate highway bridge."

It was past midnight when I arrived at Eero's townhouse, but he and Iris, his Israeli girlfriend, were just sitting down to dinner. I'd come full circle: Eero had helped me pack the van in Boston, and seeing him again psychologically wrapped up the trip.

Note: Eero's father is an architect who worked with Eero Saarinen for two years, which is how an Italian-American got a Finnish name.

Monday, September 6 (Labor Day) and Tuesday, September 7

This region is fundamentally about subtly refined inferiority complexes. Inferiority 101: Philadelphia itself is between Washington, D.C., whose power it lacks, and New York, whose wealth it lacks. Inferiority 336 (advanced graduate course in recursive inferiority complexes): Lots of folks live in no-man's lands between Philly and D.C. or Philly and New York; "NOT Philadelphia, NOT New York, New Jersey's own Rock 101.5" shouts one radio station.

W. C. Fields ("I went to Philadelphia, but it was closed") notwithstanding, Philadelphia has a lot going for it. Black, Chinese, Indian, and white citizens live, rather than just work together.

Middle-class folks can actually afford to live downtown; townhouses rent for $700–1000/month. Bars, restaurants, and entertainment appeal to wide ranges of people. The population simply isn't large enough for the total segmentation of services that one finds in larger cities ("Saturday is Nicaraguan Communist Women's Folk Music Night, Sunday is Nicaraguan Socialist Women's Folk Music Night").

ROCKY

Civic pride blossoms on every street corner with more outdoor sculpture than I've ever seen.

America's third largest art museum beckons from the banks of the Schuylkill. A huge statue of Rocky adorned the top of its famous staircase in one of the *Rocky* movies, and Sylvester Stallone donated the prop to the museum. When the museum tried to remove it, Stallone allegedly sued to force them to keep the statue there. It rests now on a South Philly street corner near Rocky's fictional home; how ephemeral is fame.

What remains is the 1920s neoclassical art warehouse stocked with piles of good stuff. Local boy Thomas Eakins gets a couple of rooms crowded with portraits. The Hudson River School is represented by a fabulous Moran Grand Canyon and a nice Andes scene by Church. The Impressionism section lacks the lively singles' scene of the Metropolitan, but a big Cézanne collection makes up for it. Those used to the crowds of the Metropolitan or the National Gallery will be confused here. Parking is free, rooms are empty, and guards are lonely. At least a dozen guards greeted me with a friendly "How ya' doin' today?"

The University of Pennsylvania is an unusual Ivy League school. First, half the students are here only because Harvard rejected them. Second, the WASP enclave atmosphere is preserved only in the architecture of a couple courtyards. Harvard had its Jewish quota and then replaced it with a "geographical diversity" objective (i.e., not so many New York Jews, please). Penn scarcely seems to have tried to hold the fort. Half the buildings bear Jewish names, and I could have sworn that half the kids strolling around campus were from my synagogue (55% are supposedly Jewish; the rest are Asian). This is not the place to tell that great Jewish-American Princess joke—no, not even the "beige" one.

Wednesday, September 8

"I don't know if this makes you feel better, but I've only been here six days and it has already happened to me twice," sympathized Elizabeth.

I must have looked a bit stunned as I contemplated the gaping hole in the side of my van. While my $700 alarm system slept, someone smashed a center window and removed all my clothing, then the cameras hidden underneath. I was behaving in an almost adult fashion until I realized that one of my slide Carousels was gone. Seventy hand-picked pictures, history.

Back at Eero's, I phoned the police and placed an ad in the *Inquirer* offering a $300 reward for the return of the slides. Philadelphia's police force hasn't yet recovered from the ignominy of the MOVE bombing, but Officers Keitt and Garrett seemed likely to restore the department credit. These trim, professional, sympathetic, young black guys looked at the stuff in my van and shook their heads.

"We wish you could say that you could park this on the street here, but you can't."

Although the loss was more than $30,000, the detectives back at the precinct declined to come out and take fingerprints. Keitt and Garrett were delighted to accept two bear snapshots—to help them identify my slides if any should turn up—and told stories of bear paranoia on childhood camping trips.

"Just run downhill," Garrett noted, "they trip and roll if they try to follow you."

I pointed out that the bears in the snapshots were standing on slippery rocks at the top of a waterfall.

"Maybe it would be better just to run."

Nobody in Philadelphia had a replacement window in stock so I pressed north toward MIT in hopes of making a staff meeting. The New Jersey Turnpike's 12 lanes have never been noted for charm, but they looked even uglier with a steady rain roaring through a massive hole in the car. The loss of my slides made me feel a bit sorry for myself, but half-hourly news updates about a German tourist murdered in Miami kept me from wallowing in self-pity. I sought comfort in philosophy as well: "Don't cry for things that can't cry for you."

The reward offer worked, by the way. An electric company worker found the carousel in the street. So I lost the cameras but got the images back a few weeks later.

After 15,000 miles, the six rainy hours to 545 Technology Square went by in a blink. As the Mass Pike rolled underneath, I thought about how good it would be to get back to finishing my Ph.D. in electrical engineering and computer science. A country-western radio station provided accompaniment: "A few more people should be pulling their weight. If you want a cram course in reality, you get yourself a work'n man's Ph.D." ("Working Man's Ph.D." by Aaron Tippin, Philip Douglas, and Bobby Boyd).

18

MIT

"I meet more people in an afternoon in a town of 3000 than I do back in Boston, a city of 3.5 million, in a month. I wore myself a rut after 14 years in Boston, going from home to MIT to friends' houses with blinders on. I eat in the same restaurants and go to the same Boston Symphony every Saturday night. When I get back home, I'll try to be more of a tourist in my own city, talking to strangers and going to new places."

Thus had I explained my new philosophy all through August. I applied it successfully on my first evening back in Boston, chatting up a grandmother from Wheeling, West Virginia, in the produce section of Stop & Shop. I was back to my old ways by the next morning.

New people and places were interesting in theory, but they couldn't compete with the reality of two hundred pounds of mail, 30 undergraduates trying to learn mathematics from me, old friends, my insurance company, a Ph.D. thesis, and this book. Exacerbating the situation was my conviction that, during my first two weeks back, I should be able to do everything I'd put off for months before traveling *plus* everything that had accumulated during 14 weeks on the road *plus* my standard MIT workload.

If one is going to be work-obsessed, MIT is about the most supportive environment imaginable. For example, one evening just after midnight I sat in my office writing problem set solutions. Raj, a fellow graduate student, was walking by just as my frustration with one problem was simmering. He came up with the right approach after five minutes. Ten minutes later, I presented the complete solution on the blackboard in our lounge. The rest of the late-night crowd, 10 nerds, blessed my solution.

As everyone turned his attention to helping Andy finish his Ph.D. project, a super-strong-for-its-weight model railroad bridge built out of thin strips of metal—Andy had figured out how to use sensors and tiny computer-controlled motors to keep beams from buckling—I reflected that, in all my years at the MIT Artificial Intelligence Lab, I'd never had to walk more than 100′ from my office to get the answer to any technical question. If I didn't have the tenacity or knowledge to solve a problem, someone else always did and was happy to help me. It didn't matter whether I was stuck designing a digital signal processor, solving differential equations, building an integrated circuit, representing complex surfaces in a computer, dividing welfare recipients into all possible family combinations, or building dozens of circuits—from phase-locked loops to high-quality audio filters.

It didn't take me too long to become blasé about the swirl of MIT life. I skipped U.N. Secretary General Boutros-Boutros Ghali's address to "leaders" from 53 nations. It didn't bother me that *The Tech,* MIT's student newspaper, glossed over Professor Philip Sharp's Nobel Prize in biology in favor of continuing coverage of sexual harassment and racial preference debates—Sharp's split-gene discovery was old news and 24 other faculty members already had Nobels. I wasn't sorry to have missed Salman Rushdie's first U.S. appearance since he was sentenced to death. I was too busy struggling with the return of my high expectations.

Was I alone in a small town for an evening? That's only natural, I only got there three hours before and couldn't expect to have made friends. Was I alone in Boston for an evening? That made me a loser, for how else could someone live in a city of 3.5 million and find himself friendless.

On the road, I was satisfied with just getting from one place to another, taking the occasional photograph or writing a few words. If I learned something or made a friend, that was a bonus that put me on top of the world. Back in Boston, the following goals seemed like a minimum: (1) know as much as MIT professors, (2) have a collection of friends who would drop everything at a moment's notice to be with me, (3) keep a girlfriend happy, (4) be as good a probability teacher as Al Drake, who's had 30 years of practice, (5) figure out how the computing landscape had been changed by the spread of World Wide Web browsers, and (6) find a Ph.D. thesis topic that would get me a faculty position ahead of 1000 other wanna-be's.

"The term started three weeks ago and I'm already five weeks behind" is a typical MIT student's lament. That's how I felt about my life. I turned 30 on

STAND ON LINE
STAY IN POSITION UNTIL
NAME IS READ, IF NAME
IS NOT READ,
TELL READER NAME

September 28th and realized that the list of things I at one time thought I could do by age 30 would now take me at least another four decades. It made me jumpy.

When I noticed how jumpy I was, I resolved to stop dating in Boston. After a month or two alone in my minivan, I had been ready to listen to a stranger, man or woman. I could devote 100% of my attention to his or her situation, and I got to know people remarkably quickly. Back in Boston, with my head filled with thoughts such as "I forgot to call Bruce back," "I'm not prepared for the lecture I have to give on Monday," and "Why doesn't Neil ever call me?" I was in no shape to give more than 5% of myself to a stranger.

I was lonely, to be sure, and not sold on the idea of sleeping alone for the rest of my life. However, I thought I would feel even lonelier spending hours skimming the surface of a stranger while thinking that I really ought to be working.

It was an article of faith in Washington, D.C., where I grew up, that small towners were narrow-minded people good for nothing except paying taxes to support our $8 billion subway and free museums. Further, one can't live 14 years in Boston without absorbing some of the prevailing contempt for those who live beyond reach of Harvard and MIT. I'd accumulated 30 years of prejudice, but it melted away during my weeks on the road. People in small towns would listen with respect to any story I told, even if it underlined fundamental differences in philosophy, religion, or politics between us. After 10 minutes of patient listening, a person might frankly note that he saw things differently, but I was never scorned by anyone for holding a different point of view.

After returning home, I had high expectations for social gatherings. I figured my great stories from the road would make me the life of the party. In reality, I'd lost the social skills necessary to survive in Cambridge, as underscored one evening when 40 people came over to my house to see some slides.

Matthew asked me what I learned on my trip.

"One thing I learned was how narrow my experience of people had been. For example, I had my first real conversation with someone with AIDS on this trip. In Utah . . . ."

Susan interrupted: "A lot of the people you know, even some of the people here tonight, probably have AIDS; you just don't realize it."

I was never able to tell anyone what I'd learned from Arthur because my introduction challenged one of Susan's cherished beliefs, i.e., that a large percentage of upper middle-class men who are neither gay nor IV drug users carried the HIV virus. She could not wait until the end of the story to put in her two cents' worth, but had to make sure that I aligned my beliefs with hers before she would let me continue.

Initially, I thought that Susan just had a bee in her bonnet. However, at two other gatherings I tried telling the same story. In both cases, a thirtysomething Jewish woman interrupted me at the same point for the same reason.

The inability of Bostonians to cope with differences of philosophy was driven home one night at the Harvest bar in Harvard Square. Bruce, Henry, and I were going over old times when Jackie, an acquaintance of Bruce's, and Roberto, her Chilean boyfriend, sat down next to us.

Bruce congratulated Jackie, a trim brunette in a stylish suit, for having just been on the cover of a travel agent's trade magazine. Jackie works for a consulting company. She gets paid big bucks to dress nicely, fly around, and tell companies how to make their benefits packages more "family friendly."

What was the subject of the article?

"It is about the difficulties that minorities have traveling."

Er . . . How is her situation relevant?

"I'm half-Japanese."

Wouldn't they have been better off choosing someone from a minority group with a lower-than-average income, perhaps someone black or Puerto Rican?

"Why do you say, that?" Jackie asked with a hostile edge in her voice.

"Most businesses' primary objective is getting money out of customers, so I would think that someone who looked poor would get worse treatment. By contrast, Michael Jackson would probably get treated better than any of us for the same reason," I theorized.

Roberto was furious.

"Are you saying that only blacks are minorities?"

To deny someone the victimhood status of "minority" was apparently an unforgivable sin. Jackie went on to relate how she'd been a victim of prejudice her entire life. She'd been teased in elementary school, treated badly by service businesses, and denied jobs. Against this bleak background, she admitted that Jews and Asians were comparatively lucky.

"We're allowed to pass by white society. If we have enough money, they let us buy houses in their neighborhoods. But they never fully accept us."

Henry, born and raised in Hong Kong, piped up, "that proves that it is classism and wealthism, not simply racism."

"That doesn't prove anything. If you get bad service, you might not chalk it up to racism." Jackie's philosophy was that any bad treatment should be put down to racism unless otherwise accounted for. Thus, nearly every day provided for her more evidence that Americans are full of bad will.

"This nation is full of anti-Semitism [a German word I don't like to use; it was coined in the late 19th century to replace the simpler "Jew-hatred" to make the feeling seem more scientific and hence acceptable to educated Germans]. Doesn't your own experience confirm this?" Jackie asked.

"I just drove 15,000 miles around North America and encountered a few people who said things that most Cantabrigians would consider shockingly anti-Semitic. However, these people had never had any experience with Jews. Despite knowing that I was Jewish, they were happy to take me into their homes and feed me. Their prejudices didn't affect their actions or their openness to learn about people. So I would have to say that it didn't matter much. I just hoped that someday they'd learn more about Jews and change their opinions."

"What about the Nazis?" Jackie asked. "Would you say that they would have been nice people if only they'd actually met a few Jews? I used to live in Frankfurt and there was one school with a few Jewish students. They had to have guards with machine guns outside because there was so much hatred from the Germans."

Jackie had a good point there. I probably sounded a bit too much like Candide. I reviewed the situation: Jackie was hurt that I'd presumed to deny her minority victim status and angry that I was too obtuse to see Americans as full of hatred. If tolerance was good in her feminist-liberal worldview, why was she upset with me for not hating my fellow Americans?

Before I could finish this thought, Henry observed that he'd "traveled quite a bit through the Far East and North America and noticed that the U.S. has very little discrimination and a lot of talk about discrimination, while the Far East is the opposite."

"A lot of clubs in Tokyo hang 'Japanese Only' signs out front," Bruce added.

Henry continued, "Prejudice isn't bad. If you've met nine Jews and have found them untrustworthy and say that there is a 90% chance the next Jew you meet won't be trustworthy, that's good. But if you say that there is no chance the next Jew I meet can be trusted, that's bad. If you are willing to give people a chance, it doesn't matter what your prejudices are."

Jackie ignored Henry's radical position and focused on me as the prime heretic. I tried to soothe her by saying that I considered Anti-Jewish prejudice a problem, just not a significant one.

"In *Civilization and its Discontents*, Freud divided the sources of pain in life into three categories . . ."

Before I could explain Freud's thesis that the pain that one gets from problems with loved ones is in another category from the pain inflicted by strangers and society, Jackie stopped me.

"I won't listen to anything having to do with Freud—he thought women had penis envy."

The range of expressed opinion in Cambridge is broader than in a small town, but the range of opinion that *any given person* is prepared to hear is much narrower. All across America, I had seen people sit down and listen to each other even when they were on opposite sides of an issue. In Cambridge, people with slight political differences can barely get through a cocktail party together.

Despite seeing some folks as narrow-minded, it felt good to be back at MIT. I remembered a 1938 comment by Karl Taylor Compton, one-time president of MIT:

> In recent times, modern science has developed to give mankind, for the first time, in the history of the human race, a way of securing a more abundant life which does not simply consist in taking away from someone else.

Alex, born 1996

19

What I Learned on My Summer Vacation

"If you are so smart, why aren't you rich?" New Yorkers like to say. "If you are so smart, how come you spent 14 weeks on the road and don't have some brilliant aphorism about the American people to offer?" seemed appropriate in my case.

Hunter S. Thompson stumbled through a drug-induced mist to come up with "America . . . just a nation of two hundred million used car salesmen with all the money we need to buy guns and no qualms about killing anybody else in the world who tries to make us uncomfortable." I know that Georges Clemenceau never had a laptop computer, yet he gave us, "America is the only nation in history which miraculously has gone directly from barbarism to degeneration without the usual interval of Civilization." *I* couldn't even summon enough ennui and nihilism to agree with Walter Holland: "Most towns are the same."

My overwhelming posttrip impression was that I had barely scratched the surface of an unknowably rich society. Every person had an interesting story; every person had learned something valuable in coming to grips with his or her circumstances. Compared to the variety of folks and lifestyles I encountered on the road, my Boston activities and social circle are but a teaspoonful of ocean water.

Most of the people I know in Boston live for professional recognition, to add initials to their name (e.g., "Ph.D.," "S.M.," "J.D.," "M.D."), for career success, and/or for social prestige and fame. In my weeks on the road, I met quite a few North

Americans who would not be out of place among my usual associates. However, I met hundreds more who lived for their families, for physical and materialistic pleasures of the day, or for religion. Many of these people were much happier than my friends. They derived satisfaction from things that have made people happy for thousands of years, e.g., children, money, religion. The typical Harvard/MIT lifestyle looked very high risk by comparison.

Professors would spend 10 years in school, then 7 years working feverishly, then get crushed when denied tenure. Scientists would spend 30 years trying to really accomplish something, but end up with only a stack of obscure papers in unread journals. Women clawed their way to moderately lucrative middle-management positions but found their career flattening out just as their child-bearing years drew to a close. Some of these aspirants would get the Nobel prize, and the rest said that they enjoyed the process and didn't need anything else. Nonetheless, I knew precious few "academic and professional strivers" who seemed as happy as Laurel and Eric (the bed and breakfast workers in Wisconsin), Ali and Michelle (Australians traveling in Montana), Shelly (young mother in Grande Prairie, Alberta), Kelly (trucker on the Alaska Highway), Lloyd (heavy equipment operator in Whitehorse), Woody (philosopher in Denali), Walter and Karin (Swiss dairy farmer and his wife, a saleswoman), Hans and Rey (bike shop owners in Juneau), Tom and Lisa (chucked it all to see America by motor home), Marty (schoolteacher in Seattle), or John (insurance agent in Monticello, Utah).

It struck me that I'd heard a lot of engineers say they wished they hadn't worked so hard on a start-up company, a lot of professors say it was a shame that they'd put their research ahead of their marriage, a lot of lawyers question their value to society, but I'd never heard anyone say he or she regretted time spent raising children. What would happen to my friends if they didn't realize their goals? Even worse, what would happen if they did realize those goals, then came to see them as not sufficient?

Thinking about all these friends growing older, unmarried, and childless, I shuddered the way I would watching a family stake their whole fortune on double-zero at a Vegas roulette table.

I started the trip timorous, lonely, and desperate to cling to old friends and family via email and telephone. I ended it confident, comfortable with being alone or with new friends, and happy to go weeks without contact from home. One of the principal reasons for this change was the fine hospitality I received all over the continent. It is very comforting to know that, should your friends and family prove wanting, you can always get what you need from strangers.

The End

DOG
WATER

About the Author

Philip Greenspun teaches at the Massachusetts Institute of Technology and is the author of five books, mostly on horrifyingly dull technical subjects. Greenspun is the founder of ArsDigita Corporation, an open-source software company, and ArsDigita University, a tuition-free post-baccalaureate computer science program.

Greenspun was born in 1963 and raised in Bethesda, Maryland. He lives in Cambridge, Massachusetts, with Alex, his Samoyed, and Pi goddess Eve Andersson, who takes care of them both.

A comprehensive collection of Greenspun's writing and photography may be found online at http://philip.greenspun.com.